net.people

net.people

The Personalities and Passions
Behind The Web Sites

Thomas E. Bleier
and
Eric C. Steinert

CyberAge Books

Information Today, Inc.
Medford, New Jersey

First printing, 2000

net.people
The Personalities and Passions Behind the Web Sites

Library of Congress Cataloging-in-Publication Data

Bleier, Thomas E.
     net.people : the personalities and passions behind the Web sites / Thomas E. Bleier and Eric C. Steinert.
         p.   cm.
     ISBN 0-910965-37-4 (pbk.)
     1. Web sites—Social aspects. I. Steinert, Eric C. II. Title.
TK5105.888.B54   1999
005.7'2—dc21   99-42511
                                            CIP

Printed and bound in the United States of America.

Publisher: Thomas H. Hogan, Sr.
Editor-in-Chief: John B. Bryans
Managing Editor: Janet M. Spavlik
Copy Editor: Michelle Sutton-Kerchner
Production Manager: M. Heide Dengler
Cover Design: Adam M. Vinick
Book Design: Jeremy M. Pellegrin
Illustrations: Joshua T. Williams

Table of Contents

Collecting Stuff & Other Diversions

The Written Word & Journalistic Endeavors

Acknowledgments

This book could not have been possible without the combined efforts of many individuals. I am grateful to our publisher, Information Today, Inc., for their continuing support, and especially to our editor, Michelle Sutton-Kerchner, our managing editors Dorothy Pike and Janet Spavlik, our editor-in-chief John Bryans, and publisher Tom Hogan, Sr. Many friends and family members provided superb advice and recommendations as we assembled the manuscript. A special thanks goes to my wife, Heidi, for her patience and encouragement throughout the writing process. Amidst everything else that was taking place, she never stopped believing in the underlying importance of our work on the book. Finally, many thanks to the thirty-six individuals who provided the real character of our book. Their insights and stories help bring the Internet to life.

– Eric Steinert

This book is the culmination of a long process, a longer one than we initially thought, but it would never have happened if not for several people. I would like to thank our publisher, specifically Tom Hogan, Sr. for believing in our idea and John Bryans, Michelle Sutton-Kerchner, Janet Spavlik, and Dorothy Pike for making it a reality. I would like to thank my friends and my girlfriend, Tori Frenkel, for their patience and encouragement as I locked myself in my apartment and rarely ventured out. I want to thank several friendly proofreaders, including my mom and dad, Carol and Michael Bleier, and Deb Wekstein, who were quick with the pen when something had to be reviewed at any given hour. Finally, the biggest thanks is to be given to the thirty-six individuals who we profiled and who took the time to send us photos and answer our questions. If they hadn't created unique stops on the Internet there wouldn't have been a reason for this book.

– Tom Bleier

Introduction

Feasting Our Eyes on the Internet

Eric Steinert and Tom Bleier signing their book deal

Back in the Stone Age of the Internet, about five years ago, we were both working as sales representatives for a small software company in the Boston area. We spent the majority of each day on the phone, calling employees of information technology departments in Fortune 500 companies around the country trying to convince them to buy our product. Although this job was no picnic, it did provide us with a salary and the opportunity to play with some of the latest technology.

Like many people stuck in corporate America, we were always trying to think of something to do on our own. One of our goals was to become writers. A lofty goal, considering neither of us had ever been published and the last writing we did was college term papers several years ago. As we talked about what future paths our careers could take, our company moved forward into the Internet age and got us e-mail.

At the time, not many of our company's clients had e-mail, so its only real use was to chat with friends and our two dozen co-workers. E-mail was fun, but not fully practical in our business environment at that point. Around the same time, all the salespeople received Mosaic, the free graphical browser for the Internet. This was our ticket to becoming authors, although we didn't know it at the time.

As a productivity tool, Mosaic was not a big help, but it did change our view of the world. Many companies did not yet have an Internet presence, so most of the graphical sites Mosaic allowed us to view were people's personal Web pages. These personal sites featured everything from pictures of the developer's friends and family to detailed information about a subject that they enjoyed, such as fish. Not a day went by in the office without someone saying to check out a certain interesting site they found. Even though each site was unique, it did raise questions in our minds, such as: Why did someone post this material on the Web? Who was this person or group of people? How did they find time to develop this site? How did they learn to build it?

In the meantime, the Internet began to revolutionize our business and our daily work routine. Now, instead of shipping software, we asked our clients to download a trial demo of it. If a potential client wanted technical specifications, media coverage, press releases, or client listings, they just checked out our company's Web site. As more of our clients became Web savvy, we ourselves would spend more time on the Web. Before long, we began to ask ourselves if there was a business on the Web that we could start.

While we never agreed on a business or Web site concept, we did agree that the Internet could change our careers. Through our hours of surfing, we found sites of people who had successfully made a switch. One was a twenty-eight-year-old environmental consultant with no children of his own who became an expert on child daycare for working parents. Another was a Canadian university administrator whose personal Web page devoted to humor came to the attention of a Hungarian gaming company who hired her to run it full-time. We then thought back to our earlier idea of transforming ourselves into writers.

From our Web surfing experience, we noticed that many people were trying to write summaries and reviews about all the sites that were suddenly popping up. It was fun to view all the awards that were being handed out, but we wanted to know more. Who was the individual behind the site? What was happening to them? Did a site about action-figure collecting really have a large audience or is the award presenter just a fan? Was the Webmaster of a translating dictionary site, a physicist, linguist, restaurant owner, or eighth-grade student in rural Iowa? This was what we wanted to discover.

Therefore, with our computer industry background and our desire to justify all the time we spent cruising the Net, we began researching the sites and creators that we found intriguing to see how we could become writers. Unfortunately, we ran into one big problem—neither of us had home computers capable of surfing the Web. We knew it wasn't feasible to view sites that could potentially change our careers from work, so we took the plunge, bought Pentium II computers, and got personal e-mail addresses. Now we felt like part of the Internet community.

As we attempted to find interesting sites by looking at award sites, links from other Web pages, and online directories, we noticed that the traditional print media was also a good resource. Between articles in magazines, books of Web site listings, and our own online browsing, we realized there would be no shortage of material on which to write a book.

This is when we began to seriously contemplate the possibility of becoming authors. Our rationale as to why we were qualified to write about the Web was that although our experience wasn't in writing, we knew the Net, and not many writers had experience with the Internet. We felt that by describing how others had used the Internet to either transform themselves or bring their interests to a wider audience, we would be able to transform ourselves into full-fledged writers.

We knew we could show how the Internet levels the playing field between companies and individuals and between experts and novices. The best example of this phenomenon is starting a business or site on the Internet, which requires nothing more than a computer and Internet access. If you want to become renown in your field, it's not necessarily about degrees or experience, but about the information you can present to a global community. Individuals actively pursue their interests, dreams, and businesses through the Web. Many people have acquired a new mindset when they look at the Web; they think of how they can transform themselves. By presenting the personal Web site creators' stories in book form, we became writers.

Now we solidified our "Internet idea." We would write the book. But we did not have a finished manuscript or a publisher. Therefore, we tried the standard method of many writers before us and sent out about a dozen query letters to potential publishers. To our pleasant surprise, we received three responses requesting us to send along more information. We were happy that one of the responses was from Information Today, Inc., and signed a contract during the summer of 1998. Where, but on the Internet, can two unpublished writers sign a deal for a book with no manuscript? After we agreed to write the book, we began our search in earnest for the appropriate sites to profile.

Each chapter in this book captures the personalities and stories of men and women who have transformed themselves through the Web. It also chronicles the movement of their sites from personal pages to well-known resources. We have drawn from a broad cross section of the general Internet population, many of whom started their sites several years ago, during the so-called Stone Age of the Web. We selected sites that were primarily run by one person and started with no corporate backing. Each site also had to be updated regularly and had to exist on the Web in some form for over a year. We wanted these site creators to discuss not only why they operate their sites and what they hope to accomplish, but also what unique opportunities their site has opened up for them.

Furthermore, we wanted to develop the book by using the tools of cyberspace. Therefore, all the initial contact was done via e-mail, and many interviews were performed the same way. During the entire writing process, we never met any of the book's participants face-to-face.

In the end, this book also became a how-to guide for building successful Web sites. Although the book is not a step-by-step lesson plan for creating the perfect site, each story does provide insight and new ideas into designing the perfect Internet space. Learning from the experiences of these seasoned creators can help any Webmaster.

These thirty-six sites and their creators come from a variety of fields and demonstrate the vastness of available sites. We categorized several sites together by subject or broad theme to give the chapters some order. These categories include: Getting Advice and Educating Yourself; Visiting, Watching, and Playing Outside the Web World; Collecting Stuff and Other Diversions; and the Written Word and Journalistic Endeavors.

The interesting aspect that we learned about life on the Web concerns the pace of change and definition of a site. While we could say a site about football is definitely sports related, what happens if it also provides a small income for its creator or considers itself a 'zine because it is "published" weekly? We quickly realized that many sites don't fit neatly into one category. There is a lot of overlap in the Web world, particularly as sites develop over time. Is a site still considered a "hobby" site or is it a "business" site because it has paid advertising banners? Is everything a Web magazine even if only one or two sections are updated weekly? Any attempt to neatly package each site into a category becomes more difficult over time.

When we started this book, we wanted readers to see the people behind the sites. Every site creator was asked what he or she did during the time they began their site. Originally, we thought everyone would be a computer person, but that was not even remotely true. We were amazed at the variety of individuals who we got to know through our work on this project. There were doctors, students, homemakers, engineers, and others. All of them were largely self-taught in the ways of the Web, extremely creative, and had a great degree of perseverance. These individuals use the Web as an outlet for their talents and interests. We often heard the stories of individuals who were told that creating a Web site was just a waste of time because no one else cares for the subject matter as much as them. It didn't take long for the reach of the Internet to prove those skeptics wrong. Through writing about these experiences, we came to understand and appreciate the real satisfaction that comes from applying oneself, mastering a new skill, and successfully communicating this with a worldwide audience.

In the process of writing this book, we each took responsibility for meeting eighteen Web citizens and learning about them and their sites. We developed a generic first round set of questions we e-mailed to a site's creator to get an understanding of a site that interested us. When we received the replies, usually within the week, we would determine whether to pursue the profile further based on the answers. We wanted to know how an individual got started using the Internet and why. The questions were specific enough to trace a timeline from before the Web site's creation, through its development, and towards the specific plans for its future. All the while we wanted to know what drove the person to focus him/herself on the site, while never actually knowing if the Internet, much less their site, was ever going to lead anywhere.

The enthusiasm shown for our introductory letter and questionnaire generated from our potential subjects confirmed our belief that we were taking the right approach. Since most commentary and writing simply took the form of additional reviews, top ten lists of the most visited sites, and arcane rankings to evaluate a site's technical features, our approach seemed almost foreign to the sites we contacted. Once they understood what we were trying to do, they became as excited as we were about the book.

Before URLs began appearing on everything from cereal boxes to commercials, the individuals profiled in our book were known mainly to their friends, family, and acquaintances. Who could have known they would become Internet celebrities? If a NASA engineer in Pasadena, a purchasing manager in Florida, or a radio marketing manager in California could have foreseen the changes that would occur in their lives through staking a presence on the Internet, would they have done it sooner or not at all?

Many of the individuals we spoke with expressed surprise at the immediate and large response they received from simply posting information. No one was expecting a significant response and some doubted whether or not posting a Web page would attract anyone's attention. However, without content restrictions or the need for advanced technical skills, many of the individuals in our book developed a loyal following by letting their personalities shine through their Web sites. Many confessed that, while they were intrigued from the beginning by the Internet, all they wanted to do was find a fun way to learn basic Web programming. One person spoke of the unexpected success of her site as being equivalent to "playing Mozart in one piano lesson."

After writing about these Web site creators, it's impossible not to understand the liberation created by the Internet. Everyone wants to be heard, and the Web has become the forum. More people are viewing and being influenced by these sites everyday. Free sharing of information is the force that has drawn millions of first-time Web visitors. This book tells you firsthand how people from all walks of life—most without even having planned it—have transformed themselves into "Net people."

Tom Bleier
Eric Steinert
March 2000

Getting Advice
& Educating Yourself

www.breakupgirl.com

LYNN HARRIS

The Truth about Breaking Up

About the Site

Breakupgirl.com is dedicated to romance advice with a humorous bent. The site includes a weekly advice column and a weekly comic strip featuring the superhero Breakup Girl. There are also discussion boards, essays, links, and an area that allows you to send out electronic postcards.

Lynn Harris never thought that advice-column writing was her calling. In fact, in college she majored in humanities with a focus on medieval history.

I wish I could tell you some dramatic story about what led me to becoming a writer, but there isn't one. Maybe it was because as a kid, I wasn't allowed to watch television and had to amuse myself in other ways. Other than that, I couldn't tell you that it was my calling or anything so dramatic. I just did it. I went to Yale University and graduated in 1990. While at Yale, I did some journalism, but not as a major because they didn't offer it as such. I was involved in campus journalism, mostly writing for the *Yale Daily News* magazine. I also wrote in high school as the features editor for the high school newspaper and acted as co-editor of the literary magazine.

What set everything in motion was an internship I had with *Ladies' Home Journal*, the summer before my senior year of college. I did everything there from fact checking to reporting to writing to loitering in the test kitchen. After I

graduated from Yale, I began freelancing for *Ladies' Home Journal* and, to help pay the bills, I accepted an office job at the Massachusetts Institute of Technology. I did the job part-time and wrote part-time. Eventually, one thing led to another and I started writing for other magazines. Approximately two years later, I quit the office job and went full-time freelance. It was 1992. My professional writing career pretty much all goes back to *Ladies' Home Journal*. I was never on staff, always freelancing.

In 1992, Lynn not only became a full-time writer, but also published her first book, although it wasn't about romance advice.

I wrote my first book in 1992. It was a college cookbook called *Tray Gourmet*. I co-wrote it with my boyfriend at the time, Larry Berger, who thought of the idea with me. It was published by an itsy-bitsy publisher, Lake Isle Press. The illustrator for that book was Chris Kalb, a college friend who is now my roommate. Chris is the person who draws, designs, and codes everything on Breakupgirl. com, so we have been working together for a long time. Finding a company to pick up *Tray Gourmet* was an unusual story. We were looking for a publisher and couldn't find one who was interested in the book.

One day my co-author's mom was walking in her neighborhood and ran into a neighbor who asked what her son was doing. My co-author's mom said he has a cookbook he's trying to sell. Her neighbor replied that her daughter is looking for cookbooks at her new publishing company. So, that's how we got that deal.

The book is still in print, which is cute. You can get it on Amazon.com, but I have no idea how many copies have sold. My best guess is a few thousand, and it's still selling. I just did a bit about it on the Food Network the other day.

Tray Gourmet didn't bring Lynn fame and fortune, but it did provide her with motivation to write another book.

I got the idea for my second book, *He Loved Me, He Loves Me Not: A Guide to Fudge, Fury, Free Time and Life Beyond the Breakup*, back when I lived in Boston. I had broken up with someone and I was miserable. I started making up games to play with my roommate. I remember sitting on my stoop in Somerville, Massachusetts, and I said, "Juliet, I bet you can say any word in the English language and I will tell you how it reminds me of Mike." She said, "burlap," and I could totally do it. Basically, I cried until I laughed. Meanwhile, I'm thinking there is something funny here. There is humor in heartbreak, and there's a book idea here. Unlike my first book, getting this book published was no great story. I already had an agent from *Tray Gourmet,* so I sent it out and waited for responses.

It was now the summer of 1995. I had moved to New York City the previous year because I wanted to be in the mecca of publishing and performing. As I was writing the book, I realized I needed something else to really pull the book together. I didn't know what to do. Chris Kalb, who was the illustrator for this new book also, has a love for comics, cartoons, and superheroes, as well as storytelling. He developed the idea of having a superhero, Breakup Girl, as the narrator of the book. That was the birth of Breakup Girl.

Even after the book was published, Breakupgirl.com was still a little ways down the road.

Once the book had been published for a while, we knew there was more to Breakup Girl than just the book. People had really responded to the book and, in particular, to the character Breakup Girl. The problem with big publishing companies is that once you're not on the list of books they are pushing anymore, they don't do anything for you. So we thought, well we are off the list, but the book is still out there. We

www.
breakupgirl.com

thought: What's currently being done is not good enough because Breakup Girl is more than just two-dimensional, so why don't we do a Web site?

We saw Breakup Girl as a character, and the whole concept was to create a place for everybody to laugh and cry. This concept matched perfectly for the Web. We wanted Breakup Girl to be interactive, to do an advice column, and to have ongoing adventures in comic strip form. The stuff we wanted to do with her was stuff you could only do on the Web. It is the particulars of the Web that make Breakup Girl so dynamic. An example is in our advice column where the site refers back to itself all the time. I make a reference to something that's in one of the comics and I link the advice to that comic strip. It is this technology of hyperlinks that literally helps build this concept. You can't do that with a TV show and you certainly can't do it with a book. It's one thing that is particular to the Web that has given Breakup Girl the life that she has.

In November of 1997, Breakupgirl.com was launched, and the amount of work to keep it updated has never slowed down.

People ask me all the time how much time I spend on my site, and I still don't know how to quantify it. Some days I spend fourteen hours in a row and then spend only sporadic hours for a while after that. It totally fluctuates. All I can say is that it accumulates to be a lot. First of all, all day Sunday I spend on the weekly column. Sunday is just for writing because all week I have to do triage. I also get anywhere from ten to fifty letters a day, and I have to manage them, print them out, and deal with them; otherwise my computer will explode. Correspondence takes time. Some letters may require follow-up, like someone wanting to let me know about a new Web site about dating violence and asking if I can link to it. I do get help from Chris and Paul the Intern, who is a real person by the way. You can see Paul in the comics on the site. The problem is that with 50,000 visitors a month the correspondence can be overwhelming.

However, it is this interactivity with the people of all ages who read Breakup Girl that I enjoy. The emails I receive are so interesting. Two of my more memorable emails include "Dear Breakup Girl: My boyfriend broke-up with me, but he won't move out. How can I start dating when he is on the couch?" If we had made up this story it would be kind of funny, but when it's real life, it's hilarious. That's one of my favorites, it's the perfect example. Another example is "Dear Breakup Girl: I'm 55. How do I start dating?"

Besides correspondence and writing the weekly column, Chris and I are basically at all times in the midst of a comic, whether he is drawing it or we are writing the scripts and figuring out what the next one is going to be. Chris mostly writes the scripts word-for-word, but we make up the plot points together. So we are always in the process of doing that. We also don't outsource anything. Chris does the majority of the Web site work. I have no computer background, at least no formal training. We are room-mates and both work from home, spending countless hours on the site. We've got press kits, I do interviews, and I do TV stuff. I work on some aspect of Breakupgirl.com pretty much full-time, but the funny thing is that I don't make my salary from it.

Breakupgirl.com has increased book sales, brought writing assignments, comedy jobs, and even a TV deal for Lynn Harris.

That's not to say Breakupgirl.com hasn't helped me make more money on my other writing assignments. I just don't think of it as distinct. I think it's just money. I do get magazine work because of Breakup Girl and I still do the magazines and freelance writing to make a living, but it's now mostly romance stuff with the Breakup Girl voice. I sometimes even get overpaid for that stuff, so it makes up for the time I put in for free at the Web site. Currently, I have a regular piece in the women's section of the New York *Daily News* every Thursday. It's not an official column. If it were, then they would own it, and we couldn't have that. In effect, I have a column but don't have to write every week. I just do.

There also is no question that the Web site has helped book sales. Since the launch of breakupgirl.com, *He Loved Me, He Loves Me Not: A Guide to Fudge, Fury, Free Time and Life Beyond the Breakup* has become a bestseller in its genre on Amazon. com. In fact, at one time it was around the 1,000th most popular book sold on their site. Breakupgirl. com has also led to a second book deal based on Breakup Girl. Little Brown will publish it in the spring of 2000. Right now the working title is *Breakup Girl to the Rescue*, but that title isn't finalized.

We also got a TV deal based on Breakup Girl. One of the people who work for Panamort television, who used to do Letterman, saw me perform and liked my act. I do an act in comedy clubs based on Breakup Girl. I hate to call it an act, because that sounds wrong. It makes it sound like a fixed script, but in any case, I do a thing where I talk about the letters I get. After the Panamort executive saw me and liked the act, she suddenly realized that the act is based on the Web site to which her sister is addicted. So, she put two and two together, reviewed the Web site, and realized that this was something that they were interested in producing. That's the story.

www.
breakupgirl.com

Freeing Breakup Girl from books and cyberspace by making her part of her standup comedy routine was not always Lynn's plan, but it's now something she doesn't want to change.

Again, no dramatic story as to why I wanted to do standup comedy, other than perhaps I'm an only child. However, I always wanted to be some sort of humorist, and now that I have been a writer for so long it's easier to have a great deal of leeway in writing in my own voice. I can write humorously, even if it's about a more serious topic. When you first start writing you can't use humor. You write what they tell you, and for me that included writing for a sewing newsletter. I really felt that with standup comedy I wanted to explore a different means of getting at the humorous voice. I have done a lot of acting. I just really wasn't interested in becoming an actor, as much as I loved it. I was sort of a drama jock in high school. I always wanted to be some kind of performer, and comedy really is 75 percent about the writing; people tend to forget that. They think they can make funny faces or smash watermelons, but standup comedy is a blend of writing and performing.

When I started doing standup about five years ago, I was doing regular standup. Now I have really squished together the two things I love, performing and working on Breakup Girl. Recently, I've started a monthly variety show at the Gotham Comedy Club here in New York called "Breakup Girl Live." The backbone of the show is that I go up on stage with a bunch of letters that I've received and dish about them, but not on a personal level. I don't insult the people. It just goes over so well because everyone can relate to everything. When people laugh, it's the laugh of recognition.

There is no way that all of this would be possible without the Web site. I wouldn't have the letters, and they are what I've been using on stage. I still work at the same clubs, and I still work the same lineups as before, but it's very different from my regular standup. What I do now is much better.

Lynn has given some serious thought to what the Internet has meant to her.

I wouldn't have Breakup Girl without the Internet. The Internet allows you to create this vibrant, consistent, and multi-dimensional world that you can't otherwise create. Let's say Breakup Girl got her own advice column in a newspaper instead of a Web site—big deal. She could write it, and it would have a different flavor than the other advice columns that exist, but she couldn't be interactive. She couldn't do the thing where you answer one person's question and link the response back to another question that is relevant or link to something that we took on in the comic adventures. Without all the explicit technology of the Internet, the hyperlinks and interactivity, we couldn't create the consistent world that people understand is possible only with the Internet. This ability to communicate back and forth—not necessarily in personal discussions, but to communicate at least in an indirect manner back and forth with people who read you—is exciting. You can't really do that on TV or in another medium.

In terms of dispensing advice about relationships, I think it is easier to do what we set out to do and succeeded to do, which is to create a conversation about relationships that is not gender specific, because the Internet is not. I know that there are statistics about the demographics of the people who use the Internet, but basically the Internet is accessible to everybody. It gives you the opportunity to take this co-ed audience, tap into it, set yourself up as a co-ed site, and have people feel comfortable there and understand that the site is for everybody. I think that is a unique feature of the Internet. I think it is the unique element of Breakup Girl. I don't think we could quite have done that with a newspaper column.

Lynn's future is not just more books, TV deals, and comedy routines. She wants to keep enhancing the site that has made all this possible.

We would love to add so many things, but we just don't have that much time. We do want to keep doing exactly what we are doing, but we would like to add features. It would be nice to interview different celebrities every month, do more live chats—and I don't mean like a chat room necessarily because that is well handled elsewhere, but a chat with some sort of celebrity or expert where you can ask a question before or during the discussion. Enhancing the interactivity is a goal. In an ideal world, we would update the site daily. Weekly is not bad, frankly. We are pretty proud we do it weekly, but I mean if we did it exclusively full-time, there would be no end. We just sit and dream of all the things we could do, if we had the time.

I look back and cannot believe how fortunate I am. I just can't believe how much I love my job. Gosh how did I do this? I mean, I really love it. It's so cool.

CHAPTER 2

Welcome to
CareGuide.com
your personal caregiving resource

www.careguide.com

OLIVER MITTERMAIER

The Finder of Caregiving

About the Site

Careguide.com, also known as careguide.net, consists of two areas. One area is devoted to childcare providers and one area is for eldercare providers. Each section allows you to search by state, county, and city to find the appropriate care provider. You can also submit your information and get free referrals if you do not want to search for yourself. Other information the site provides includes a monthly column, general resources, and guides for picking a provider, plus a message center that allows viewers to read about other peoples' experiences.

I'm always asked if I have any children. I do not. I also don't have any parents that are in need of third-party providers.

Why Oliver Mittermaier is asked about children and parents is not because people want to know about his private life, but because of the career he built for himself. As the co-founder of careguide.com, he built a site to help people find childcare and eldercare providers for their family members.

Many people that I know came to the Web business from the outside. In other words, they were not initially involved in technology, software, or the Internet, but sort of discovered a need for something and then looked at the Internet and the opportunities presented there and decided to give it a shot and create something new. I imagine that this is probably something you'll find a lot.

Oliver discovered the need when he was helping a colleague at work.

About three years ago, at the age of twenty-five, I was working for a company that specialized in energy and environmental projects in developing countries. My college degrees are in energy and environmental consulting, so it was a natural fit. It is a big company with a lot of employees and, obviously, a lot of parents. A friend of mine there had a three-year-old son and was searching for daycare for him. She was the corporate librarian, so of anybody in the company, you would think she would know where to access this type of information. We talked about her finding daycare, and she seemed incredibly frustrated and anxious about this whole process. At that point, I suggested she take a look at the Web. Surely there is something out there, I told her. If you go to Yahoo! and type in daycare San Francisco, you will probably come up with something, and it might be a place to start. Sure enough, we did this together and absolutely nothing showed up. I proceeded to help her by going to a local bookstore to see if there was some kind of local guide to daycare, since it seemed to be a pretty common need. Again, I found nothing.

Meanwhile, another friend and I had both been interested in at least doing something along the lines of creating Web sites. We spent a lot of hours talking about this daycare problem and how it would be great if we could use the Internet to solve this dilemma. We began to collect some information by going to the state licensing boards, making a few calls, and looking in the yellow pages. This was the information we used for creating a little database locally for the bay area. We then learned the basics of how to set up a Web site, and we built the site.

In less than a year, Oliver and his Web site partner, Michael Goldberg, built a site so popular that they had to decide if they were going to do careguide.com full-time.

Before we knew it, we were getting traffic. We got our first hit report. We were getting between fifteen and twenty thousand hits for the first or second month that we were up and running. We looked at that and thought, wow! At that time (in 1996), that was a lot of traffic.

www.careguide.com

We also started getting a lot of e-mails from parents on the East Coast—we were just listing West Coast childcare providers—asking for information on daycare in their area. So we started expanding the site, and the traffic kept growing. The site was up a good nine months, and my partner and I had pretty much come to a crossroads. My partner, Michael Goldberg, was working in the gourmet food industry and I was doing my consulting and travelling a lot, so we both had to decide if we were going to continue to do this. If we were, it had to be done full-time, because it was becoming very time consuming. At this time, I also was getting ready to consider whether or not to take an assignment that would station me in Egypt for a couple of years. This also forced me to deal with the situation.

So we did a little research and, with the bit money that we both saved, decided to jump into it full-time. We wanted to see if we could develop this revenue model of providing free listings, but with the addition of going to the individual providers and offering them enhancements for a certain amount of money. At that point, I think we were charging five or six dollars a month, something outrageously low like that. On the childcare side, we now charge twenty dollars a month. Our whole operation has changed considerably from the time when it was the two of us working out of my old apartment, just moving along as a very lean little operation.

As a small operation, Oliver and Michael had to learn business management and technology as they proceeded.

Basically, I think we were pretty good at dividing and conquering. My partner has a lot of small business experience, and I had worked for large companies. He took over a lot of the financial issues, such as accounting and things like that. My background lent itself a little more easily towards computers and software, which became more my responsibility. Actually, at the time I started the site I did not know HTML. It wasn't like I had ever taken a class, but the turning point in my understanding of page building was really when somebody explained to me that you could actually view the source of any page through your browser. That was the greatest teacher right there. Unfortunately, it is a little harder today because it no longer is just straight HTML, but back then it was pretty easy to at least create the interface.

The database portion was always something that we knew we would have to take out of house; therefore, we hired some programmers to design the back end and the search functionality. I feel the site is pretty neat from a technological standpoint. It's a dynamic site. Every time we bring on a new subscriber, we don't actually have to be creating HTML page, it is all generated dynamically and that was done right from the start.

Now that things were moving along, Oliver and Michael wanted to become an even bigger presence on the Web.

Suddenly, we found ourselves doing careguide.com full-time and spending a lot of time on the phone and meeting with people. It worked out really well, at least for the first year and a half before we realized that if we really wanted to take this to the next level we had to do something different. At the time, the biggest constraint was just manpower. We launched into the eldercare product, in addition to the childcare database, and the core of the company was still just the two of us. Granted, we had some temp help that came in on certain days, and most of the technical stuff was getting done out-of-house, but it was still just a completely overwhelming prospect for the two of us to lead this alone, especially with the way the Internet was growing. If you look back, four years ago the name Yahoo! wasn't very commonplace, whereas now it's everywhere.

Therefore, we decided to approach investors to grow. It is one of those situations where the investor community is a very tight community. It is difficult to get them to listen, if you are real outsiders like us. We had no previous experience in doing this kind of thing, so it was really a function of working that network of family and friends and talking to people, asking if they knew anybody who might be interested in investing in this idea. This task was made a lot easier because we already had a proven concept, granted on a much smaller scale, but the model was already there. It was just a function of let's add more resources and scale the whole thing up so we can truly call ourselves a national resource.

Our grassroots approach of proving to ourselves that we can actually build the site from the ground up, rather than coming up with the concept and then finding a group of investors or an institution to buy into it, obviously made a lot of sense to the investors. They realized it was just a function of getting some more bright people on board who can buy into this concept. We were successful and got investment capital in the beginning of 1998. This allowed us to add employees, who now total fifteen including us, and to increase our advertising.

Careguide.com began adding eldercare listings before they received investment capital, but with the infusion of money they could successfully grow this part of the site as well as the childcare piece.

The idea of expanding into eldercare was developed because a lot of the licensing boards that provide information on the public government level for childcare providers also license eldercare providers. We also found that referral agencies do both. Furthermore, benefits managers of human resource departments at big companies say childcare and eldercare are the two big issues that confront their employees. It made a lot of sense for us to grow in that direction. Although, at the time, I had as little understanding as most people do about the differences

www.
careguide.com

between assisted living and home healthcare or what exactly hospice care is and other eldercare issues.

What helped most about allowing the eldercare piece to seamlessly integrate with the childcare part of our site was that the decision-making process of a parent looking for daycare is very similar to that of an adult child looking for a provider for his/her parent. The only difference is that on the eldercare side, it is even more complicated, because you have the whole financial component and the health and medical issues. Most importantly, where we really saw the advantage of the Internet in this situation was that many people live in a different city, if not a different state, than their parents, so the task can be more daunting. The classic example of suddenly being confronted with the issue of having to find some kind of provider, whether it is a home healthcare provider or nursing home, and where and how to start can be very intimidating. The biggest scare for us, of course, was whether we were ready to bite off that next chunk, which has definitely been a challenge.

Since Oliver started careguide.com three years ago, his responsibilities have changed.

My daily work has definitely changed in a really big way. I feel my Internet career is probably the classic story of what happens to, for the lack of a better term, entrepreneurs, or people who come up with an idea. You get it off the ground and then suddenly realize that in order to make things work you need more people—and with more personnel, more hardware, and such comes some sort of structural change. I giggle about it because looking back only three years ago, I didn't imagine that we would actually be running a corporation. I guess it is the American dream to a certain extent.

It's been incredible. It has been a really exciting ride, but it also has been a hell of a learning process. I didn't go to business school, although I took business classes in college. I had the basics in accounting and finance and things like that, but it's not like I'd ever really studied what I'm doing. Michael and I have gotten through everything by using common sense, and it's working.

It's really phenomenal to think that I'm twenty-eight years old and doing this. In my former job in the consulting world, generally you hire somebody because they have a lot of experience and you're interested in their ability to advise you on how to find a solution to certain problems. As a young person in that world, you're always at a disadvantage, although you might have a lot to contribute. It's seniority that rules. In the Internet world, one of the most satisfying aspects is that young people such as myself can really grow quickly into an expert. Now, when I go to certain associations with whom we have partnered, I'm actually giving presentations on Internet marketing to people who are a good fifteen to twenty years ahead of me with respect to basic business experience and general marketing experience. However, when it comes to the Web, they are so far behind that there is so much that I can show them. It is great to be able, at a relatively young age, to be the kind of person that can actually show other people how the Internet business works.

careguide
www.careguide.net

Home | Child Care Directory | Resource Center | Parents Speak Up! | Bookstore

Search choices: <u>State:</u> Massachusetts <u>County:</u> Suffolk <u>City:</u> Boston

How old is your child?

Infant	Toddler	School Age
• <u>Less than 2 Years</u>	• <u>2 Years</u>	• <u>5 Years</u>
	• <u>3 Years</u>	• <u>6 Years</u>
	• <u>4 Years</u>	• <u>7 Years</u>
		• <u>8 Years</u>
		• <u>9 Years</u>
		• <u>10 Years</u>
		• <u>11 Years</u>
		• <u>12 Years</u>

QUICK SEARCH TOOLS

HOME   STATE   CITY

Home | Child Care Directory | Resource Center | Parents Speak Up! | Bookstore

Tell Your Provider You Found Them On CareGuide!

 Interested In Being Included in CareGuide? <u>Click here</u>

 <u>Click here</u> for free child care referrals

 E-mail us at <u>care@careguide.net</u> or call 415-474-1278.

 Help Us Serve You Better by <u>filling out our on-line survey</u>

Facilities listed by CareGuide are listings only - **not recommendations**. All information about the facilities has been obtained either from the facilities themselves or public/private available sources. CareGuide does not guarantee the information about these facilities nor do we license, endorse, or recommend any of these providers.

www.
careguide.com

Oliver has always appreciated the responses of his viewers.

We get thousands of e-mails per week and a little under four million hits per month, which translates into, I believe, 700,000 page views a month. Granted, that's discounting graphics and all such elements. On a daily basis, I know we process hundreds of referrals. I was recently on vacation, which confirmed that I cannot go on vacation without my laptop because I know upon my return I literally would have 1,000 e-mails in my mailbox after being gone for only one week.

A really satisfying thing about being in this particular niche on the Web, versus having a database of car dealerships or fast food restaurants or something that I'm sure would be really interesting and popular for a lot of people, is that we definitely interact with a group of people on a very personal level. We collect a tremendous amount of information about people's health concerns, incomes, and backgrounds. When it comes to child and eldercare, people are so desperate for help that they are willing to basically say, here's who I am and I really need help. I enjoy being able to participate in this part of their lives. It is fulfilling to know that either through surveys or e-mails, our site is helping. It is not unusual for people who find something successfully through our site to e-mail us and say, "Thanks a lot. You can't imagine how much easier you made my life. I was so panicked about what to do and I managed to figure it out from the information that you provided."

Careguide.com's audience has grown with the Web, and Oliver feels their head start is something other companies or individuals will not be able to replicate.

Most of our audience growth has occurred over this last year. In large part, it is directly associated with the amount of money we can spend online. The Web has changed drastically. I think that if we were to take the approach that we took three years ago to try to start this kind of business now, we wouldn't be able to do it. We were very fortunate that we had this idea relatively early in the Web's life. Just by putting in a lot of time and having a vision, we were able to set the foundation for something that, with a little more capital, was able to really take off.

More and more sites are springing up that are trying to imitate us, either on a regional or local basis, but it takes a lot to promote yourself, and that's our advantage. We spend significant amounts of money every month advertising the site with the big search engines. Nowadays, you must have relatively deep pockets to be able to sustain your exposure and be able to go to the search engines and make those key word buys so that when somebody types in Senior Care Nursing Home or something close to that, people can find you. It has definitely worked for us. That is really what pushed our recognition to this level, because if you go to most of the major search engines, if we are doing our marketing correctly, you should be able to find us relatively easily when you punch in those key-words.

We are also establishing an identity by working together with other partners by re-branding or private labeling our site for their users, because we know that ultimately what we are doing is using the Web as a vehicle to connect consumers with these other providers. In order to do that you need to focus on your distribution, which is the name of the game. Examples of this are Web sites like thirdage.com or women.com, where what we have done is repackaged our content and made it available to their users. Therefore, if you go on women.com you'll have access to a senior care guide. Once you get into it, you'll realize we are serving it up. The idea there is you need to be able to get your information in front of consumers. Our site is like any other kind of publication or any other medium where what you are really bringing users is information about specific providers or bringing providers qualified leads that might be potential customers.

Promotional spending has increased this year at careguide.com, as has traffic, but Oliver is keeping his feet firmly planted in promoting his Web site exclusively through the Internet.

The big money and the big players are crazy about the success of a company like Yahoo!, but advertising our brand outside the Internet is just not cost-effective. Even though, through investment, we have more money to spend on promotion and marketing, off-line advertising, such as placing an ad in *Working Woman* magazine or something like that, doesn't make sense. I'm sure that is going to change sometime down the road. Right now, there are some really good arguments that we don't need to advertise in those arenas. An example is if we were to spend money on TV ads, our ability to target that audience is relatively slim; plus, you now have to rely on that user to remember careguide.com and remember the URL when they are sitting in front of their computer the next morning at work. Currently, there are a lot better ways to drive users to our site, such as targeting the search engines, co-branding, or utilizing other applications in the human resource community.

www.
careguide.com

All in all, Oliver is just happy that they started their Web site first.

The nice thing about the Internet is that it will always remain, just by virtue of the fact that it is pretty much open to anybody to create their own site, an interesting mix of commercialism and individualism. You'll always be able to find sites about whatever interests you might have, but today I don't think we would've been able to do our site the same way that we did originally.

When we started three years ago, finding considerable amounts of capital to really get your site promoted and going wasn't something people even considered. Now, most companies that are looking for commercial success are forced to do this. I know our early entry on the Web played a huge role in our success because we had the opportunity to educate our consumers and the public in our language and show them that we've been doing this for a while and we understand how this works. Today, the Internet is becoming a much more competitive environment, and a head start can only take you so far. It definitely has helped in our ability to make it to where we are today, but no one knows what the future holds.

GARY FOREMAN

Economizing for Life

About the Site

The Dollar Strecher (www.stretcher.com) provides time- and money-saving information via a regular column and newsletter. The site features a library of topics ranging from getting the best deal on a car to designing a household budget. Visitors can access articles online, find out about subscribing, submit questions, and purchase book compilations through the site.

While the Internet delivers around-the-clock shopping capabilities and urges people to spend, spend, spend, it never expected to have Gary Foreman telling readers how to save, save, save. As the consumer advocate of the 1990s, he has quickly become the Ralph Nader of the Internet.

I tend to think the origin of my interest in saving time and money actually goes back to my father. My dad was a Depression-era child born in 1917. His parents had good times through the 1920s on a family farm in Wisconsin. However, they had to struggle to keep it during the 1930s, when my father was a teenager. That memory left an indelible impression on him. Throughout my childhood, Dad believed that one should pay cash for things. You didn't borrow. If you could find a way to delay a purchase for a while, then you did. All of this strongly affected me. My father taught by example—he fixed his own cars, did the home repairs, and lived his life in a simple manner.

I was a certified financial planner during the 1980s and worked in that field until the late '80s. After that, I worked as a purchasing manager for a few years. Today, I write on a full-time basis about how people can save time and money.

Dollar Stretcher is an Internet creation that began as an outgrowth of the weekly column I've been doing for three years. Around 1996, I was doing research on the Internet, as many people were doing around that time. I thought it was only fair to give something back, so I realized the Internet could help distribute my column to a wider group of readers. Before long, I found myself sending copies of whichever column I'd written that week to an expanding group of friends and friends of friends. After a while, my occasional mailings grew into a real list numbering in the hundreds. Then, when that list included a thousand or more individuals, I started collecting articles from other writers as well upon which to build on my general theme of saving time and money. That effort eventually became the Dollar Stretcher newsletter. It's not only a true Internet creation, but also a real life story of the power of people.

I discovered that the Internet is a great place to do research around the issue of saving time and money. You search for information about how to economize, whether it is saving money on electricity, grocery shopping, or getting a good deal on an automobile. In the early days of the newsletter and before the widespread popularity of the site, I had a little more time to spend with newsgroups. Dollar Stretcher is now a full-time occupation that keeps me busy sixty hours or more a week.

I first focused full-time on Dollar Stretcher in July of 1997. I started the Web site in the beginning of 1996, while I was still working as a purchasing manager. Since then, the growth has been quite satisfying. As it is, we're growing at about 250 percent a year.

Gary's background in helping people to make sense of their finances and working with families trying to get the most out of their earnings demonstrated for him the real value of his own advice and its impact on people's lives.

I understood that there is a need for people to save time and money. All you have to do is review the statistics on debt load and bankruptcies, or take a look at how fast we're all living. At the same time, the Internet is a very good way to get into a business with a very low cost of entry. Unlike so many retail operations, I don't need to have a storefront. You can test something on a part-time basis on the Net, without investing huge sums of money or time, and still see how successful it is. So much of business is exploring and experimenting to find out what works and what doesn't. I found that the Web site speeds your usual experimental phase of the business cycle. It makes it so much easier for readers to provide you with feedback, and for your potential customers to let

www.
stretcher.com

you know how you are doing. You have all the needed information to change your approach and focus your message. In the non-Internet world, if you go through a half dozen cycles back and forth during the course of a year, then you're really moving along. With the Internet you can go through the same essential learning curve in about a week's time.

Meanwhile, I had a rough outline of where I wanted to go with my Web site, but no actual business plan to develop it. The dynamics of writing an Internet newsletter change so rapidly that it really doesn't make sense to write down a plan. I know where I want to be six months from now in terms of growth, and that's about my horizon. I'd rather experiment and find what works and just go with it. Fortunately, being a small operation, I'm the only employee of the corporation. I don't have the responsibility of having to respond to lenders, venture capitalists, and that type of thing. I outsource a lot of work to freelancers. All the Dollar Stretcher writers are on the outside contributing on a regular basis.

From my business experience, I know to use strategic partnerships as much as possible as a way to grow the site. Wherever I can, I'll work with other sites that have common interests, such as frozen meals or advice about bulk food shopping. Fortunately, my topic of saving time and money is broad enough that there are a lot of possibilities. There happen to be many different aspects to the various topics of getting the most out of your time and money. I can work with a site that specializes in something like freezer meals, or one that specializes in automobiles, or home mortgages. I can work with them and, in some cases, they can provide content to me. I gain valuable exposure to their marketplace, as well.

The other element that has helped is to write on a regular basis, and use my column to attract visitors. I also try to get my column placed where it makes sense. I syndicate it myself, which saves me from having to split my revenue with a publisher or tailor my writing to suit his/her current requirements.

The focus of our newsletters and the Web site is to help people. Our motto is "living better...for less." What we want to do is give people different concepts and ideas so they can try to apply some of those to their lives and do better with the resources that they already have.

I'm one of those learn-as-you-go guys. My degree is in business management. I know just enough to get by; just enough to know when I need to get some help. Fortunately, I've been blessed with good people to whom I can go for advice. I'm probably working on the whole thing about seventy hours per week. I'm pretty much always working on Dollar Stretcher—whether it is the newsletter, the column, or my site—which easily makes for twelve-hour days. I don't work on Sundays. We're currently growing at about 12 or 13 percent a month. That calculates to about 300,000-350,000 unique addresses per month coming on board.

At this point, we're at a modest profit, but the site is growing so rapidly that I expect the revenue to grow much faster than the expenses. Naturally, we have normal office-type expenses, but the biggest items are related to site hosting services and upkeep of the site. It takes a lot of work to provide a weekly online newsmagazine. And with the technology continually changing, there's always something new that requires expert help.

The weekly column goes out to about thirty different places that currently carry it—Web sites, newsletters, that kind of thing. The online newsletter goes out every Monday. I try to keep it less than 40K. A lot of e-mail readers seem to have problems at that level or with larger size files. Working within that size file allows me to run about three stories per issue. Beyond that, it's just too big. We're presently at 51,000 subscribers. Meanwhile, the Web site will contain everything that's in the newsletter each week, plus some additional material that I couldn't fit in the newsletter. To update the Web site, I'll take those three stories and the reader's tips and develop them into a theme. I'll add additional tips and an additional five to seven stories each week. Then the site is refreshed every Monday.

In terms of meeting our expenses, we have a sponsor for the newsletter. With the Web site we track individual page views, and we can do more than your typical banner. If someone wants to create something with text, something that's a little unique, a bit bigger than a banner, that's fine. Readers don't seem to mind it. It seems like with a simple banner, a lot of readers are blinking over it completely. If they see a picture, or something a little different that doesn't look like a banner, they're more likely to focus on it for the five seconds necessary to actually impress something on their minds whether they want to click through or not. Advertising space is all sold on a per exposure basis. My perception is that some of the late players on the Web, or some of the bigger players, are starting to carve out a niche. Before long, in order to be a genuine Web attraction, you're going to need ten million page views per month. I think the Internet is going to be less a search engine business, and more of a portal business.

Gary tapped into a niche of his own that focuses on accessing information to save time and money.

I receive and respond to between 500-1,000 e-mails per week. We do a lot of reader response items. Each week, we run a section

www.
stretcher.com

called, "Can You Help This Reader?" Also, we highlight two or three topics, such as the best way to find inexpensive paint, how to obtain the best value on ground beef, buying leaner versus fattier ground beef, and such. We then invite people to send us what they know on these topics. It's not uncommon for a "Can You Help This Reader?" question to draw 200 or 300 responses all by itself. A few weeks later, I narrow down all the responses to the best answers and include two or three of these features in the newsletter. Quite often I even create a separate page if there's sufficient information about that one particular topic. Considering this and all the routine business e-mails, reading and responding to the mail could be a full-time job in itself.

When it comes right down to it, I must admit that I relish the interactivity. I happen to be blessed with truly great readers. After all, I recognize that no one person can have all the frugal living ideas in the world. In fact, we had a question a few weeks ago regarding a young woman who had a miscarriage and no medical insurance. This unfortunate situation resulted in four thousand dollars in hospital bills with no financial aid. She was looking for ways to solve this problem. We posted this dilemma in the "Can You Help This Reader?" section.

We got responses from billing clerks, managers of hospital billing departments, people who negotiated for insurance companies with hospitals, even doctors. They provided various options that were available to this woman, including ways that she could work with the hospital or resources that might even pay part of the bill for her. It was amazing just realizing all the different options that this woman had. Where could you get that outside of the Internet? In *The New York Times*, it wouldn't be possible for them to do that level of reader-response service. I welcome the e-mail that I receive from readers. Let there be more!

Plus, you must understand that I've got a soft heart. I hate to see people struggle with their finances. I've had people work for me who were getting dunning phone calls from bill collectors, that type of thing. I know how disruptive that can be to a person's life, to a person's marriage. We get a lot of people saying, "I'm in over my head with credit cards." "How do I get out?" Or "How do I maximize grocery savings?" These issues arise constantly. In general, the topics are very varied. If Dollar Stretcher can help a little bit, it definitely feels good knowing a positive impact can really be made at the grass-roots level.

Another issue that I run across is that people feel like they're living at too fast a pace and they can't keep up with it. I think they feel like the treadmill is going around and is getting increasingly out of control. I can tell from the tone of the e-mail we receive. We've run a series of very popular stories for stay-at-home moms. A lot of the e-mail I get talks about mothers who want to pursue their career. They talk about rushing from daycare to work. Then, they live "fast" at work and rush back to daycare. They talk about their lives rushing by them, and all the while there is no satisfaction. These mothers turn to this series as a way to slow down the pace and bring some satisfaction to their life through timesaving tips.

In the context of Gary's professional background, it would be difficult to design a more appropriate means to help others and directly impact so many individual lives.

If you review my professional background, it's based on trying to get the most for your money. As a financial planner, you're trying to maximize the use of resources, everything from estate planning to budgeting. As a purchasing manager, you're trying to maximize your purchasing power. Honestly, everyone that has known me says that I've been frugal my whole life! I'm not completely sure why, but it comes to me naturally. I've also been writing, although not professionally, since grade school.

It's nice to be able to create something that can help so many and get the help out there through a medium like the Net. Like most people, and I fancy myself as being a little bit creative, you enjoy seeing the final product that you have accomplished. If you're a writer, you like seeing your work in print somewhere; you like to think that people are reading it. It's a joy seeing it out there. I enjoy seeing the traffic increase; I view that as a vote of confidence. I guess the most challenging aspect of writing is knowing which opportunities to attempt next.

There are so many opportunities on the Internet. It's difficult to use your resources and not spread yourself too thin. Where do you spend your effort? Where do you spend your dollars? For instance, take one aspect like marketing. For me, the opportunities are the general print media, co-branding, cross-linking, and using my column. I try to create experiments that are relatively inexpensive in terms of time and money. When I find one that works, I just keep doing it. I don't have the financial resources of some of these enormous sites. If I had a few million dollars to throw in and experiment with, that would be a different business.

I've been really lucky to have some great opportunities made available as a result of the site. In particular, I've been approached by a publisher about writing a book. The publisher would not have known about Dollar Stretcher had it not been for the work of a regular contributor. This contributor started with an

www. stretcher.com

e-mail list featuring a discussion group on freezer meals. Then she was approached to do a book. Her book is called *Frozen Assets*. When her book was being prepared for publication, the publisher invited me to do a blurb for the book cover. The whole thing started with me running one of her recipes about once a month, which was good for her circulation and naturally provided some good information for my readers. One thing led to another. That made the publisher aware of what I was doing on the Web. This resulted in my book, called *The Dollar Stretcher*. It will consist of about twenty-five to thirty-five previous columns concerning a variety of issues.

Gary doesn't just write about saving time and money, he truly lives it. It's a lifestyle that has been passed from generation to generation.

Kids gain so much knowledge from their parents. My own kids are seven and eleven. I can talk to them a whole lot about saving money. However, they learn mostly by example. If they see me fixing a lawn mower to save money, that action speaks louder than any words. This is true for any values in which you believe. If your lifestyle reflects these values through your actions, then your kids will learn them too.

theFreeSite

www.thefreesite.com

MARC MCDONALD

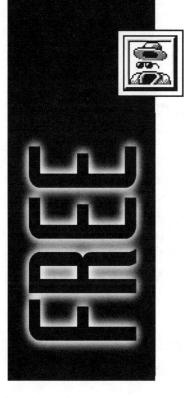

There Is No Better Deal

About the Site

The Free Site (www.thefreesite.com) is divided into more than two dozen categories and provides visitors with free graphic utilities, software, and even manufacturers' samples like toothpaste and shampoo. Those looking to create their own site will find Web space, screen savers, graphics, fonts, and email services, all at no cost.

Marc McDonald works eighty to ninety hours per week, but only gets paid for thirty-two.

I'm a journalist during my day job. I work for the *Fort Worth Star-Telegram* as a copy editor. It's a good career in which I've invested over twelve years. However, today print journalism seems very old-fashioned, and the promise of the Web beckons. It's like a great, new frontier out there. I want to have the Web's definitive site on the topic of freebies: shareware, graphics, e-mail programs, and literally hundreds of other things. To my knowledge, I've succeeded in that my site is the Web's largest and most awarded freebies site.

I work thirty-two hours per week at the newspaper. The balance of my time, I work on the Web. I put in fifty to sixty hours per week on the site. It's really all I do, outside of sleeping and eating. I should take about a month off, just for my health's sake.

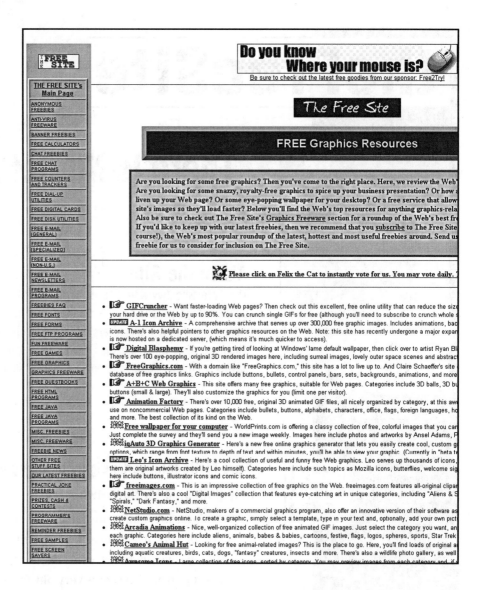

I spent a lot of time online before the World Wide Web. I used to frequent many of the old, defunct bulletin board systems and I had huge long-distance phone bills to show for it. I also spent quite a bit of time on Prodigy. Their message boards were a wonderful way of corresponding and debating the issues of the day, sort of like the way Usenet began. With the advent of the Web site, my involvement with computers increased dramatically. Half of my time was previously spent playing computer games. Now I do nothing but work on my Web site.

Initially, The Free Site was part of a larger Web site that Marc maintained. Dr. Webster's Web Site of the Day was based on the Cool

Site of The Day model which, from early on, proved to be a successful formula. The site, known for its reviews and Web site awards, developed a very loyal following amid a crowded field.

Dr. Webster became one of the Web's most high-profile awards. I knew I was succeeding when Yahoo! Internet Life began featuring my selections; they were kind enough to say: "Courtesy of Dr. Webster." It was after a year of doing Dr. Webster's that I decided to offer my visitors a few extra sections. I had quite a regular audience coming in daily.

In running Dr. Webster's, I was always trying to figure out how to make the sites I recommended more appealing for visitors. Instead of just having a big list of past picks, I thought about categorizing the selections by topic. While I never had the time for doing that, I did notice that many of the site submissions that I was receiving involved freebies of one type or another. So I made up a section of freebies that was basically past award winners. It just took off from there. After a while, I noticed that the freebies section was the most popular part of the site, even more popular than the parent page, Dr. Webster's. I ended up focusing on it exclusively, and it became The Free Site.

I enjoyed working on Dr. Webster, but there just weren't enough hours in the day to devote the necessary time to it and The Free Site, which was building traffic very quickly. Even today I'm not 100 percent sure that Dr. Webster is permanently closed. I stopped doing picks and still haven't decided whether or not to reactivate the site. I received many e-mails from people who missed the selections. I get daily messages to this day from some of the more loyal fans who want to see the site back in action.

Looking back, I should have spent less time on my awards site and more time on The Free Site. The awards site was fun, but the whole cool site of the day genre is really worn out and the site never really took off, traffic-wise, the way The Free Site did.

It was while running the Dr. Webster site that Marc learned key strategies for drawing in viewers and future advertisers.

Since Dr. Webster was my first foray onto the Web, I had to learn while proceeding, regarding traffic. I received very little traffic during the first six months. I spent a huge amount of time plugging the site into every search engine, index, and list of links I could find. However, for the most part, traffic remained stagnant. I found as I went along that I was getting traffic through link backs. I would give a site an award and they'd post it on their page, thus bringing in traffic for me. As time passed and more

www. thefreesite.com

sites received awards, I found my traffic building. An early obstacle to this whole process was the lack of initial recognition. The first few dozen sites I awarded had no idea who Dr. Webster was. It was only after a year, when I was more established, that people recognized the award and were thrilled to get it. Part of what helped my credibility was the fact that I did a full, critical review of each site awarded.

Although I'd be the first to admit I'm no computer genius, I do know how to write. Many sites I see on the Web have terrible writing, even if the site's design is great. Ultimately, people are looking for information on the Web. Therefore, if a site features good, crisp, informative text, that's a real plus.

I'm not really that much of a tech person. I've studied C programming and can do a few basic things, but that's definitely not my strong point. For me, the tool that helped the most was the emergence of sophisticated Web authoring programs. I originally coded Web sites with Windows' simple Notepad text editor. Nowadays, many top programs make the whole process of creating and updating a Web site much less time intensive.

Understanding the underlying logic of The Free Site's success offers a lesson in how to establish Internet brand identity.

I've often wondered why an author would bother creating a great program and release it for free. I think operating The Free Site has given me some insight into this. The Web is still like this vast untamed wilderness. Everyone is racing around trying to stake his/her claim. If you want to establish a name for yourself and build recognition, then releasing a must-have freeware program is a great way to do that. The key is to build an audience first and worry about revenues later. If you have a lot of people using your freeware program, revenues will come sooner or later. For one thing, it gives you a platform for advertising.

My main focus for the first two years was simply to get as much traffic as possible. I didn't even give any thought to making money. I just enjoyed having a site that pulled a lot of traffic. To this day, I get a bigger thrill out of that than I do making money, honestly. Of course, I do also enjoy the many kind notes visitors send me.

Focusing from the start on building traffic resulted in extremely good results for The Free Site as time passed.

I get approximately 40,000 visitors per day on the site's welcome page. Traffic has increased steadily, month by month, since the site's inception. I have yet to experience a month or even a week in which traffic hasn't climbed from the previous month.

Holidays are also good for pulling in extra traffic to The Free Site. I usually have a holiday-freebie-themed page, and this helps pull in new visitors. I had an April-Fools-themed freebies page last year, and it was even featured on Britain's BBC-TV. Needless to say, I saw record traffic of 40,000 visitors in one day while, at that time, I was getting typically about 20,000 visitors daily.

Marc receives between 100 and 150 e-mail messages daily from visitors to the site.

Some e-mails contain suggestions or concerns that a particular offer is invalid. I make sure all the content is very fresh. Of the hundreds of offers I list, I always confirm that there are no scams or offers that don't deliver what they promise. The site is regularly updated by making sure that the dead links are pulled. Even though there are software programs that automate the process of finding dead links, to do a good job, you've really got to do it manually. Also, I always pull any listings that don't deliver what they promise. I get many e-mails from people telling me how much they love the site. In fact, I actually wish more people would write in and tell me what I'm doing wrong or how I could improve things.

I had quite a few scared people write in when I did an April-Fool's-themed freebies page. I had a gag on that section that launched a pop-up JavaScript window that scared people into thinking they'd gotten a virus. The vast majority of visitors, though, enjoyed the joke, based on my feedback.

I really have a pretty general, broad audience. I haven't done any formal surveys, but I've gotten literally thousands of e-mails and notes on my message board and guest books, so I do have an idea of who my audience is. And I've found that audience pretty much covers the spectrum, including all ages, nationalities, and occupations.

The most loyal in my audience are those who're trying to learn how to build their own Web site. They're often delighted that a resource like mine exists to show them how to get all these great free goodies for sprucing up their site.

These folks, current and future Webmasters alike, flock to The Free Site as a direct result of all the Web-related tools Marc

makes available. He has also built an informal network to make additional advice and information available.

There are many Webmasters with whom I share reciprocal links, and we're always swapping Webmaster stories, tips, and suggestions. My circle of online friends and Webmasters probably totals around 100. However, it's friendship in a different sense than your typical friends. On the one hand, I trade many e-mails with these folks at all hours, particularly late at night. I correspond with them more often than I do with my real-life friends. On the other hand, I've never seen these people or heard their voices.

For the past year, a major topic has been the issue of piracy. It's a big problem that haunts and troubles us all. We correspond a great deal on the topic of how to deal with pirates. I'm always being alerted by many of my Webmaster friends about sites that have pirated my content. They know about these pirates because I share reciprocal links with them. Then, the pirate sites come along and copy my contents. Also, many Webmasters who know me notice that, after a listing on The Free Site, they're finding themselves linked on many sites with whom they've never corresponded. They visit these sites and, if they notice pirated content, alert me.

It's one thing to take a little inspiration from another site. But it's quite another to steal text and graphics wholesale from a site. I even discovered one site that called itself The Free Site and stole my design, my graphics, and listings. The only difference was an added pornography section. I even got a few e-mails from my visitors, wondering if this site was my affiliate and asking me why I was associating myself with adult content. The Free Site has a family-oriented audience. It was quite annoying, to say the least.

In addition to the free graphics, screen savers, and software that are always popular with the Webmasters and technically oriented visitors to The Free Site, it's a little ironic to discover which freebie generates the most enthusiasm among Marc's core audience.

The part of my site concerning free product samples, non-computer related manufacturer samples like detergent, draws the most traffic by far. I think The Free Site's product samples section's popularity is tied into the same spirit that causes people to grab anything and everything they can at a convention. I've seen people at conventions stop by every booth and grab every pencil, poster, sticker, and anything else they can. Plus, it's a fact that well-maintained, valid lists of samples are few and far between on the Web. Most lists are badly out of date, as sample listings come and go quickly and you must keep on top of them to make sure they're current.

I get a lot of people who are on a budget. Visitors to the site such as students, retirees, and others love getting samples of toothpaste and other money-saving items. People are fascinated by the idea that they can simply fill out a short form and get something, anything, sent to them in the mail. Everyone loves freebies. People truly love getting samples in the mail, even if it's junk that they won't use.

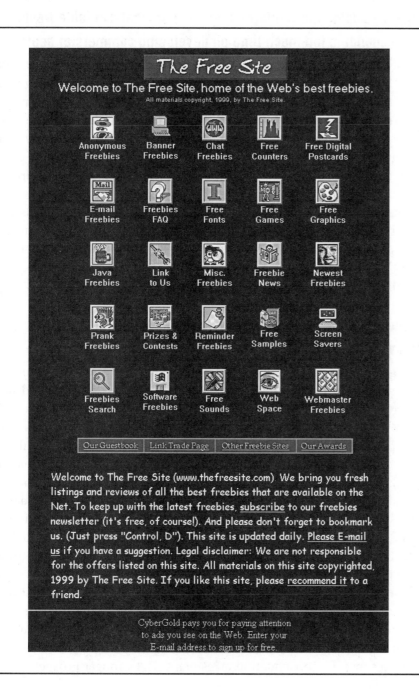

www.
thefreesite.com

While The Free Site never earned a penny during its first two years of operation, the site is today earning revenue from banner ads and ads in the newsletter that is sent out via e-mail to 100,000 subscribers. The newsletter includes updates on free samples, contests, and holiday-themed freebies. Marc intends to concentrate on developing the site further by adding more information on additional available freebies rather than spending too much time on developing commercial deals.

Only about 5 percent of my time goes into exploring revenue deals, and I have many ambitious plans for the site itself. Time is the only thing that limits me on what I've been able to do. At the same time, I don't want the site to come across as this big commercial venture. Mainly, I want The Free Site to remain relevant. I'm not interested, at this point, in partnering or selling the site. I enjoy working on the site too much to not have full control over everything. After three years of hard work on this site, it's starting to pay off well for me. I can only see this increasing.

I see the Web five years from now as being dominated by large, massive corporate sites. As an example, in 1910, there were about 5,000 automakers in the United States. After that, there was a big consolidation resulting in just a few major makers. I don't know if the Web will turn out that way, but I'd suspect there will be a big shakeout eventually.

Meanwhile, the expertise and effort required to build a site has changed over the years.

It's getting more difficult to impress visitors these days. You need more and more technology. And it's difficult to do a technologically sophisticated site and create its content all by yourself. The technology is getting more complex. Web sites should no longer be created, as they once were, with simple text editors. They can be created in this fashion, but odds are they won't draw an audience. I remember when backgrounds first appeared on Web pages. I thought it was really amazing to see a page that had a nice background, instead of the typical boring default gray. Now, I don't even bat an eye if a site offers stuff like real-time video or virtual reality modeling language features.

The whole concept of a one-person site may be obsolete eventually, as technology grows more and more complex. Web surfers are getting more jaded. They're expecting more and more of Web sites. Sites that were top-of-the-line two years ago may not even draw any visitors these days. It's increasingly difficult for one person to build a site and create the content that's required for it to appear on many bookmarks.

Unless I'm mistaken, this is a common pattern in all industries. As industries mature, consolidation takes place. The stronger prosper while the weak disappear. Even corporate America has, for the most part, stumbled on the Web. But they have the backing and the resources to get their way. So, eventually I see perhaps 1,000 major sites emerging as the place where almost all Web traffic goes. There will be smaller, independent sites around, but they'll get few visitors.

Marc McDonald will continue to leverage his writing and Internet expertise to keep The Free Site as one of the single best resource sites on the Web. With a recent feature on CNN, the site is only helping to fuel the growth of personal Web pages, and, one day, maybe even Marc's own Webmaster career.

It is my ultimate goal to be able to run the Web site full-time as my primary job. It would be great to be my own boss. The money would be much better. Plus, I'd have the real possibility of writing what I want, without editorial constraints. The Free Site, with its large audience, could open doors for me to develop other topics. My goal is to survive and prosper in the long term.

www.
thefreesite.com

LOCKERGNOME

CHRIS PIRILLO

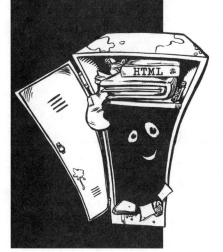

High-Quality E-mail Newsletters * Windows 95/98/NT/2000/Millennium * Subscribe Today for FREE!

www.lockergnome.com

A High-Tech Twist on Life in the Heartland

About the Site

Lockergnome (www.lockergnome.com) is a Windows 95/98/NT newsletter distributed via the Internet. The newsletter, delivered by email, features advice and reviews for anyone wanting to get information about Web resources or instructions on creating a site. The site includes directions for subscribing, technical tips, and weekly digests of past newsletter.

Des Moines, Iowa, may not be the most likely place to manage a daily Windows 95/98/NT newsletter emailed to more than 135,000 subscribers worldwide, but for Chris Pirillo, age twenty-five, it's what Silicorn Valley is all about.

When people meet me they don't always understand what I do. Even if I explain it, they still don't understand. If I said, "Okay, I drive a truck for a living. You can understand that, can't you?" You can understand someone physically driving a truck on the roads, the highways; you know what truckers do. But, when I say that I publish an electronic newsletter, a lot of people are dumbfounded. "Well, how do you send it out? How is this done? How do you make money?" There are lots of questions. I didn't have these answers when I began. I've only had one formal computer class, which was a BASIC programming course in high school; everything else has been self-taught. I've never really read any type of computer book, either. I simply turned

45

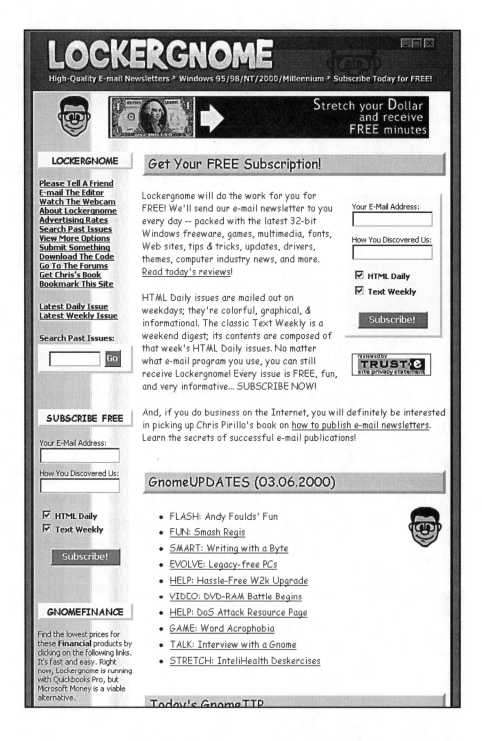

on the computer and played a bit to see what I could do. I'm not a programmer; I'm more of a user.

Before the Internet, I worked with computers as much as humanly possible. There weren't a lot of computer-related resources available at that time. I suppose I started "seriously" working with technology with the Commodore Vic20. I believe I was in the fifth grade at the time.

I went to the University of Northern Iowa (UNI) at Cedar Falls and joined a great fraternity, Tau Kappa Epsilon. I was an English Education major, which really means I'm only qualified to teach people about nouns and verbs. Although I wanted to begin my own business after graduation, I had no idea what that business would be specifically, or how to go about starting it.

However, while wanting to get a business started, Chris, the aspiring entrepreneur, had to consider his greatest blind spot.

I'm not a really good leader in the sense that I can inspire others. I have a tough time relying on someone else to keep the passion behind the business going. From the time I decided to launch an online business, the people who worked with me at UNI were rather annoyed by the fact that they didn't have a lot of input. I really wanted some concepts that would take advantage of the Net and its incredible power to reach an audience, but their ideas just weren't all that innovative or timely.

I found that there was a lot of talking about a lot of things. My friends and I would sit around talking for hours in the Student Union munching on hamburgers and whatnot. Unfortunately, a lot of what we talked about was just that: talk without action. Originally, I wanted to open up a computer lab to the general public. Nobody helped. Plans fell through. Then, I wanted to do online resumes for UNI students. Nobody helped. Plans fell through. So the concept of doing something was there, but as to what it would be, we weren't sure.

I knew that the Internet was a powerful medium but, of course, had no idea how I could harness that power. I started online in 1992, since the UNI had free access. Through playing around with friends, I learned how to do basic Internet things. We were primarily using it to communicate with each other, but therein lies the power.

One night at Teke house, my fraternity, the whole business idea came together for me and just presented itself, almost as an epiphany. I wanted to publish using the Net to reach an ever-expanding audience. After that, I took matters into my own hands and worked on a business plan like my life depended on it. I was making sure things were done exactly as they should be, such as filling in all the details, asking all the questions, doing the leg work, nodding my head, and making decisions.

www.
lockergnome.com

Chris developed a very good understanding of the Internet on his own. He decided to use the technical knowledge he had gradually acquired and his degree in English Education to create an easy-to-read information resource on the Web. The Net would provide a very cost-efficient means of reaching people worldwide so he could afford to experiment with different formats.

There are still many people who don't understand what they can do with computers. That presents a large problem to a certain population that is online at this time. However, I knew exactly what I wanted to do. I wanted to reach first-timers, those people putting together home-based sites, and others looking for useful technical resources on the Web.

Chris decided his high-tech newsletter would have a decidedly low-tech name. A high school teacher used to call Chris gnome because he's short. While not thrilled with midget, munchkin, and other names this writing teacher came up with, the nickname gnome appealed to him. Standing by his locker a few days later, Chris chose to join the two words into one, lockergnome. Years later, the cute name coined in high school would serve as the official title of a fledgling Net startup.

The newsletter was born largely because I could not find a similar type of service anywhere online. I figured that since I couldn't find it, then I might as well make it. The original purpose of Lockergnome was to deliver high-quality information at an affordable price. In the newsletter, I review stuff that is available for the Windows platform. Essentially, that is the contents of a typical Lockergnome issue. Lockergnome features the very best of what is on the Internet, whether it's shareware or freeware. If I review it in Lockergnome, my readers know it's high quality.

I write and publish the newsletter from my apartment—from the time I get up in the morning, pretty much on and off all day. My work is here, and when something needs to get done, it gets done. As far as hours, the first several months required my attention all day, every day. Now, it's probably about five hours a day, seven days a week. It's very difficult for me to escape it. Lockergnome is centered around myself, which is a good and bad thing at the same time. Meanwhile, I'm always being asked why I don't sell the entire thing, and make a quick profit. Lockergnome isn't exactly a traditional business. It would be difficult to simply walk away from it.

I distribute two different formats of the newsletter. An HTML daily edition goes out Monday through Friday. Then, 90 percent of the information from the daily issues is compiled for the text of the weekly issue, which goes out every weekend. In each issue, I usually feature a thirty-two-bit program, a fun download, a font, a desktop theme, a tip or trick, a system update, and computer-techie news. However, I found that trying to locate news lately has been difficult. Much of today's news is all about business, money, and mergers. It's incredibly boring to me. I believe that we as a computer-user population have hit a large lull in the technology news sector. I should add that discussing business-related topics is difficult for me because I have trouble commenting on something in which I'm not the least bit interested.

At this time, I'm not aware of any other service like Locker-gnome's. There are Windows 95 and Windows NT Shareware newsletters; however, they are not read nearly as heavily as Lockergnome because of my unique approach. I take a very personal approach. Like any writer, sometimes I have good days, and sometimes I have bad days. While some readers don't like my occasional obnoxious style, there is a definite group that lets me know they appreciate my straightforward approach.

I use my Web site to provide subscription information, along with samples. Since it's information driven there aren't tons and tons of eye candy. It's designed to show you the information, get you subscribed, and then send you off on your merry way.

In terms of carving out a niche, Chris's folksy approach and easy-to-read format have paid off.

Lockergnome is one of those subscriptions about which people have repeatedly said, "This is the only newsletter I get." Or, "Out of all the newsletters I get, this is the first one I read." Or, "This is the last one I read because I always save the best for last." This isn't my ego speaking; these are my subscribers' words. That's where the power of Lockergnome truly is. Without users, my newsletter has little to no value. It's one of those things that people rely on, pretty much on a daily basis, to help them navigate this strange new world.

Many of my readers have described Lockergnome as something that features the best of the Net, minus all the technical garbage and junk being dumped into email accounts on a daily basis. People get used to seeing the reliable Web tools I show them, so they learn that Chris Pirillo delivers the best of what's available. "I'm going to click on what he sends me." Therefore, when I review a product, program, or Web site, it gets a tremendous amount of click-throughs. Very few independently run sites or newsletters on the

www.
lockergnome.com

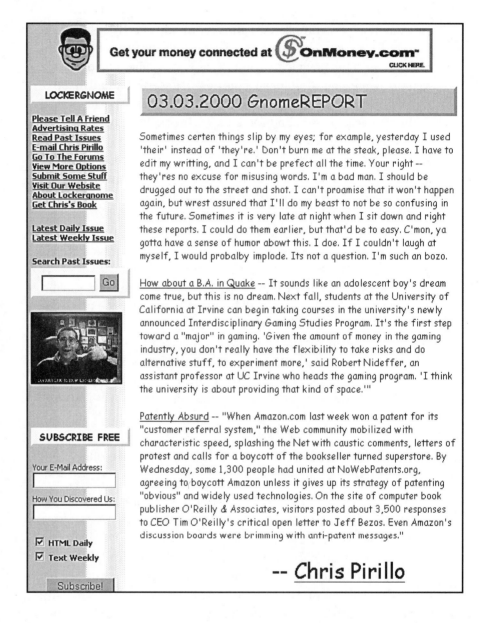

Internet can brag about that. I suppose it's where Lockergnome's reputation really stems from; that's where the magic really is. What people do with what I write or how they act upon the information that they receive are the important concepts for anybody who is trying to do business online. When you've got content online, you want people to get it and follow through with it.

Lockergnome attracts readers from nine years old to ninety years old. Their common bond is wanting to learn, which is nice since that has been my motivating principle all along. Typically, they want to learn more about the Internet, or tips and tricks about their own PC. With my newsletter, they can get the inside scoop on something, my personal recommendation, download the latest gadgets or system updates, fonts, etc. I truly believe that my readers have that common feeling, the curiosity, the will to learn, the desire to learn.

My expertise is not necessarily self-proclaimed, but I've gotten to the point where a lot of people trust what I say, which is simultaneously a good and bad thing. There is a lot of pressure that is placed upon me that wasn't as apparent at the outset of the newsletter. Now that I have 135,000 readers, those stresses are only going to increase. I'm taking it with as much stride as possible. My head can only get so big, I think.

While much of the newsletter's content is technical information or advice, the beginning of each newsletter includes interesting news, something that I happened to do that past week, or something that was just plain odd. Since the HTML newsletter comes out on a daily basis, some people are annoyed with me talking about personal stuff that I do. However, my reviews are very personal; that's my style. I use a liberal dose of humor, as much humor as I can possibly throw in there. Some people are really turned off by that. That's fine. If they don't want to read me, it is their choice. If someone doesn't want to read Lockergnome, I'm not going to lose sleep over it. I don't mean to be rude, but I can't please everyone. I've been down that route, and it's impossible to sustain.

The Northern Iowa Lockergnome charm seems to be having its effect.

My subscribers like to believe that I'm not writing to 135,000 people; they believe that I'm writing only to them since the newsletter is written in an extremely personal manner. Everything that is compiled in Lockergnome has been through my experiences. But for every person who is annoyed by the personal touch, there are a hundred other people who want to have that personal touch. This is probably because most Web sites aren't very personal, especially major shareware Web sites. They pretend to be your friend, but they're not.

www. lockergnome.com

Chris was becoming so good at consistently delivering the personal touch that, about one year into things, he received an email from Tony O'Seland, a Lockergnome subscriber in Oklahoma. The transcription follows:

"I will offer a dollar to go into the operating kitty of your publication. I realize this isn't much, but if the rest of the subscribers will offer a dollar, you will be able to keep up with the technology required to continue to do the fine job you have presented for free. In fact, I'd like to present this as a challenge to the rest of the list! I'll put up the first dollar and challenge everyone else to do the same!"

I thought to myself, "Wow! That would be a lot of dollars." But I didn't call them donations; I called them challenges. Within just a few weeks, hundreds of people actually took the time to write me with personal comments and letters, and even a little bit of money. That was nice, since the subscription itself is free. Hopefully, it will continue to be that way.

What impressed me most was not the money, but that the subscribers took the time to mail something to me. This is a huge leap, especially doing this first on the Internet. This company is 100 percent Internet and you wouldn't expect the Net to create such a response.

To this day, I've received a few thousand handwritten notes from all over the world. It amazes people when they see this enormous box of Lockergnome challenge letters. Based on this amazing experience, non-profit organizations have since asked me how I managed to pull off the whole thing. Well, I provide a good, solid product. I provide something that people like to read and about which people enjoy telling others. In fact, the letters and challenges are still appearing. The biggest single challenge I received was $100.00 from an American character actor.

Currently, advertisements are the only way that Lockergnome is really making money. Right now, with the HTML version of Lockergnome, we have the ability to put graphical and rich media banner ads in there. Presently, I'm earning as much on a monthly basis as I would with a teacher's salary, and the opportunity for more is far greater because I'm turning a profit by keeping my daily business costs low.

I could never sell Lockergnome outright because I would have to go with it. I'm not going to sell myself and I'm not going to sell the mailing list. If someone started to write in place of me in Lockergnome, the dynamic would completely change. They would have a different writing style and different editing abilities. It wouldn't work to the same degree, unless I was at the controlling helm making sure that the good stuff got through and things got written correctly. The, not-yet-patented, Pirillo approach is a key aspect not to be forgotten. That may be part of my controlling nature, but that's the way I am. I can't apologize for that.

Several other email newsletters, whether Windows related or not, have copied some of what I do. When someone submits something to Lockergnome, I'll always give that individual credit. I can't take credit for finding everything that I feature because others have found great sites and downloads. I've learned to be careful to give credit where it is due.

Even after as much demonstrated success as I've had—publishing on the Net, getting married, pursuing my own business—a lot of people still come up to me and say, "How can you do this kind of work? How can you make money?" I'm tired of this line of questioning. First, I'm having fun. Second,

I'm making enough money to survive on a month-to-month basis. Most importantly, I'm not stuck in a dead-end job. I've got a lot of opportunities before me. I have a lot of different ways to do things and continue to grow the site. For as many negatives as there are, there are overwhelming positive things about it.

All right, now that I'm married, I'll admit, I need to get more serious about the making money stuff.

Fielding all the questions and suspicious inquiries, Chris faced the toughest battle of all—convincing his own parents that Lockergnome was going to be a credible professional pursuit.

Interestingly enough, I was not able to convince my dad of an email newsletter's worth, despite how well things were going. About three or four months after starting Lockergnome, I was still trying to explain to my dad all of the particulars of how this is what I want to do and why it is going to work. He still didn't understand, and with worries like: "How can you do anything on the Internet? People aren't making any money, and yada, yada, yada." He's a big Seinfeld fan. He's also a math guy, and a CPA. He just wasn't convinced of its financial viability.

One day, my Dad and I went to Best Buy, a local consumer electronic store. My Dad was looking for a camera. So he went back and looked at cameras while I perused the software aisles, looking for the latest stuff. There was a guy holding onto a package and, out of the nowhere, I just said, "That's a really great software package, very useful." Now, I usually don't walk up to someone and say things like that, but I felt very strongly about the software that he was going to buy, Partition Magic. He said, "Yeah, I've been thinking of getting it, but I'm really not sure," and so on and so forth. So, we talked for around fifteen minutes about how he would use the software, and all the problems he might run into. He was still hesitant and not convinced of how it could be put to use. I said, "Just get it. You won't be disappointed." Following up, I asked, "Are you on the Internet?" He replied that he was. Pulling a business card out of my wallet, I said, "Here, let me give you this. If you have any problems with the software, just email me." He seemed assured. "Oh, Ok, no problem." He looked at the business card, and then he looked up. "Oh, is this you?" I'm thinking to myself, "Would I hand out my dad's business cards?" He said, "Oh, Hell, I've been a subscriber since January!"

At that point, seriously, he completely flipped out! He could not believe he was actually meeting me. He said, "I thought you were some eighty-year-old doctor who knew everything about computers. I can't believe you're as young as you are." He called over his wife and the rest of his family and introduced them to me. He continued to carry on and even asked for my autograph! I was just amazed that he was so thrilled to actually be meeting me and talking to me. And this was only about five months after starting Lockergnome.

I just had to call over my dad. I said, "Dad, you've got to meet this guy. He's a Lockergnome subscriber I just ran into." At that point, I think Dad realized what was happening. He was beginning to understand what I was doing with Lockergnome, how I was communicating with people, and that I was going to eventually make money. I wasn't just sending out a newsletter, but actually connecting with different people on as much a personal level as possible.

I'd like to believe that if such a thing happened with any of my other subscribers, they'd react the same way. People are thrilled to simply get mail from me. They look forward to getting their daily HTML Lockergnome delivered.

The Internet opened up possibilities for Chris that he could have never imagined.

Working on the Web has enabled me to meet "Weird Al" Yankovic, somewhat of a childhood hero of mine. I've been listening to his music since the seventh grade. I know it sounds odd, and I have other musical interests, but Weird Al and I have a similar sense of humor. I even created a fan Web page for him. When I realized that the band's drummer, Jon "Bermuda" Schwartz, was online, I emailed him. He wrote back saying that he would tell Al about the site I created. I was amazed and overcome with the idea that this could really happen. About a year later, they were touring through Iowa, and I emailed Jon and asked him if I might be able to get backstage passes. He replied that he would get me free tickets and a couple of backstage passes. So, that summer, I got to meet Weird Al.

A lot of things have happened with Lockergnome since it began in August 1996. I don't know if I'd want to do anything differently; it's been a very good few years. The positives outweigh the negatives as I continue to develop the site. I like to think that I'll let people judge for themselves. That's the way things are done in Silicorn Valley.

CHAPTER 6

Horse Country

www.horse-country.com

KRIS CARROLL

N E
W S
Cyberbarns

Jr Riders
Journal

Life's Lessons from the Saddle

www.horse-country.com

About the Site

Horse-Country (www.horse-country.com) offers a wealth of equine information to riders and enthusiasts. This site features information on safety, veterinary tips, horse welfare, and rescue updates. It also helps younger riders develop a better appreciation of science and biology.

It is not uncommon for young girls to become very interested in and caught up in the world of horses. The majesty and beauty of the animals captures their attention. For Kris Carroll, age fifty-one, sharing the wonders of the equestrian world with children of all ages has become a way of life.

My mother dropped me off at the barn when I was kid and picked me up in time to take me to college. Actually, I was dragged to college against my will. With a couple of tries, I managed to earn a Bachelor of Fine Arts in photography. However, it was due to my upbringing around horses, and the time I spent grooming, feeding, and caring for them, that now helps to define how I interact with the world around me. Ever since I was a child, I have seen horses as gentle and thoughtful creatures. Riding has provided me

Gymkhana, Pony Rides
Activity Pages

Horse Country: Gymkhana Quizzes

To play match correct number from the graphic with the names of the points of the horse, then click 'Am I right?' If the answer is correct, it will be stored until you are finished and ready to email. If the answer is incorrect, you can try again. When you have all the correct answers, (always check your answer even if you know it's right) finish the form at the bottom of the page and submit them to be posted in the Blue Ribbon Winners Circle. Good luck!

Java Script
This page requires a JavaScript enabled browser and some knowledge of horses.

Novice Points of the Horse

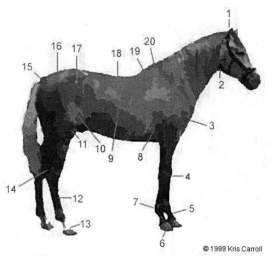

© 1999 Kris Carroll

(help tip: open a second browser to view while completing the quiz
or download, then print this graphic to organize your answers)

back [____]
[_____]
[Am I right?]

hock [____]
[_____]
[Am I right?]

barrel [____]
[_____]
[Am I right?]

hoof [____]
[_____]
[Am I right?]

cannon [____]
[_____]
[Am I right?]

knee [____]
[_____]
[Am I right?]

chest [____]
[_____]
[Am I right?]

pastern [____]
[_____]
[Am I right?]

coronet [____]
[_____]
[Am I right?]

poll [____]
[_____]
[Am I right?]

with a profound understanding of life itself. This has determined who I am, how I set my priorities, and continue to learn.

From 1987 to 1996, I was a graphic designer and illustrator supervisor. I opened the first computer graphics studio at the University of Washington for the department of pathology, School of Medicine, moving much of the research publication work from the darkroom to the computer. I'm completely self-taught and started the studio with a MacSE and Superpaint. The more I learned about the technology around me, the more I explored. I used the time to learn about the Internet, email, newsgroups like rec.equestrian, and the World Wide Web. The Internet was and is an incredible revolution in mass communication. Suddenly, there were no barriers to publication. Through my work, learning all I could about the programs and applications available to me, dreamers and non-geeks like me could experiment.

Before computers were ever around, kids played dream barn games. I recall that in the book National Velvet, the main character, a young girl, had a collection of paper horses cut out of magazines. She dreamt of training, racing, and riding them, as I did as a young girl. After I bought my first horse, late at night when I should have been sleeping, I would sketch out barn designs, and make a long list of names I might call my stable.

Horse Country began in my imagination when I first played the computer simulation game Myst, initially released in September 1993. I knew I wanted to take a similar approach, and design a game intended to introduce kids, both boys and girls, to the world of horses. I decided to sketch on paper a walk-around learning environment for beginners, as well as experienced riders. In April 1994, I began sharing my ideas with family and friends who encouraged me to approach people in the software game world with this concept.

In the early versions of Horse Country, I mapped out an educational component that I later used in prototype Cyberbarn games to encourage players to explore technology, math, and science by way of their virtual involvement in the equestrian field. The Cyberbarn games allowed players to board and virtually care for a horse, then progress to owning barns and equestrian businesses. These kids acquired key lessons of responsibility and organization in a friendly and safe environment on the Net. Whether managing the feeding, coordinating the vaccinations, or gaining insight into the costs of running a working stable, the games helped facilitate the learning of real-life skills.

I maintain Horse Country at a level of technology for kids to learn and develop their interests. As they acquire skills, I add

www. horse-country.com

new features. The pen pal listing began in May 1995. When the list reached critical mass with thirteen kids a short time later, I set up the Junior Riders mail list in July 1995. The next month, I introduced the concept of the Cyberbarn game. Games were limited to forty barns to keep the player-run registries and event schedule manageable. Digest subscriptions were limited to barn and business owners, about seventy kids.

With the site's popularity, my job at the university and Horse Country meant eighteen-hour days. I would go online at 4 AM to deal with pen pals and the kids in Australia. Then I would immediately return online when I arrived home in the evening to deal with game email and digests until midnight. Recently, I moderated my effort a bit. I'm putting in a mere ten hours per day, with no income or weekends off. From March 1995, until I had to close the games section of Horse Country three years later, I was online twenty-four hours a day, and seven days a week for the kids. All right, I confess that I did take a one-week vacation in May of 1997. I put about 200 percent of myself into this site. I regret having to close the Cyberbarn games; however, at that point, I was literally burning myself out and my family along with me.

Kris could never have anticipated how quickly her site would attract visitors from all over the world. Though temporarily an inactive part of Horse Country, the Cyberbarn game component was so popular with visitors to the site that Kris was spending several hours a day managing the progress of all the players.

With the game, each barn owner can have a Web page and learn to write it him/herself, and expand the farm being run to include boarders just like in real life. Barn owners or boarders could run businesses and associations with related Web pages. Real-life research was encouraged; kids were taken seriously and were challenged with disasters. A mail list brought each game community together in one or more daily digests.

Each of the Horse Country Cyberbarn games ran under a name. Horse Owners Club for Kids (HOCK) was established in August 1995. I walked this group of players through set up and the development of a smooth working game, modeled on any real-life regional equestrian community, but with the added feature of the Web to keep them organized and a digest to establish communication.

Riding Equestrians in the Northwest Sun (REINS) was established in June 1996. The game began as an all-western or stock seat game. It never reached full capacity, so it was changed to an all-purpose game, though it always retained a strong western style. It was more relaxed, had a less hectic show schedule, and was a haven for players with heavy school schedules and real-life pressures.

Since it was no longer possible for me to personally mentor every player, I established the mentor-boarder program. Experienced barn owners accepted responsibility to mentor new players who moved into the barn as boarders. This was just like real life. Each barn owner forwarded digests to their boarders, posted for them, taught them the rules, helped them run events and associations, and prepared them for owning their own barns.

I walked the first kids through the basics, from email to tagging standard HTML by hand. Following that learning curve, the players acquired key skills and the ability to work with tables, frames, forms, and chats using the Internet. Many have now sought out the chance to learn how to scan in material to their Web site and are creating their own graphics. The kids have personal Web sites their own clubs, and some even have community pages. Those first kids taught the next wave of players and so on, with me in the background.

All of the game subscribers participated through email posts to the digests and authoring Web pages. Players designed their stables, acquired their horses, hosted events, and opened equestrian businesses or associations just like real life. Horse shows, races, and field events were announced by posting the class lists. A Web page served as a calendar for all announced events. A designated player posted a list of dates in the digest as a reminder. Competitors could email a list of horse/rider entries for each class, race, or event, along with a virtual check to cover show fees. Winners were then selected by random drawing. Prizes were awarded and the results posted in the daily digest notes and on a competition results page. Timely posting of results and learning to host reasonably sized events were part of the learning process. A show or race association secretary was assigned to track the winners for high point awards. Game play could be suspended if a player held up point tally. Each aspect of play, like real-life competition, was subject to rewards and disappointments, taxes, and license fees. The moderator or players assigned reality checks, ranging from a stolen tack trunk, veterinary emergencies, floods, windstorm damage, and staff problems to computer system failure and insurance cancellation. We considered every possible scenario in the game's overall design.

By June of 1998 the Horse Country games I designed and ran included over a thousand active barn owners and boarders. However, with no budget and no programmer, despite enormous interest in further building the games, I

www.
horse-country.com

crashed and closed the Cyberbarn games. It came down to a question of self-preservation. I had run out of hours in the day.

The site also features a very popular newsletter called Junior Riders Journal, which offers young riders advice and serves to answer questions from readers.

Horse Country received a special email message from one family who wrote in about the positive impact the site had on a young friend. They thought the site was very impressive and printed dozens of Gymkhana activity pages from Horse Country for seven-year-old Kelly. Kelly had been adopted for Christmas through a Florida chapter of Big Brothers/Big Sisters. Kelly's favorite "thing" is horses. The family noted their surprise since Kelly never had a ride or a personal experience with horses. Junior Rider Journal subscribers from all over the world joined in the "adoption" to make young Kelly's holiday a horsey dream come true.

Horse Country benefits kids directly. How many eleven-to-fifteen year-olds, on a daily basis, use their understanding of genetics, biology, medicine, soil management, nutrition, and structural mechanics? I don't tell the kids what to think, but I do teach them how to learn and give them good reason to do just that. Meanwhile, the site is also heavily moderated, since I keep a pretty close eye on the kids and their Net manners. Senior kids mentor and moderate also.

There are also adult professionals who occasionally help me and offer advice concerning specific issues. Dr. Jessica Jahiel, who was a member of the United States Pony Club curriculum committee, and Dr. Charlotte Newell, D.V.M. regularly write in Junior Riders Journal. Plus, U.S. Pony Club hunt representative and artist Claudia Coleman offers a Horse Country feature to critique drawings to teach art and a deeper understanding of horse conformation. Additional help with more technical questions is always available via email from horse trainers, breeders, and adult competitors.

Although Kris raised children of her own, Horse Country has, in a sense, allowed her the chance to play a critical role in the lives of children all over again, a role she takes very seriously and cherishes.

I especially enjoy watching the kids acquire skills and grow. Some started as fourteen or fifteen year-olds and are now beginning college, taking computer courses, pursuing pre-vet or equine studies programs. I receive letters and notes from many kids telling me what a great introduction Horse Country was for them to the world of science, biology, and equestrian studies, in general. It is incredibly rewarding just knowing I've helped to open up this whole world for these kids.

Jr Riders JOURNAL

Cyberbarns

Young Riders Group and Bookshop

International Pen Pals

horse-country.com

Gymkhana Activity Pages

JRJ 1999 Calendar Page
I.ride@horse-country.com T-shirts

Gymkhana: Interactive Quizzes
Novice (N) Intermediate (I) and Advanced (A) Challenges

Time to check out Summer Riding Camps

rec.equestrian FAQs

Horse in Art
Associations
Barn Cat Pages
Catalogs Galore
Clothes Horse
Colleges and Camps
Eq Safety
Horse in History
Horse 'n Hound
Groton House Farm
International
PNW Barns
Riders Library
Horse Racing
Horse in Science
Horse in Sport
Tack Shop Talk
Trainers Talk
Vet Rap
Web Resources
Welfare and Rescue

Horse in Art

About Horse Country | Awards | Press | Parents | Kids | Site Stats |
Kid Sponsors | Other Sponsors | Privacy Policy Statement |
Premiered online February 27, 1995. Updated daily

 and

This site is best viewed with Netscape Communicator or Internet Explorer

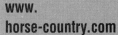

www.
horse-country.com

As a mother, Kris is well aware of the many challenges and pitfalls young people face, so she also tries to do what she can to make sure Horse Country always stays a safe and nurturing environment.

I am worried about the world kids live in, with the high teen suicide rates, guns in schools, and the realities of two working parents. The whole thing, as I continue to learn first-handed, is truly nuts. What I know, and perhaps their parents don't know, is that electronic communication has a steep learning curve. To take advantage of this incredible new resource, kids need Internet manners, respect for the property of others, and strong communication skills. Someone must do this job, and it has ended up being me. Plus, many adults think they protect kids when they discourage them from pursuing so-called unrealistic dreams. Based on my own personal experience, I always counsel them to "go for it" and pursue their dreams. Every attempt has teaching value.

For Kris, Horse Country has permitted her to be mother, counselor, and Internet guide all rolled into one.

I have a twenty-five-year-old daughter who finished college and has worked and lived in Europe most of the last three years. I'm married to a research scientist with a background in molecular biology and genetics who mines the databases for therapeutic proteins. I have a cat who spends her days tormenting two Hungarian pointers. As for riding, my first love is foxhunting, but I've concentrated on dressage for the past five years. I'm paying off some vet bills and catch riding until I can afford a horse of my own again. Most people would think I'm a fool for giving up my own dreams for these kids. I didn't plan to do that; it just happened. I've talked about selling the site. Financial stability is critical when you consider the good you can do for all the new kids coming online.

Although she spends anywhere from twenty to sixty hours a week on the site, Kris has yet to be compensated for her work.

At first, I was overwhelmed with the original version of the site, including running the Cyberbarn games. In making that time commitment, I put my family and myself at occasional financial risk. Today, I do some freelance work to support Horse Country out-of-pocket. Ironically, after a little over three years and a lot of legwork, still no horse industry sponsor or software developer has stepped forward to support these games that I've worked so hard to design. Many software companies talk about games for girls, but they really mean stuff that appeals to parents' and grandparents' wallets. Meanwhile, I am currently working on a Cyberbarn game guide for hardcopy publication using 100 MB of archives taken directly from my experiences with Horse Country.

Horse Country is the longest running equestrian site and the first online site to target girls. Science and technology will play a big part in the careers of the next generation; no one should be left behind. Before I created Horse Country, there was nothing organized in a fashion that encouraged a community to form, especially one with kids from all over the world. Now, kids who like horses, whether their family can afford them or not, will find a home on the Web. I just never expected the site to be as popular as it became. I'm still surprised so many came and stayed for so long.

www.
horse-country.com

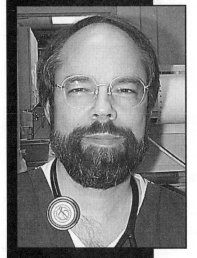

CHAPTER 7

CYBERDOCS
the doctor is always in

www.cyberdocs.com

DR. KERRY ARCHER

The Doctor Who Still Visits

About the Site

CyberDocs.com (www.cyberdocs.com) is a site that allows you to either immediately contact a board-certified emergency physician or schedule an appointment with a doctor who specializes in a particular field. A virtual house call is then arranged, and the interaction between the doctor and patient can occur via either an online chat or audio/video conferencing. If your diagnosis requires medication, Cyberdocs can arrange for delivery of prescription medicines to almost anywhere in the world.

Doctors doing house calls is a thing of the past, but with the advent of the Internet, Dr. Kerry Archer, a forty-seven-year-old emergency room physician at Salem Hospital in Salem, Massachusetts, saw an opportunity to get back in touch with patients.

The concept of CyberDocs was born as the result of many conversations held between Dr. Steven Kohler, an emergency room physician I met at Salem Hospital, and myself, regarding the possibility of establishing a clinical service on the Web. This service would provide online, interactive, consultative medical care for a defined subset of minor medical problems. Our feeling was that there would be a significant number of Web users who, with the prevailing trend toward patient self-empowerment, would find the concept of interacting with a physician without having to travel to an office to be a very useful and convenient adjunct to conventional office-based medicine.

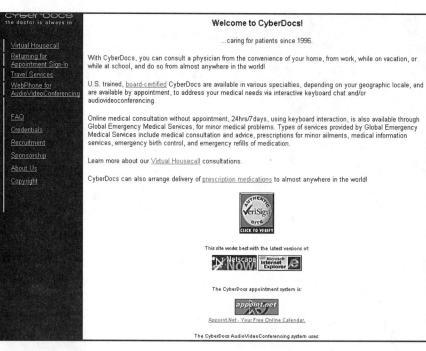

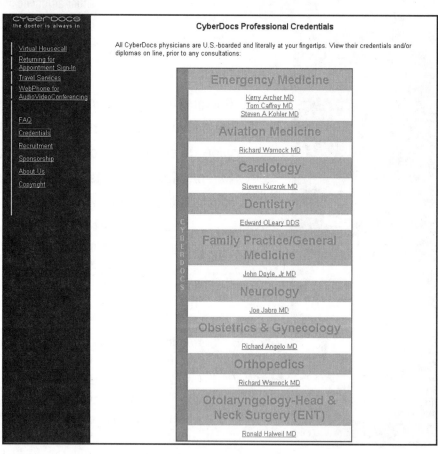

We created CyberDocs as a concept that could help extend a physician's care beyond the physical constraints imposed by distance and time. It was felt from the outset that it would serve as a valuable enhancement to conventional medical care, but was never intended as a substitute for it. In keeping with that philosophy, we have set about building, from the ground up, a workable programming substrate that allows a physician and a patient to communicate in a secure, SSL-encrypted, "live" format that includes keyboard interaction and an option for videoconferencing as well. It was always felt that CyberDocs would be, in many ways, a reflection of traditional fee-for-service medical care, and that patients would value the convenience sufficiently to be willing to pay for such a service.

Dr. Archer is always a doctor first and foremost, but he was not a technological neophyte before he embarked on CyberDocs.com.

I had my first interaction with computers in my junior year in high school. I attended a summer program on the nervous system, sponsored by the National Science Foundation at the Foundation for Research in Boston. As part of that program, we operated a small Wang desktop computer that used punch cards for data entry, but computers never made much of an impression on me until I became involved in the early 1980s with computer bulletin boards and FidoNet. For a short time, I ran my own bulletin board system that dealt with topics of interest to the general PC computing community and tended to be quite technically oriented. I remember being very excited the first time I was involved in an online keyboard chat with one of my early visitors. Subsequently, I became exposed to the Web, at first via Telnet, then via Mosaic and its progeny. With my realization of the vast interconnectedness of it all, came the first thought of "putting my mind out on the Web," and melding aspects of medicine to Web-based connectivity.

In September of 1996, Dr. Archer and Dr. Kohler turned their idea of giving medical advice via the Internet into reality by launching CyberDocs.com. Although many people were skeptical that people would pay for medical advice on the Internet, CyberDocs has been getting patients since the beginning.

We are currently averaging approximately 80,000 hits per month and perform approximately 100 virtual house call consultations per month. To date, only a small percentage of patients

www.
cyberdocs.com

have come to CyberDocs via my emergency practice. Given that emergency medicine doesn't generally provide ongoing care to patients, but rather refers them back to their primary care physicians, it would be expected that the majority of patients would come to us via the Internet. As CyberDocs grows with additional physicians who perform primary care and who have conventional office-based practices, I anticipate that a larger percentage of patients will tend to use CyberDocs as a convenient mode of interaction with their own physicians.

We also receive a lot of e-mails each week. I don't keep count, and although some e-mails are memorable, confidentiality issues preclude discussing any specific e-mail here. I can say that we have received e-mails from a diverse number of countries, including patients in South Africa, New Zealand, Japan, Scandinavia, Korea, Brazil, China, and Australia.

Interestingly, the most common "disease" entity CyberDocs has treated historically has been male pattern hair loss, medically called androgenic alopecia. Finasteride is a treatment we commonly prescribe for this condition, if clinically deemed appropriate by the attending physician, and with certain provisions.

We have noticed that whenever CyberDocs is addressed in a newspaper, magazine, or television show that our hit count increases significantly, perhaps attesting to the surprising impact of conventional, non Web-based media on informing the public about the nature of our services.

From the start, the site has always transformed itself, whether it was changing the physical look or utilizing the newest and most appropriate technology.

The site initially looked quite different than it does today. Originally, it was mainly red, white, and blue with numerous animated GIFs. Various pages also contained classical MIDI music. We received a fair amount of negative e-mail from patients who had limited bandwidth or who didn't enjoy classical music, so when we revamped the site into its present form, we omitted those things.

We have switched our online conference engine from HTML to Java and back to HTML, for various performance reasons. This is an example of the technological changes we have done over time. We recently developed the site in Active Server Pages, transitioned our databases from MS Access to SQL 6.5, and have just implemented audio/video conferencing capability into our appointment-based consultations. Our chief programmer has been Steven Pellegrini, a multiple-skilled Web developer who coordinated the fine efforts of a variety of support personnel at Wing.Net and has been with the project since the beginning.

My responsibilities involving CyberDocs have remained several and become somewhat more diversified as the project has evolved, including assumption of more administrative duties than I might otherwise wish, but my primary commitment continues to center around the clinical development and enhancement of CyberDocs. Although I must admit, the hurdles to developing this site have been numerous.

The translation of the CyberDocs concept into a working site has proved to be a prodigious effort, mostly in terms of having to simultaneously micromanage so many different aspects of the project. Whether it is working with the programmer to code and debug the Web site, setting up the e-commerce aspects, dealing with the media and attempting to explain the uniqueness of the CyberDocs concept, conforming to individual state policies regarding telemedicine, or answering e-mail inquiries, the list never ends. Furthermore, with every iteration of the site, numerous additional issues arise, all of which compete with the scarcest resource of all—time.

I spend an average of twenty to thirty hours weekly on the site, although this can vary. This typically takes the form of providing online medical consultations, with the rest spent on online development issues relating to the Web site.

Developing a medical site can present some unique dilemmas ranging from insurance and regulatory boards to patients attempting to deliberately get inappropriate prescriptions.

As with any new modality in medicine, getting insurance can be tough. Medical insurance companies are naturally cautious about the implementation of Web technology to patient care, and we share that concern. Our liability carrier is quite forward thinking and has expressed its support while enunciating general guidelines for minimizing risks. The regulatory boards have been largely noncommittal in terms of commentary. They are as interested as we are in the provision of high-quality patient care, and our communication with various regulatory boards has simply focused on that general concept.

As far as a patient faking symptoms to possibly get a prescription, ultimately, you never know if they are telling the truth, although after practicing medicine for many years one's discernment of clinical conditions, not to mention human nature, improves. In an office or hospital, a patient might equally well describe symptoms that are not quite factually based. Moreover, in medical coverage situations when patients call

www.
cyberdocs.com

their doctor after hours, another physician who typically doesn't know them well may be providing coverage for the doctor's practice and interact with a patient solely via phone. A patient in such a circumstance might similarly describe nonfactual symptoms to the physician in an effort to obtain certain types of medication. Therefore, the question of a patient's ability to provide nonfactual or misleading information to a physician is always a concern, no matter what the medium of their interaction. In any event, we maintain a list of non-prescribed medications on the site, which makes clear that dissembling would be a waste of time and effort.

The logistics of running a doctor's office that is always open can be taxing, but so far CyberDocs has successfully handled the volume.

There is a dual format for CyberDocs. Patients may either obtain an on-demand consultation without appointment, or they may elect to obtain an appointment-based consultation. Emergency physicians who are always available provide the on-demand consultation. The appointment-based consultations are handled by a variety of other specialists in various medical fields.

For the appointment-based consultations, a patient would generally not have any waiting time, assuming the doctor is on schedule with the preceding online appointments for that day. Given the present volume that CyberDocs is seeing, appointment-based waits are simply not an issue. Time zone differences are handled automatically by the appointment software the physicians and patients use, so a satisfactory appointment time can virtually always be found. There have been a few times in the past when our patient volume for on-demand, non-appointment-based consultations has required a short waiting interval between consultations, but this is unusual. Moreover, the physician is able to go back and forth between patients in different virtual offices, if circumstances warrant.

Presently, we have approximately twelve physicians providing consultations using the CyberDocs system, with many more who have expressed their intention of using CyberDocs to provide online consultations for their patients. It should be noted that the registration format for physicians to enroll in the CyberDocs system is similar to a conventional medical staff credentialing process, which is quite thorough and requires some time to complete. This past month, we had four physicians complete their credentialing, and there are several others who are in the process. We receive inquiries on an ongoing basis from physicians throughout the United States, and recently from other countries as well.

Besides adding doctors, CyberDocs is attempting to build its features and profits.

Among many enhancements that are being discussed, we are looking at the possibility of providing more convenient methods of acquisition and integration of medical data within the CyberDocs system, so that the consulting physician will be provided with a truly enhanced methodology for data retrieval and review. We are additionally discussing possible plans to make CyberDocs a system that can be used by physicians on a global basis.

Currently, CyberDocs is paying its costs. Before, the site was financed out of our personal pockets. Our startup costs to develop a useable site at the beginning were in the neighborhood of around $20,000. As development has proceeded, however, those costs have mounted. Our projections indicate profitability within the next twelve to twenty-four months. However, we would still be interested in possible venture capital funding if a suitable source were to present itself. Ultimately, I am looking towards making CyberDocs.com my full-time job.

The founders of CyberDocs.com feel there are many instances that have shown the need and usefulness of sites like their own.

We have had patients who, while traveling abroad, have used our services to obtain United States formulated prescription medication within twenty-four to forty-eight hours for minor ailments, or for refills of crucial medication that they were taking. In an Internet-less society, these people could not have done this, and would have had to fend for themselves in a foreign healthcare system. By virtue of the Internet, we have referred patients in other parts of the world to world-renowned specialists for care of their medical conditions.

Dr. Archer firmly believes delivering medical advice via the Web is the wave of the future.

Virtually all feedback from other physicians who have actually taken the time to carefully examine the nature of the types of limited medical services we provide on the Web have been quite positive and encouraging. Naturally, as with any new development in medical care, there are detractors, but as the quality of information exchange continues to improve along with improvements in bandwidth access for physicians and patients, I believe even those currently skeptical of Web-based telemedicine will be led to re-examine their views.

www.
cyberdocs.com

CHAPTER 8

Way Cool Weddings

www.
waycoolweddings.com

CARL & KIMBERLY WHITE

Matrimony Made Easy

About the Site

WayCoolWeddings (www.waycoolweddings.com) is a guide to wedding sites and resources on the Web. The site highlights personal wedding pages on the Web, offers a wedding-of-the-week feature, and also offers a wedding-of-the-year award. Visitors searching for advice will find links to various wedding service providers, as well as helpful tips and suggestions.

Carl White first met Kimberly in 1989. While they were both living in Philadelphia, Pennsylvania, Kimberly attended a party Carl was hosting. Love must have been in the air—a relationship took root, and a five-year courtship began. During his twenty-sixth birthday dinner on August 19, 1994, Carl proposed to Kimberly. At the time, neither could have guessed that their ensuing engagement and wedding would become the stuff of Internet history. It all began when Carl decided to post information on the Web about their upcoming wedding for their guests.

Way Cool Weddings really got its start as a pretty straight-forward guide for all the people coming to our wedding, stuff like directions, menu for the reception, formal wear, rental places, and such. Basically, it was all the usual things you need to think about in planning a wedding. We thought it would be really cool as well as very useful to post the information where

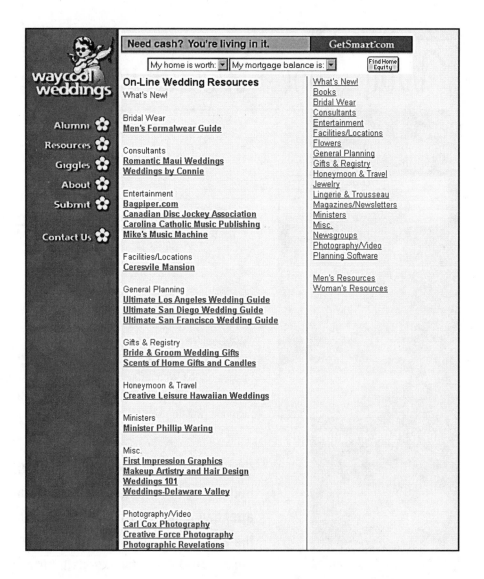

everyone could get to it easily. We started on that project in June of 1995. While the wedding itself was set for August 26, 1995, the immediate feedback we got from guests was really encouraging and very positive. We felt that through our effort in creating the site, we were providing a real service to all of our loved ones, since it gave them some additional information about us as well as a chance to RSVP online regarding the wedding.

However, not many husbands-to-be suggest to their fiancées that they set up a live broadcast of their wedding on the World Wide Web.

Before we knew it, the entire process began to take on a life of its own. The site quickly grew to include photos, video images, a guest book—and, in August, the world's first wedding broadcast live on the Web.

The success of our Web site started only after our wedding and its broadcast. We began to think of other things that we could do online. We wanted to share with others the great experience we had using the Internet for our wedding planning. It was through that process that we started Way Cool Weddings to encourage others to create their own wedding sites. While we were the sixth such site at the time to do this type of thing, today there are literally hundreds of wedding-related sites on the Net. There are actually Web rings of personal wedding sites, people who just create sites that link to each other.

My wife and I wanted to do something original and were determined to take a different approach. Yet after the incredible success leading up to and including our wedding simulcast, we came down to one persistent question, "What can we do now?" We decided to have a site that highlights other wedding sites. Now, it has grown into this monster. I really feel like I'm contributing to the Internet community. I receive emails from around the world commenting on what a great resource my site is. It's really all about the "people" part of it, not the business part. I want to be in touch with the people who are making their way, step-by-step, through the marriage preparation process, just as Kimberly and I had done. Successful wedding planning is about learning what options are available.

But it was Carl's hard work and early arrival on the Internet that helped to establish Way Cool Weddings as a destination site in the wedding industry.

With the start of Way Cool Weddings, I would spend every Sunday night working to post new material for the week. I would spend about four hours furiously surfing the Web, just searching for wedding sites to review and new material to feature. Things have really changed due to the growing popularity of Way Cool Weddings. Now I get about two dozen sites that contact me weekly, hoping to be featured on the site.

Carl's work in the technology field with US Interactive gave him the chance to follow the Web during its initial development stages.

I became interested in the Internet in late 1994. I was working as a creative director developing CD-ROM titles and thought the Internet was something that was important to my growth in the multimedia field. Currently, I work at US Interactive designing user interfaces for various software applications. I think the design work I do helps me provide Way Cool Weddings with a professional presentation. I have a

www.waycoolweddings.com

professional advantage, in that respect. Somebody without my background would have to pay to make the site appealing to a general audience and consistently pull in traffic to the site. I think I have a site that is clean, simple, and easy to navigate. I've actually been told that by people in the industry.

I saw my work on the Web as nothing more than a hobby, a means to informally pick up a new skill and have some fun. Heck, it would be cool to do this Web stuff. Before I knew what was happening, the site took off, along with the Internet as a whole. The whole thing snowballed, and it was really all very surprising.

Despite not having experience in the wedding business, Carl's early work on the Web and the connections he made earned him an invitation as a keynote speaker to address WedCon, the industry convention in New York.

There was a tight-knit group of some of the early movers in the wedding industry who put together an annual conference. The majority of them were professionals. I was on the other side—the guy getting married. Since my personal Web site got so much exposure, and I started Way Cool Weddings, I was working with these people regularly and was asked to give a presentation at WedCon. Although there were about six wedding-related Web sites in 1995 when I began, I was the only one who didn't begin with a business that was later brought to the Web. We worked together a lot, shared information that was available on the Net, and helped to grow the community that has since developed. With so many people online now, it's not the same closely intertwined group anymore. Many sites are now popping up and linking together content that is already out there.

The WedCon convention drew together all those involved in the industry. And, here I am, the average guy, talking about how I planned our wedding. A lot of people at WedCon had direct wedding industry experience. However, I was neither a professional speaker nor one who had ever pursued weddings as a business.

My technical background helped out tremendously. I actually had a live connection to my Web site, and showed some of the video coverage from my own wedding. Although I really struggled through it, my presentation ended up going very well. It seemed strange to actually have a line of people waiting to talk with me afterwards.

I had to remind myself what I was really at the conference to do, and not just get immersed in the experience. There were businesses selling bridal gowns, portrait photography, catering services, musical entertainment, and all of the other traditional wedding services. At one point when on stage, I thought to myself, "What the hell am I doing here?"

I was asked to speak again at the convention the following year, but declined since I didn't have the time to prepare and make a presentation.

In his effort to maintain a close personal connection with future newlyweds who were just getting started on all the details of planning their wedding, Carl focused on adding enhancements to the site so he could answer individual questions.

We're using some of the money that we raise in banner advertising to implement better things for the site and make the updating process easier overall. I have less and less time to maintain it, and with some nice scripts, specific aspects of the site can be automated. The resource area was really easy in the beginning. I would get one entry, "Hi Carl, I'm a caterer in Hawaii wanting to tell people on the Net about my services." Back then, just a couple of people per week would write to let me know about their wedding-related service or product. However, now I often get a dozen entries per day. It gets to be impossible to keep up with the different people, their businesses, when they contacted me, and so forth. There are people in the wedding industry who learn about the site, and say, "I just have to get my listing on there." I know this for a fact. But, as I've traveled along the learning curve, we're now making these folks do the work by submitting the information and details about their site. The submissions now come to me ready to be posted. I only need to approve it. Having the vendor do a lot of the front-end work will save me hours of time in preparing the entry. I can spend nine or ten hours over the course of a month just doing routine editing alone.

www.waycool
weddings.com

Recently, I decided to outsource some of the business aspects of running the site, which really has worked out great for me. My full-time job does not allow me the time to solicit advertisements for my site. I also don't have time to manage it. Without the extra help, I'd be struggling to make the contacts and do the contracts. In terms of selling advertising, I'm represented by the Women's Forum, which specifically targets companies with female-related products and services. The arrangement has really worked out well and helped make my site successful. However, I could not survive off of the revenue. Right now, I'm focused on investing the money back into the site to make sure it stays true to its beginnings. At the same time, I am working with some programmers to do back-end stuff to automate some of the interactive features.

Currently, we're close to about 100,000 individual viewers per month. Since the debut of the site, we've found that figure has only been on an upward trend. I've had a lot of fun operating the site, and continue learning more and more about the Internet while enjoying it.

CHAPTER 9

Community Church & Daycare

www.ganandacc.org

REVEREND RUS JEFFREY AND HIS WIFE, SANDRA

A Ministry Without Borders

About the Site

The Gananda Community Church Web site (www.ganandacc.org) includes a description of the ministry, their mission statement, and a calendar of events. As part of the daily service of the church, the site features a virtual office and chat area for parishioners in the Rochester community it serves.

After his formal training at a theological seminary, Reverend Rus Jeffery found himself in a challenging situation.

My first assignment as pastor was in a rural area of Ontario, Canada. I felt isolated as a pastor in this remote part of Canada. It was around that time when I started getting involved with using the Internet, to reconnect with people online. It was a great chance to communicate with people again, since I was not located in a large city. I soon discovered all kinds of valuable resources for my work as a pastor. At the same time, others in the ministry started dropping me e-mail notes, wondering where they could find resources on the Net and, as a result, the Pastoral Resource Center was born. The site represents my first venture into the world of Web pages.

Rus sought out a broad range of ecumenical resources, including crucial support services for people in ministry as well as families seeking pastoral assistance.

I decided to develop the site to help other people in ministry quickly locate interesting and useful sites on the Internet. I have an interest in helping others get the resources they need. I personally understand the burden facing many pastors, which is burning out while in the ministry due to insufficient support or available resources. As a result, I really want to encourage pastors and others in the ministry in whatever way I can.

The Internet opens up the world as far as communicating with other people and colleagues in ministry. It uses technology to reach out and touch people, which is the basis of our goal as administrators anyway. Technology really streamlines everything.

In 1996, Rus became the senior pastor of the Gananda Community Church in New York. Making the transition from rural Canadian countryside to suburban Rochester posed a new challenge.

Upon assuming the new position, I knew everyone would be really busy and life would be hectic. As a result, the question arose: How do I avoid burning out while also not becoming a nuisance by knocking on everybody's door each night. I decided to step back and review the situation.

In today's busy society, it's a lot easier to keep in touch with people over the Internet. The majority of people here have an Internet connection at home and at work. Keeping connected becomes a way of maintaining our vision among the leaders. The Web site I developed for the ministry, Ganandacc.org, became another way to let people know we are always able to connect in some way. It is creating more freedom. This ministry and our parishioners are pretty much on the cutting edge. The people in Rochester to whom I minister love the constant accessibility.

E-mail makes up a large part of our leadership training in Gananda, New York. We have a ministry leadership team that consists of people nominated and elected by the full members of the church at the beginning of each year. In many cases, the people in these positions hold various leadership positions such as treasurer, worship leader, or head trustee. Our Web site and the Internet serve as a way of keeping our mission and vision statement in the forefront of the minds of our leaders, and it's a great way for me to keep in touch with them in the area of encouragement and ongoing training. People also enjoy the fact that they can send a message to their pastor anytime and will always get a response. It saves a lot of unnecessary time in telephone tag and answering machine messages.

Basically, our momentum comes from the very fact that as a church ministry, we are really at the forefront by using the Internet for all facets of ministry. It's a form of communication. It's also a great resource that enables us to reach more people than we've ever thought possible.

Aside from the e-mail aspect of the Internet, we recently added a virtual office, which includes my business card, an in-basket to leave files for my attention, and even a way for parishioners to page me on the Internet. Recently, we added a calendar of events, a chat area, and a way for people to post prayer requests. This office allows anyone to quickly see if I'm online. Other leaders in the ministry use the office for transferring files, such as PowerPoint slides used for the words of the songs we sing during services. Instead of sending large file attachments via e-mail, we simply use the file section of the virtual office.

www.
ganandacc.org

The impact of Rus' efforts is clear to his parishioners.

I was at one of our leader's homes recently. He was saying, "I've never had this much contact from my pastor in all my life." "You are training us every single week." The Internet allows meeting them where they are. We have one meeting per month involving the ministry leadership team. If there are pertinent matters, e-mail is sent. Also, the virtual office provides them with twenty-four-hour access to ministry news and announcements. The Internet, and our Web site specifically, is a great way of encouraging others, and listening to—or I should say reading—what is transpiring in their lives. There's a standing joke in the ministry at Gananda. If you're going to be involved in leadership, you've got to have an e-mail address.

While Rus has successfully used the Internet for his work with parishioners in both a rural and an urban setting, inviting only encouragement, reactions from fellow church officers have run the gamut.

The feedback I've received from other pastors has been varied. Some say I really should not be doing any of it. I guess they see me as the maverick; it's simply different from what is usually accepted as common practice. That general opinion becomes the old style of thinking. Integrating technology into one's daily work is not the standard kind of church committee thing. It can be frightening for the traditional pastor. I will often hear, "Well you shouldn't be using a computer in the ministry. It's a tool of the Devil." I just reply, "Do you have a TV?"

Not too long ago, I was at a meeting of a group of churches, the Susquehanna conference with which we're affiliated. There are about twenty-five churches in this conference. I was speaking with one of our superintendents and asked him about the vision statement. "How many of your pastors in this conference can quote the vision and mission statement." He replied, "Probably not many." I said, "Right, because it's not in front of them all the time."

You can ask anyone of our leaders at Gananda, and they can tell you what our vision and mission statement is because at least once a week they are receiving it in a leadership thought that I send to them. The benefits far outweigh any of the comments from those who sit back and say you shouldn't actively use technology in the ministry when I know that I can get together with any of our leaders and, instantly, we can talk about concerns. We can talk about the ministry; we can discuss topics like whether or not we are making sense in what we do as a church.

By its nature, the church is based on historic traditions and rituals. People somehow imagine that we're supposed to be back in the 1960s and that we're not really supposed to reach outside of our doors. If people want to find us, then they need to come to the building. However, people don't just come into church. Gone are the days when you just open up the doors on Sunday morning and everybody's just there waiting to enter. But, by using the Internet, people know they can send me an e-mail and can rely on me to always respond. It becomes a way of being relevant to the world in which we live and meeting the genuine needs of the people we serve. I like to tell people that Sunday morning is truly a very small part of what we're all about.

It's gratifying to know that there are people who are really interested and want to know what is going on at Gananda. I have great dialogues with other pastors. I tell them what we're doing via the Internet, and they are impressed. Then I inform them that it's only twenty bucks to get online. They tell me their concerns about it not being acceptable to their people. My reply is always: "If you really want to have an impact in the twenty-first century, you need to be budgeting this. You need to be looking at this."

There are many issues that are restricted to the committee level in other churches around the nation. We don't have committee meetings every night. We don't need them. I don't need to call the ministry leadership team together to unload on them. I'll just send reports, letters, or other ideas out via e-mail. Then, when we do come together, we can actually talk intelligently about all through which we have been journeying.

Since his early days of reaching out to parishioners in rural Ontario, Rus has been very successful in bringing more and more people into the ministry.

Research has shown that more people in their late teens and early twenties are getting their religion from the Internet. We cannot ignore this. We cannot assume the traditional thinking that everyone will be coming to our church door. We must use this technological resource.

Rus maintains strong links with other pastors. Having earned his Master's degree at Asbury Theological Seminary in Wilmore, Kentucky, in 1993, he maintains close links with his professors, and is the moderator for the Asbury mailing list, a vital resource and means of communication for the school's graduates.

I receive e-mail from people in ministry overseas looking for encouragement, information on ministry, or wanting to know of which denomination we are a part. If the ministry in the Gananda Community Church, one half-hour outside of Rochester, can have an impact on somebody overseas or elsewhere in the United States, then

www.ganandacc.org

that's wonderful. That progress is really happening. I discuss this with our leadership and explain how our ministry is reaching outside Gananda Community Church. It's all a matter of using the tools that are there to impact people's lives.

I know there are a number of church sites on the Net, but I'm not aware of them doing what we're doing. We're actively using the Internet as a training tool for educating and developing our leaders. That's where we see the greatest impact. The Internet is a great tool that continues to amaze me. Well, part of me just likes being on the cutting edge. We're now in the planning stages for a new building that will be fully multimedia, including computers with dedicated Internet connections. We will truly be a multimedia church!

Rus continues to build his role as the senior pastor by reaching out to both the Rochester and virtual communities that he serves. Through the Internet, he communicates with a growing audience and hones his skills as a counselor, a speaker, and a writer.

One aspect that our parishioners love about our Internet presence and Web site is the opening jokes at the start of services, because I'm the moderator for a newsgroup called Net.Humor.Religion on UseNet2 service. I approve all UseNet2 postings. Due to this, I'm now getting tons of material, so much so that I'm working on a book called *When God Laughs*. It's going to look at God's sense of humor and is also going to be a collection of humor. This is humor that the Internet has helped to generate and I allow everyone in the ministry to share.

I think our site's popularity is building simply as a result of my involvement in other areas of the Internet, like the Net.Humor.Religion site. As a result of this involvement, people are discovering that I'm a pastor with a sense of humor, which encourages new people to seek out the Web site to discover more about my ministry. It is creating more freedom while broadening the impact of my work. People love the humor and often let me know how nice it is to find a pastor who understands that church doesn't have to be boring. Looking back to when I was still in seminary, I took a class on healing, and we spent a number of sessions looking at the effects of humor on people and its many benefits. I think we take ourselves way too seriously at times. After all, laughter is the world's best medicine.

Rus continues to extend his dialogue with people far outside Gananda's immediate doors. The Internet has helped introduce the reverend and his family to new cultures.

Probably one of the most interesting people I've met is Vladimir Trousov from Kaliningrad, Russia. Vladi is not in the ministry. He's actually a Web page designer whom I met on another list I subscribe to called Autorace. (Racing is a favorite hobby of mine.) One day he sent me a private message, and we just started up a conversation. We talk about many things and, from time-to-time, we do discuss items of faith as well. We keep in contact on a regular basis, and my three sons think it's great having friends in Russia.

All of this wouldn't have been possible if Rus had chosen the typewriter.

Before going into the ministry, I actually spent ten years in radio. I was a radio announcer. The technology was there for me to use. I left the radio business at about the time that computers were becoming more commonplace. When I left radio and went back to school, I told my wife that I needed to either get a typewriter or a computer. We decided on the computer.

Links!

Racing!

Search Engines & Back Links

Christian Resources

Illustrations

Fun Links

Mail Lists

Software Links

Space...The Final Frontier

Virus Safety

Wesley Info

E-Mail
Pastor Rus

Welcome! Since June 27, 1996, you are visitor

`4486`

This counter brought to you by the fine people at

WEB counter

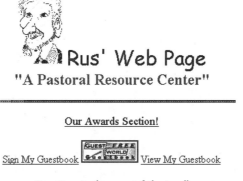

Rus' Web Page
"A Pastoral Resource Center"

Our Awards Section!

Sign My Guestbook   GUEST FREE WORLD BOOK   View My Guestbook

Greetings in the name of the Lord!

Welcome to the *"Pastoral Resource Center"* for the Internet. This page came about as a result of my involvement as List Moderator for the *"Asbury Theological Seminary General List."* As moderator I not only take care of message traffic control, but I also try and direct fellow ministry workers to some great resources available via the Internet. I was getting tired of always writing the same information over and over again in messages, so this page was born. Now when people ask for resources, I simply say "visit my home page!"

This page is here as a resource tool for you, the ministry worker. If you have any suggestions for how this page can help you

www.
ganandacc.org

Visiting, Watching, & Playing Outside the Web World

www.viking
underground.com

DAN HILDRETH

A Football Team's Biggest Fan

About the Site

Vikingunderground.com (www.vikingunderground.com) follows the Minnesota Vikings of the National Football League throughout the year by providing daily news and weekly columns. The site also lists email addresses of other fans around the world and provides a bulletin board for posting comments. On the site, you may also buy merchandise and view photographs and statistics of all the players and games.

What began as a family bonding experience in rural Iowa turned into a hobby that twenty-six-year-old Dan Hildreth of Burnsville, Minnesota, cannot escape. However, that is just the way he wants it.

Every Sunday since I was five years old, I would sit in my father's recliner on cold winter Sundays at our Iowa home, anxiously awaiting my favorite football team, the Minnesota Vikings, to take the field as we watched on our console television. I was either outfitted in my favorite purple Vikings T-shirt or my purple terrycloth robe. Vikings football games were always an event at my house, with even my younger sister getting into the act by placing a quarter on top of the TV each Sunday betting against the Vikings. Once the game ended, we all enjoyed a homemade, family-style dinner prepared by my mom. It was more than just a football game at the Hildreth home. It was a time for the family to get together and have a good time.

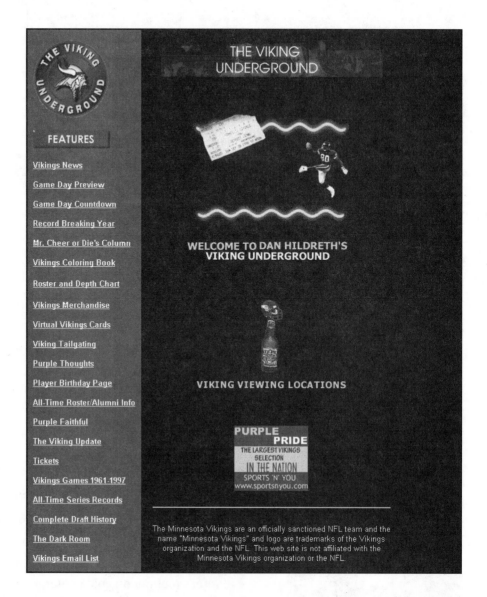

When Dan got his first computer, he wanted to exhibit his passion for the Minnesota Vikings outside of his family.

I had my first computer for exactly three months before I published my first Vikings page on the Internet. I was attending college at Iowa State University and living in Ankeny, Iowa. I started a small site for fun with a few photos taken by my wife at the Vikings' training camp in Mankato, Minnesota. I then added facts, statistics, and other information that I found interesting as a fan. That was in August of 1995 and the original address was http://www.commonlink.com/~dhildreth.

Having absolutely no computer background when I began my site, I was forced to teach myself everything. I learned HTML through a lot of trial-and-error, spending literally hundreds of hours to get to the point where I was able to put something together that people were actually interested in viewing. As the years went by, I continued to add and build more information, which eventually led to changing the address to www.vikingunderground.com. The reason for the name change was to gain better exposure because domain names tend to be easier to remember and have a more professional feel.

Dan, like many Webmasters, is devoted to his site, having worked on it consistently for three years. However, unlike many other Web developers, he has yet to make any money from the site.

I update the daily news, which is the most popular section, 365 days per year. I have missed maybe seven days in the last two years; those days were during the off-season and there was no news to be found. Overall, I spend in excess of twenty hours per week working on the site. The work entails updating existing sections as well as developing new areas. The daily news is the most time-consuming. I obtain my information, in many cases, directly from the Vikings public relations department and supplement that news with local media outlet reports.

Between 40,000 and 70,000 visitors view my site each month. Furthermore, I receive forty to fifty e-mails per week regarding the site. One of the most memorable came from a serviceperson in the Air Force based in Japan. Through my list of e-mail addresses of other Viking fans across the world, called the Purple Faithful, he was able to make contact with another serviceperson on base and they were able to watch games together. I am also aware of one instance where a couple of Vikings fans met on my Purple Thoughts message board, which is an interactive chat area and the second most popular section of the site, who are now currently engaged to be married.

I have never made any money from the site advertising or otherwise. I just enjoy knowing that thousands of people visit the site everyday and knowing that I have something to contribute that interests them. I also enjoy computers in general, and the site has been a great opportunity for me to expand my current skill base, which ultimately has translated into a real full-time job as the Webmaster for MLT Vacations in Minnetonka, Minnesota. I know I wouldn't have gotten this job otherwise, because the experience working on the Vikings site gave me the ability to handle my current position.

www.
vikingunderground
.com

Dan's altruism does not end with providing Vikings fans an unparalleled site at no cost. He also likes to help others through his site.

I feel that I have some influence in credibly projecting a positive image of the Vikings organization with the audience that I have been able to build. I have been fortunate enough to help raise money for the Vikings Children's Fund through the sale of Viking Underground shirts and by promoting their various events, which has also been a source of enjoyment for me. Last year, Sports N You of Burnsville, Minnesota, agreed to begin production of Viking Underground T-shirts and polo shirts. A dollar from each shirt sold went directly to the Children's Fund. The sale was a success, and the check will be presented this year.

Dan has received a lot of recognition for his site, including being named the official fan club site of the Minnesota Vikings by the Minnesota Vikings.

The relationship that I have with the Vikings organization would not have been possible if it weren't for the page. I have been able to work very closely with the Vikings over the last year and a half. They have been very good in getting me information and recognizing my efforts on the site. I was thrilled when they gave me the designation of the official fan club site of their organization in April of 1998. I believe the Vikings gave the site the "official" tag for all the work that I have put into it over the last three years and the quality of the product I have been able to produce. I also feel that because I had everything compiled already, they realized it was the next logical step.

Outside of the Minnesota Vikings recognition, I have also done three or four radio interviews about the site, including one on Minnesota Public Radio. There have also been approximately ten articles written about the site. These articles have appeared in the *San Antonio Express-News*, *Star Tribune*, *St. Paul Pioneer Press*, *Monday Night Football*, *Twin Cities Internet Guide and Directory*, *Beckett's Football Magazine*, *The Net Magazine*, *Internet Guide to Sports*, and *The Des Moines Register*.

Dan has also received a World Wide Web award as the top personal page for 1996 from Net Guide.

The page views have gone up dramatically since I won the 1996 Net Guide Awards, which was a great experience. My father and I flew to Los Angeles for the awards and had a wonderful time. After the Net Guide Awards I realized that I had something special and worked twice as hard to make it even better. Other than leaving my dad's coat at the airport in Kansas City and having to have it flown to Los Angeles in time for the ceremony, everything went very well. Walking onto that stage in front of hundreds of people, with my Web site displayed on thirty TV screens behind me, was something I will always remember. It was quite an accomplishment, and I was happy that my dad was there with me to share in it.

Dan gets great satisfaction from knowing his viewers of www.vikingunderground.com and the Minnesota Vikings really appreciate his site.

My biggest perk is meeting people from all over the world who visit my site and seeing the Vikings recognize it both during the game on the scoreboard and in their weekly press releases. The Vikings display the address on the scoreboard at all of the home games, and there is a Viking Underground banner that hangs in the end zone each week. The banner was paid for by visitor contributions. About forty visitors from my site donated nearly $500 to get the banner constructed.

Recently, there was a Viking Underground reunion that was organized by one of the most loyal visitors to my site, Mindy Luczak, a meteorologist from Fort Wayne, Indiana. Over sixty fans from the site, including myself, attended. Mindy did a wonderful job of organizing it, and it was a great success. The reunion was held over the Labor Day weekend in Minneapolis.

In the following paragraphs, Mindy describes how she organized the reunion:

"The Viking Underground reunion started out as an idea among some of the regulars in the Viking Underground chat room last December. We all decided that we joined together on this site because of our common interest in the Vikings. We enjoyed debating the football issues in the chat room and decided that it would be great to get a group of us together to meet face-to-face and enjoy our favorite pastime together. I was chosen to organize it since I put together the out-of-state fans' petition to keep the Vikings in Minnesota. I gathered interested viewers' addresses and phone numbers over the off-season and, in April when the schedule was released, we set the date of the reunion for the first home game on Labor Day weekend.

www.
vikingunderground
.com

By the deadline of mid-May, we had sixty Viking Underground people from twenty different states ready to attend the first annual reunion. Most of the correspondence was done through posts on the Viking Underground or through e-mail. I felt we were able to set up a Viking fan's dream weekend. We had tickets to the game, a block of reserved hotel rooms, tours of both the Vikings' practice facility and where they play their games at the Metrodome, autograph sessions with both current and former players, and two organized evening socials. On game day, we had a tailgate before the game and were all allowed on the field for player introductions. Even with all these great activities, I consider the real success of this reunion to be the fact that for probably a third of these people, who had been lifelong Viking fans, this was their first Vikings' home game. Needless to say, plans are already being made for the next annual reunion."

Vikingunderground.com has not only made Dan a star, it has helped introduce several other people to Vikings fans, including Todd Carlsen and Brian Maas.

I tried to incorporate as much fan involvement as possible in developing the site, which has led me to be able to co-op the work of fans worldwide. An example of this is that while NFL Europe was in session, I was able to get player interviews from Vikings fans in Europe. Two other Vikings fans who write consistently for the site are Todd Carlsen, who does game, season, and draft previews, and Brian Maas, who writes a weekly column for the site and also takes the majority of the pictures that are used. Each of them tell their story as follows:

"My name is Todd Carlsen, and I first discovered Viking Underground two and a half years ago while earning a finance degree as a student at the University of Minnesota, Duluth. Right away, it became my favorite Web site, and I began writing for it about six months after I discovered it. Without a doubt, I think it is the best Web site of its kind on the Internet.

I work in the investment finance industry, but I combine my love of football and analytical skills to follow the NFL closely. With Dan's input, I write weekly scouting reports on upcoming opponents, NFL draft reviews, and Vikings season previews. I'd like to think our reports are of a professional quality. We have definitely been ahead of the professionals on a number of occasions. At the season opener two years ago, the Vikings played the Tampa Bay Buccaneers, and we were the only ones to declare that the Buccaneers were over-hyped. Several national magazines even picked Tampa Bay as Super Bowl contenders. The Vikings easily defeated them, so we were right on target."

"My name is Brian Maas, otherwise known as Mr. Cheer Or Die. I'm a pharmacist and serve as a clinical manager for PCS Health Systems in Minneapolis. I grew up as a Viking fan, watching Joe Kapp and fellow North Dakotan Dave Osborn play on the tundra-like field of old Metropolitan stadium in the late 1960s. You can see me at home games wearing my trademark purple sunglasses and my "Cheer Or Die" shield, which has earned me a front-row spot in what I call the "Thunder Zone." I began writing weekly columns for Viking Underground in November 1996 and have been writing weekly, including the off-season, ever since. At the same time, I assumed photographic responsibilities for Viking Underground. I have photographed Viking players at away games in Chicago, Phoenix, and the Meadowlands in New Jersey, as well as at home games, mini-camps, and training camps.

Since 1996, I have also begun organizing special events, such as the popular Viking Underground tailgate parties. During the 1998 opening tailgate against the Tampa Bay Buccaneers, over 100 Viking fans representing twenty-four states and three foreign countries were present. My recipes from these tailgates can be found on the Web site. Recently, my Metrodome Horseradish Burgers and Pomegranate-Grilled Lamb Chops were selected for inclusion in the nationally published John Madden's *Ultimate Tailgating Cookbook*.

Dan and I also assisted former marketing director Stew Widdess, in setting the largest single-game attendance record ever at the Metrodome on September 22, 1996, when 64,168 fans attended the Vikings' 30-21 victory over the Green Bay Packers. This record was made possible by placing bleachers on the field and filling them with Viking fans from various Viking fan clubs around the country. Only fans that visited www.vikingunderground.com knew of the special seating. The extra 600+ seats sold out in four hours."

Being a fan with creative input used to show his team to the world has taught Dan a lot about the Internet.

It has meant a new career path and a lot of fun for me. I learned that the Internet is a powerful tool if you have something to say and people are interested. Having 4,000-5,000 Viking fans visit my work everyday has meant a lot to me over the last three years. It's not a "build it and they will come" situation. On the Internet, you must build it and it must be good or they will find their information somewhere else. My general philosophy on the site has been to work harder and spend more time than anyone else would be willing, and so far, this has worked well.

www.
vikingunderground
.com

Twenty-one years after first sitting in his dad's recliner and watching Minnesota Vikings games from his house in Iowa, Dan has a different view of the field because of the Internet.

I am a season ticket holder, courtesy of being the official fan club site of the Minnesota Vikings, and I go to every game with my dad. I love going to games with my dad on Sunday. We have a great time. I also make it a point to forget about the site on Sundays during the game, and to have fun and enjoy the day.

Gridiron Grumblings™
THE EZINE OF NFL COMMENTARY
...as much ATTITUDE as you can handle!

www.gridiron
grumblings.com

JOHN RAKOWSKI,
JOHN GEORGOPOULOS,
ROY T. CANKOSYAN, JR.

Gridiron Guru

About the Site

Gridirongrumblings.com (www.gridirongrumblings.com) is dedicated to providing information about the National Football League. It features several different columns of commentary, which are updated regularly. It also has many weekly features, including columns on various topics, a question of the week, game predictions, and a RealAudio™ taped broadcast called WGRD–Gridiron Grumblings Radio! Aside from commentary and weekly features, there is a links section, readers survey, NFL chat room, replies to incoming email and a free fantasy football game.

American football is a rough sport, where playing when hurt can make you a legend. It was one player, commonly known for playing while injured, who cemented John Georgopoulos's interest in football at a very young age.

Larry Csonka, the Miami Dolphins hall of fame running back, started my interest in football. When I was about eight years old, I read an article in the magazine *Dy-no-mite* about him. Csonka was such a tough player that he regularly played with a broken nose. Ever since that article, I've followed football religiously. I have also worn Larry Csonka's number on my uniform T-shirt, number thirty-nine, for every team I've ever been a part of, regardless of the sport.

Ironically, when I was ready for organized football, I went to a high school that did not even have a football team. I was a student at the Bronx High School of Science, which is famous for producing Nobel Prize winners, not football players. Therefore, to satisfy my football playing cravings, I played in pick-up leagues during high school and then through college. It wasn't the best, but everyone I played with loved the game and loved to play.

Now, I'm thirty-three years old and a football nut; just ask my wife, Doreen. She abandoned all hope of me ever being productive on a Sunday, which is NFL game day. I love watching games, analyzing them, and talking about them. Although I can't say I ever did anything unusual to see a game, I did once take a math exam for someone in exchange for some New York Jets football tickets when I was in college.

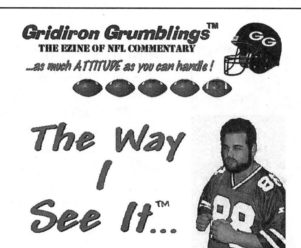

Gridiron Grumblings™
THE EZINE OF NFL COMMENTARY
...as much ATTITUDE as you can handle!

The Way I See It...™

Well, Super Bowl XXXIV (or 34 to us non-Romans) is now history. How will it be remembered? As one of the most thrilling, if not *the* most thrilling Super Bowl? Or will it be remembered as the final chapter of one of the most **"fairy tale"-like seasons** in NFL history? For me, this Super Bowl will remain the summary of this wacky season-- the way it should be, I guess... First of all, let's talk about the first 30 minutes of the game. What a collective **bundle of nerves**! Three missed/botched field goals, the complete deviation from each team's established game plan, the inability of the Rams to put the game away early. Why were the Titans so eager to **abandon** Eddie George and their running game? By not making use of George and their grind-it-out offense, the Titans gave the explosive Rams' offense more opportunities to take the field-- except that the Rams didn't seem to want **to win the game**! I mean, **six** trips inside the Red Zone and only *nine points*? Can I just say two words about that? **Marshall Faulk**. Why wasn't Faulk given a couple opportunities down low? The guy is arguably your main playmaker on offense, set a record for combined yardage from the line of scrimmage during the regular season, and he gets practically no shots inside the Titans' 20? Between Vermeil and Fisher, I haven't seen such a botched game plan since Wade Phillips **benched** Doug Flutie in the AFC wildcard game... At halftime, after restocking on **pizza, beer and, for dessert, light beer**, I had resigned myself to a dreadful second-half of football when something amazing happened: despite being down 16-0, the Titans decided to run the ball. Using George and the running ability of McNair, the Titans rallied around fallen comrade **Blaine Bishop** and physically dominated the Rams. The Titans asserted themselves and dominated **both** lines of scrimmage as they caught up to the Rams, 16-16 with just over two minutes to go. But in this second-half of remembrance, the Rams remembered two things: that they had the NFL's best deep game and that the Titans play man-to-man defense. Warner hit Isaac Bruce with the 73 yard bomb-- Bruce caught the underthrown pass and outraced the entire Titan secondary to paydirt. Where are all the guys now who **crap on the Prevent defense**? In any event, the Titans had one more shot, and they made the most of it. Sloppy, undisciplined play by the Rams' D (three penalties for 25 yards) helped the Titans a great deal... but you got the impression that the Titans would come up short, since Tennessee was now relying on McNair's arm and not his legs; indeed, there were at least two passes where he clearly lacked the touch required to get the ball to an open receiver. In the end, however, he used his marvelous athletic ability to escape the grasp of *two* Ram linemen and hit Mason for the completion to the Rams' 10, setting up the dramatic final play. There are those who will criticize the play-calling, saying that the Titans should have gone for the endzone-- or that McNair should have allowed the play to breakdown before taking off for the endzone on his own. **Hogwash**. The play was an excellent call-- how many times have you seen that short slant go for a TD when the middle LB (or SS) *misses* the tackle on the WR, who then scoots away? Give credit where credit is due: Mike Jones made a great open-field tackle in an age where basic tackling fundamentals are about **as common as Clinton telling the truth**...

No, Super Bowl XXXIV was not the most exciting Super Bowl from start to finish (I would still vote Super Bowl XXV, Giants-Bills, that honor)-- but it certainly ranks right up there. Not a bad way for the the NFL to kick off the new century. Not a bad way at all.

How do *you* see it? Just click here to let us know!

Published: 31-Jan-00

BACK TO
GRIDIRON GRUMBLINGS

Of course, I have a favorite team, which is the New York Giants. I can remember rooting for Ron Johnson and Spider Lockhart in the 1970s. Although I am also quite the Dolphins fan as well since, as I mentioned, my favorite player of all time is Larry Csonka.

This enjoyment of professional football led John to start a National Football League (NFL) draft Web page in May of 1996.

The site was launched, as a goof, in 1996 as a review of the NFL draft. The original URL was http://www.redbay.com/gridiron. I had come up with the name Gridiron Grumblings in 1987, when a couple of college buddies and I were watching a New York Giants game. I was being very critical of the coaching, and one of my friends accused me of "grumbling" about everything, even though the Giants were winning. Given my penchant for alliteration, I started "billing" myself as the Gridiron Grumbler. The rest, as they say, is history.

The first Web page was actually an online extension of a newsletter I had been writing for the eight owners of a fantasy football league for which I was the commissioner. This league, nicknamed the Mighty XFL, is a league in which each owner picks current professional football players for their team and then uses actual game statistics each week to determine their standings.

When I put this page on the Internet, I only expected that I would do a NFL draft review once a year, just for fun. I felt it was also a good way of teaching myself HTML and Perl. The first online issue contained a short essay on how to conduct a fantasy draft, along with the question, "If you were building a NFL team from scratch, around whom would you build your team?" I received an overwhelming number of letters complimenting my writing, and that encouraged me to do a follow-up.

As John decided to expand his Web site by increasing the amount of content and the frequency of updates, he decided to look toward other members of his fantasy football league for help.

I do Gridirongrumblings.com with two other guys I met in college, who are part of the Mighty XFL, John Rakowski and Roy T. Cankosyan, Jr. Although they weren't directly involved in the first posting of Gridiron Grumblings, they did have indirect input, because it was through the fantasy league that I first perfected the Gridiron Grumblings style. John Rakowski goes by the name the

www.
gridiron
grumblings.com

Statmaster on the site. He holds a B.S. in computer science. Roy Cankosyan, Jr. goes by The Instigator on Gridiron Grumblings, and has a business degree. I go by Head Honcho, and have a B.S. in computer science and a B.A. in biology. We all went to Fordham University in New York City.

The site's original form was a constant experiment. Frankly, it wasn't very attractive because we were always trying out the latest techniques. We tried it all—image maps, Java applets, background music, heavy animation—and we finally decided that less is more and that our content was our best asset. This was especially true since all the effort applied to use the latest techniques did not equate to either increased viewership or a better product. Thus, the simple two-frame layout that exists today was born. We are proud of the fact that none of our pages take an eternity to download, yet our readers still find us interesting.

All of this experimenting takes time.

My writers spend five to ten hours per week preparing their articles. I spend between twenty-five and thirty hours per week on the site. In addition to writing my own columns, I edit the other columns and do the entire HOME coding for the site. I also spend a couple of hours per week soliciting sponsors, tinkering with the look and feel of the site, and checking out new software and technology.

It wasn't until we started receiving mail, asking us for help in answering NFL-related questions or help in reinstating Instant Replay, that we knew we had achieved a following. Today, we receive an average of about 100 emails per week during the NFL season. We always try to encourage our readers to send us their thoughts and opinions. Some are very memorable. There is one Dallas Cowboys fan who wishes the most horrible scenarios for me, since he thinks I insulted the virtue of his beloved team. Another email suggested that since I'm from New York and don't like Jerry Jones, I must be a communist and should be very careful the next time I visit Dallas.

The most memorable are the simple letters that thank us for the site. One email was from a United States soldier in Japan who said our site brightens up his day. Another was from a gentleman in Scotland who said our site reminded him of his favorite sports bar in Chicago during a Bears-Packers game. Letters like that make it all worthwhile.

We publish Gridiron Grumblings all year, and the hits depend on whether or not the NFL is in the news. During the NFL season, 150-200,000 hits per month would not be uncommon. At any time, our hits have increased roughly 100 percent compared to the same time the previous year.

Winning the Lycos Top Five Percent award helped to increase our hit count, as did being listed as a top NFL site by the major search engines Excite, Infoseek, Magellan, Web TV, and Pointcast. Also, being listed in the Netscape Netcenter's "What's New and Cool" section helped us get a lot of visitors.

John added some unique touches to his site, a weekly radio address from the Web site called WGRD—Gridiron Grumblings Radio! and a weekly football fantasy game.

I started WGRD because I love to hear myself talk! Actually, WGRD was created because I read in a trade magazine that sites using RealAudio tend to retain customers. Therefore, I learned how to record and encode sound for the RealAudio player. In the beginning, WGRD had only ten to fifteen loyal listeners; however today, many weekly broadcasts later, we can count several hundred listeners as Grumblers.

WGRD also created other opportunities for Gridiron Grumblings. Other broadcasters, most recently, Mike Toebe, of KQAM Sports Radio in Kansas, have heard WGRD and decided to invite us on their shows for guest appearances. Today Kansas, tomorrow the world!

The RealAudio broadcast has also become a favorite of fantasy football aficionados. This large interest from fantasy football players in our site led us to do some reader surveys, which indicated that fantasy football was the number one thing on our readers' wish list. When I found this out, I decided to leverage my twelve years of fantasy experience and develop the structure of a unique fantasy football game. We introduced our free fantasy football game, MVP of the Gridiron, at the beginning of the 1998 season. It brought us several hundred new subscribers each month. Currently, we have a little over 1,200 people signed up and playing.

MVP of the Gridiron is just one facet of MVPgames.com, which is an offshoot of Gridiron Grumblings. When I began designing a fantasy football game for our visitors, I got help with developing the scoring rules from John Rakowski, the Statmaster from Gridiron Grumblings, but I needed help implementing the game. I turned to a good friend, Lorenzo Colasante, of the computer consulting firm Solar Productions (www.solarproductions.com), and he agreed to help build the MVPgames.com site. I have high hopes for MVPgames.com, because we are also planning to add fantasy games for baseball and basketball. Of course, we are also

www.
gridiron
grumblings.com

hoping to turn MVPgames.com into a revenue-producing site within a year or two.

Gridiron Grumblings gives its viewers a lot of information, and John is not done adding to the site.

All of our features receive roughly the same number of visitors, but I think that the Fantasy Forecast, Sunday Soothsayers, and The Way I See It generate the most reader mail. Fantasy Forecast discusses issues dealing with fantasy football games utilizing real NFL players and statistics. Sunday Soothsayers makes game outcome predictions using the Las Vegas gambling lines. John, Roy, or I have written this column in the past, but because we all have taken on weekly columns, I began an off-season search this year for new Sunday Soothsayers writers. I chose two good buddies, Vincent Ponticelli and Thomas Scarpati, who won their 120-man football office pool two years in a row. The Way I See It is my own weekly commentary on different topics about the NFL.

However, if I could create the site all over again, I would have included Fantasy Forecast from the start. Fantasy football coverage seems to have fueled most of our 200 percent increase in readership this season. Fantasy football is so hot right now, and I believe our forecasters, John and Roy, have done a great job of mixing analysis with humor in their column. The guys also dispense free, personalized fantasy advice, which most other sites don't do. There also is the crossover with the MVP of the Gridiron fantasy game, which sends several readers to the site.

In the near-term, I'm working on adding video to the site. I'd also like to see our sister site, MVPgames.com, expand its offering to include fantasy games for baseball, basketball, and hockey. Both projects seem to be moving forward.

As for the long term, it would be nice if Gridiron Grumblings became the flagship site of the most attitudinal sports news network bent on world domination. In fact, we have already begun developing our next e-zine, Pro Baseball Weekly, at www.probaseballweekly.com.

As expenses rise for Gridiron Grumblings, John's goal to increase revenue has not been to make money, but to cover costs so that he is able to spend more money on the promotion and technology of the site.

My friends think I should write a book on how to create a successful Web site for less than twenty dollars a month. When Gridiron Grumblings first began, my monthly costs were roughly twenty dollars per month, not including my Internet access, which was also approximately twenty dollars per month. I was able to keep costs down

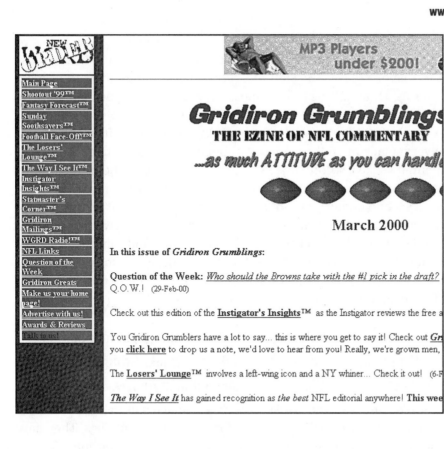

Main Page
Shootout '99™
Fantasy Forecast™
Sunday Soothsayers™
Football Face-Off!™
The Losers' Lounge™
The Way I See It™
Instigator Insights™
Statmaster's Corner™
Gridiron Mailings™
WGRD Radio!™
NFL Links
Question of the Week
Gridiron Greats
Make us your home page!
Advertise with us!
Awards & Reviews
Talk to us!

Gridiron Grumblings
THE EZINE OF NFL COMMENTARY
...as much ATTITUDE as you can handl

March 2000

In this issue of *Gridiron Grumblings*:

Question of the Week: *Who should the Browns take with the #1 pick in the draft?* Q.O.W.! (29-Feb-00)

Check out this edition of the **Instigator's Insights**™ as the Instigator reviews the free a

You Gridiron Grumblers have a lot to say... this is where you get to say it! Check out *Gr* you **click here** to drop us a note, we'd love to hear from you! Really, we're grown men,

The **Losers' Lounge**™ involves a left-wing icon and a NY whiner... Check it out! (6-F

The Way I See It has gained recognition as *the best* NFL editorial anywhere! **This wee**

www.
gridiron
grumblings.com

because I was doing all the programming myself, and I worked long hours to get the job done. My monthly expenses have risen only slightly to about fifty dollars per month, but the site's revenue covers that fully.

In my opinion, getting advertising is the most difficult task facing the Internet publisher. In the beginning, when Gridiron Grumblings only cared about publishing quality NFL commentary, solicitation for advertising accounted for roughly 10 percent of my time. As we started to build an audience and incur expenses, hunting for advertisers accounted for 80 percent of my time. Oddly enough, when we hit around 75,000 monthly impressions I contacted Flycast Advertising, an Internet-based ad agency that brokers ad deals between buyers and sellers, and they rejected us as a client because our monthly impression count was too low. A few months later, when our impressions had reached 100,000 a month, I contacted Flycast again and this time they accepted us. It was like 100,000 impressions was the magic number. Now with Flycast as our ad rep, I'm back to devoting 10 percent of my time to advertising and 90 percent to writing and coding.

With all of that considered, if we're lucky, we clear a few bucks by year's end, but nothing major. All of us are basically doing this because it is a labor of love. The staff of Gridiron Grumblings all work in other fields as white-collar professionals. They take no pay for their work on the site. All money taken in by Gridiron Grumblings goes to paying expenses and promotion. Unfortunately, working this site will probably never replace my full-time job. Although if you take into account time spent, it is like a second job. As I mentioned, I spend about thirty hours per week on Gridiron Grumblings, in addition to the forty hours per week I spend on my "day job" as an Internet applications analyst. I must keep the "day job" because, after all, I have a wife, a newborn son (who will be a future draft pick of the New York Giants) and a mortgage to pay. Although if CNNSI or ESPN need a quality subsidiary for commentary, they can give me a call and I'll see what I can do to make the site my full-time occupation.

Even with all the time and effort John and the others put into the site and with the number of viewers they get each week, Gridiron Grumblings cannot get NFL teams to take them seriously.

Several public relations assistants have contacted us to let us know that there are no press passes available for Gridiron Grumblings. They have also said we can have no access to players or coaches for interviews. It seems that nobody takes Internet journalism seriously. For example, during the past two seasons, we requested press passes from both the New York Giants and the New York Jets and haven't gotten any. The Giants haven't even bothered to respond, while the Jets essentially said that only "traditional" press is issued passes. They say this despite the fact that Gridiron Grumblings is read by more people than the New York Jets' own official team paper.

Even though we have little contact with NFL people, we are regularly contacted by other media, such as radio, print, and other Internet sites for our opinion on NFL matters. So our reputation is beginning to create opportunities for us.

In the end, John feels he is forging a new path, not only in football commentary, but also in publishing.

The idea that several folks consider us "gridiron gurus" is a testament to the power of the Internet. After almost three uninterrupted years of publication, Gridiron Grumblings has become synonymous with quality NFL commentary, something that would have cost hundreds of thousands of dollars in the world of print media.

In my opinion, the Internet represents the latest, best opportunity for hard-working people to make their fortune. Imagine what it would have been like to be on the ground floor of radio or television broadcasting. Think about if you were one of the first newspapers in your town at the turn of the century. That is how I view the Internet—a chance for the trailblazers to define a new medium.

www.
gridiron
grumblings.com

CHAPTER 12

BALLPARKS.com

www.ballparks.com

CORY SUPPES

A Man for All Sports Seasons

About the Site

Ballparks.com (www.ballparks.com) is a site that lists pictures, facts, and histories of the places professional and amateur sports teams play baseball, basketball, football, hockey, soccer, and the Olympics. The list of sports facilities is not limited to only each team's present stadium, but also shows the same information about their former and future facilities. The site also has a virtual mall for purchasing sports-related gifts and a map section that allows you to click on a map of the world, drill down to the appropriate city, find a stadium, and get directions to that stadium.

All over the world, millions of people watch sports. People trek many miles to see their favorite teams. Cory Suppes, a thirty-six-year-old father of three in the San Francisco area, is one of them. Cory's interest, however, extends beyond the actual game to the buildings where the teams play.

I have always wanted to be a sports "architect." I love all sports, but am fascinated by how these very quiet buildings turn into absolute nut houses when they are filled with players and fans. The transformation of these places into arenas where people absolutely worship their teams intrigues me.

I still remember my first visit to an arena, the Calgary Corral hockey arena, when I was about seven years old. I watched the Calgary Centennials junior hockey team, which featured a goaltender, John Davidson, who later played professional hockey and become a national announcer. My first stadium visit was when I was about ten

107

years old. I went to McMahon Stadium in Calgary, where my Edmonton Eskimos football team played the Calgary Stampeders. My first ballpark visit was at age twenty-six when I was flown to Los Angeles on a business trip and went to a game at Dodger Stadium, where the Philadelphia Phillies played the Dodgers. During that game, Mike Schmidt, the hall of fame Phillies third baseman, hit one of his last home runs.

After going to so many sport facilities, I thought that I could design and build a better stadium than anyone in the world, which would house all sports. My stadium would house soccer, football, track and field, hockey, basketball, indoor soccer, indoor football, and boxing, and would even contain a golf course. I know I was the first to think of having a sliding floor with natural grass that moved outside the facility to allow it to grow. My idea was to

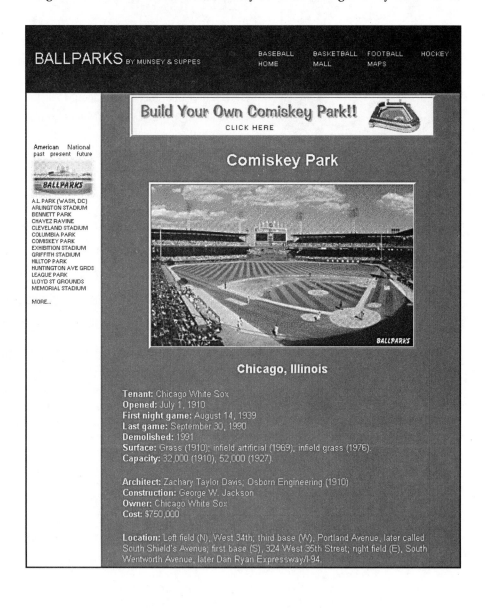

have a football game transpiring on the top level and a hockey or basketball game occurring under the sliding floor at the same time. The facility would also have smart traffic and parking, plus the capability to house non-sports activities like conventions, hotels, shops, and restaurants. The seats would have plug-in radios to listen to the play-by-play and order pads for food. Now facilities are going up using some of these ideas. Oh well, I missed out on some patents.

Cory realized that he would probably never build his own stadium, so he wanted to become a chronicler of sports facilities.

My first goal was to do a book on all the facilities. It would be a series called, "The Places We Play In." I would start with baseball and continue with football, hockey, and basketball. The books would be similar to the wonderful books in the series called "A Day in the Life." It would mostly be a coffee table picture book that would provide the reader with a feel for what it is like to be in a sports stadium in another part of the world. I am not a wordsmith; I am more of a visual person. I hoped to be the first to create such a book, since there really isn't anything like it already published. I wanted to be able to sell them at the stadiums and to offer them to the teams and players. Unfortunately, due to my lack of resources and contacts, the book was truly a pipe dream.

As computers became easier to use and the multimedia programs became much more cost-effective, I decided to investigate making a CD-ROM with all the material that I collected over the years. After speaking to a computer friend in December 1995 about how I could accomplish this dream, he said that I should explore using the Internet. This was a good idea, because with the Internet I would be able to change anything instantaneously, while with a CD-ROM or even a book, change is not possible. As I started to surf the Net using American Online, I found a site that was running for a few months that basically did what I intended, but only with baseball. I noticed the URL was www.sfo.com, which meant that the Internet service provider was in San Francisco. In May 1996, I contacted the Web site's owner, Paul Munsey, via email and told him that I was interested in forming a partnership. Paul responded by asking what I had in mind and I replied with some of my ideas.

We got together that week and started brainstorming. Paul wanted to work on baseball only and improve the pages there. I was thinking much larger. I wanted to cover all sports arenas and even other facilities like convention

www. ballparks.com

centers, bridges, churches, and skyscrapers, until I discovered how much work it would take. Scaling back my plans to just sports buildings, I said that I would have football up by the start of the football season, followed by hockey and basketball. Unlike baseball, for which there is a wealth of information about their ballparks, football, hockey, and basketball stadiums are not as romantic; therefore, collecting the necessary information is a much tougher challenge. We agreed to become partners and acquired the URL www.ballparks.com in September of 1996.

Even with the challenge of collecting all the information, it was very important to me for the site to contain different sports. In my opinion, there is a bigger sports fan base out there than just baseball. Again, because I am such a huge fan of all sports, I decided that we needed to be able to follow all the sports from season to season. This way, our site was always "on." Also, if we were just one sport, we could easily be duplicated, but with the size of the site now, covering over 550 facilities and over 1,500 dedicated and related pages, it would take someone with an awful lot of determination to compete with us. We also realize that the big boys—ESPN, CBS, CNN, Sports Illustrated, ABC, Fox, and NBC—have all the money they need to close us. We believe that if we keep building, we might foster a relationship with all of the above and not be a competitor to any due to the fact that we do not delve into teams or players.

Therefore, utilizing Paul's recipe, which allowed him to micro-create the look and feel of the baseball section, I was able to macro-create the entire site. To this day, Paul continues to explore the details of each ballpark's page, while I continue to work on the other sections and build its bulk. I am also constantly exploring potential partnership arrangements with other Web sites and traditional sports companies. I want this site to be the center of the Internet universe for all sports facilities.

Each one of these profiled buildings is a city unto itself, where an incredible amount of money and people resources converge. One of my goals is for Ballparks.com to be the Webmaster for these facilities, in which we could distribute their information online and interconnect to the other facilities. This would enable them to do what they do best, which is run their facility. An overhead savings would occur for them because they would not have to employ a programmer to do this work. We could then tie in tickets, scheduling, bookings, and even cost savings for travel, hotels, restaurants, and merchandise and food services into our site.

Although Cory is still working on becoming the official Webmaster for all these different sports facilities, people inside and outside the facility business do acknowledge his site.

Paul was in contact with some of the baseball teams and even arranged a meeting with the San Diego Padres, who were very kind in that they met with us in their office and gave us some artist renderings of their proposed new stadium. We were then treated to a tour of their ballpark, Qualcomm Stadium, formerly Jack Murphy Stadium, and given free tickets to the July 3rd fireworks show. I was in contact with the people in charge of the Staples Center in Los Angeles, a new basketball and hockey arena, who told me that NBC used our site for a half-time feature of a NBA game in which they showed the facility from our site. One problem though, we did not have the newest renderings with the Staples Center name on the facility. Other correspondence included talking with people in St. Paul, Minnesota, who are working on the new Wild Arena, and being interviewed by Facilities Management Magazine regarding the Toronto Skydome. (Paul and I had very opposite views of that facility.)

The site has also allowed us to interact with sports and Internet people ranging from HOK Sports, Ellerbe Becket, Ticketmaster, CBSportsline, Universal Studios, Lycos, Alta Vista, Yahoo!, and people writing books and articles such as this one. We have had people come by in desperation mode to ask for information and pictures and, for the most part, we have been able to steer them in the right direction or help them directly. A couple of students have even asked me questions for research papers. I've enjoyed speaking with a couple of older players of football and hockey, who wrote to tell me about their time spent at their respective home stadiums. Even the radio announcer for the professional hockey team, the San Jose Sharks, checked in once to make a friendly correction.

What's amazing is that almost immediately after posting our site, we started receiving email from people who either added, corrected, commented, or complained about what we were putting up on the site. In the beginning, I was averaging twenty-five to thirty emails per week. Today, I am averaging 105 emails per week. As we started getting people from the newspapers, radio, and magazines emailing requests for more information about our site, and then getting write-ups in *The Wall Street Journal, U.S. News & World Report, CNN Interactive, Toronto Star, Houston Chronicle*, and the *Los Angeles Times*, we knew we had something good.

www.
ballparks.com

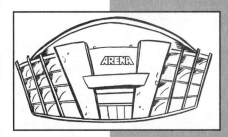

Cory is very ambitious, as he tries to constantly add more facilities to Ballparks.com. The site is very time consuming.

I spend about thirty to forty hours per week working on the Web site. This time is in addition to the time I spend at my regular job as a project manager for a hazardous waste company. My weekly Web site duties usually involve answering the email that I receive containing additional information about a particular stadium. Unfortunately, some of these additions can take anywhere from one to three hours. People send me updates, pictures, new facts, corrections, articles, insights on new projects, questions, and even stories of when they used to work at a particular stadium. I always respond to all email, whether it is positive or negative. I believe in repeat business, and I want people to return. If they can take the time to say something to us, then I believe we should respond in kind.

I've had only three negative letters in which the writers found something wrong and were very rude with how they expressed it too me. One letter was from a Marine sergeant who was based in Korea. He and I began by actually threatening each other with constitutional rights and freedom of speech all regarding the moving of the Cleveland Browns football franchise to Baltimore. I think he started emailing his buddies and they started contacting me to make a change in how I had the links set up at the Cleveland Municipal Stadium page. He did not want anything to do with the Browns moving to Baltimore and stated very strongly that the Browns franchise and all its history would remain with Cleveland and not be moved to Baltimore. After researching the agreement with the NFL, I decided that he was right and removed a link from Cleveland stadium to Memorial stadium in Baltimore and vice versa. The great thing is that we do get many, many positive letters telling us about how our visitors love returning to the site and seeing the new changes.

Along with answering emails, I add new pictures, articles, and new vendors to our virtual mall. I correct coding problems when they are found and I expand the map search section, which allows a visitor to click on a map of the world, drill down to the appropriate city, find the right stadium, and (if the stadium is found) get directions. Each one of the individual maps takes between one and two hours to create. I use four separate programs just to create one map page. I also work on future sections of the site that I have in mind, such as the soccer section and Olympic section. Other new projects include adding a NCAA basketball section, a racecar and horse track section, and development of the golf section. My major project for this year is to create a dynamic calendar for each facility. I designate Friday nights as the time I upload all the changed information.

Cory has been trying to leverage the fact that Ballparks.com gets a lot of visitors into partnerships and profitability.

We get approximately 1,000,000 page views per month, but because we use two different ISPs and only one has a counter, the number might not be that accurate—it might be much larger. An example of something we cannot count is if someone does a search and comes directly to a facility from what I call from the "side door" instead of the "front door," then we are not able to count that hit. Usually the baseball season puts a spike into our count just because of the nature of the game; people are always searching for different pieces of trivia and data. Currently, the most popular page on our site is baseball's Oriole Park at Camden Yards, the home of the Baltimore Orioles. People also like to view the old and new facilities areas, the sections that get the most visitors overall.

The site is paying for itself and has allowed us to invest in newer technology so that we can automate the site and offer jazzier features. We run the site from two local Internet service providers. Paul's baseball parks piece is at one ISP and my football, hockey, basketball, Olympics, soccer, maps, and mall sections are at another. Each has a monthly fee resulting in a combined total of forty-five dollars per month, which Paul and I divide. Each year, we also have

www.
ballparks.com

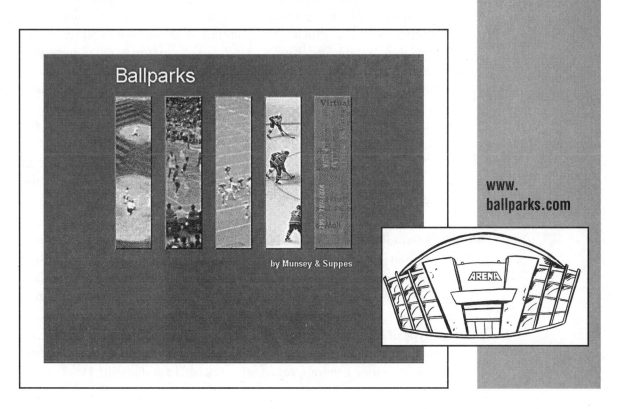

Ballparks

by Munsey & Suppes

to pay a subscription fee for our URL, which is fifty dollars per year. The only other cost involved is for upgrading software or hardware, or for buying informational material for our research. These costs are paid for out of our own pocket. The largest expense is our time, which is spent updating our site and then uploading it to the Web. Unfortunately, advertising alone does not make much money and, therefore, we explored other revenue generators. We receive revenue from our virtual mall, which gives us a percentage of every sale via our site but, of course, we would still like to earn more money.

We used part of our profits to contract out professional programming to provide our site with some specialized items. Those items include our virtual mall program, some JavaScript, and now a program to provide a virtual calendar for all of our listed facilities. In the beginning, I did all of my own programming. I am self-taught and enjoy the challenge of learning new software. I was able to pick up HTML by seeing how other people did it and "cutting and pasting" it to fit my vision. Now that the site has become so large and I am involved in so many other projects, hiring someone to help code certain projects makes sense.

Regarding partnerships, I have been in the process of putting together a business plan to present to some venture capitalists who have approached me to upgrade and move this site forward. I am currently positioning the site to co-brand and partner with many different sites to provide content for them. I am also in the development stage of my virtual ticketing/virtual reservations idea, which I have submitted to the United States Patent Office as a patent provisional. I already have three customers that expressed interest in that idea. I have also spoken to Madison Square Garden, the New Jersey Meadowlands Complex, and the New Jersey Nets, who seem interested in my virtual view/tickets idea. Recently, I went to Kansas City and met with the top two sports architectural firms in the world, HOK Sport and Ellerbe Becket, to develop a working relationship. Also, approximately seven game manufacturers expressed interest in developing a relationship in which we would provide virtual images for the backgrounds of their games.

Ballparks.com has redefined Cory's future.

I started this site basically to display all the information that I collected over the years. I wanted to present it in a format that no one has ever used. It is our "living book" that is now becoming more than just a book. It is becoming a central meeting place for all kinds of people with a passion for this type of information. As I created my sections, I have started to develop an entrepreneurial mindset of how else this site could be used to potentially make money, thereby reinventing my career and myself. I love sports, computers, organizing large amounts of information, and visualizing all the ideas that this site could produce.

The Internet has leveled the playing field between the big guys and us little guys. I have grand dreams of going after the monopolies out there and I think that by combining the awesome power of the Internet with today's database systems, we should be able to successfully compete on an equal level.

www.
ballparks.com

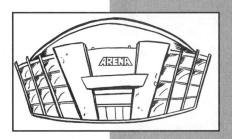

www.coolrunning.com

DAVE CAMIRE

A Running Repository

About the Site

Coolrunning.com (www.coolrunning.com) is a site dedicated to road race running. It lists many upcoming local, regional, and national races across the United States of all different distances, from 5Ks to ultra-marathons. It also lists the results of most of these races. The site provides either online registration or the ability to print out entry forms for many of the listed races. Additionally, there are columnists, daily news pieces, weekly features, a kid's section, an online mall, a health and fitness area, and a running club directory.

Some people believe television ruins children's lives by making them sedentary. Dave Camire was influenced by television, but it had the opposite affect on him. He became more active!

In 1968, at the age of twelve, I saw a report on the local news about the Boston Marathon. The concept of running 26.2 miles intrigued me. The next day, I was out training. I haven't stopped since. Right now, I run about fifty miles per week and participate in about ten to fifteen races per year.

Although I didn't run on any official teams in high school or college, I ran during that time to stay in shape. My high school did not have a cross-country team, and I was too busy working my way through college to find time to participate on a team. Since those years, I have run in many races. Some of my proudest accomplishments include running a 2:36:21 marathon and being on the team that won the 1989 Boston Marathon Men's Open Team title.

I have also been very involved in my local running club, the Greater Lowell Road Runners club. I was the editor of the club's newsletter for fifteen years and was the recipient of the Road Runners Club of America national journalism award for outstanding club newsletter. I formed and managed the club's racing team for six years. During that time, we won four national cross-country men's masters titles, and the club won the very competitive New England Grand Prix three times. I also served as club president, secretary, and membership chairperson at various times. Furthermore, I was responsible for starting the BayState Marathon, which is the organization's biggest event. This all led to me having the great honor of being one of the first five inductees into the Greater Lowell Road Runners Hall of Fame.

Through all his years of participating in the running community, Dave was trying to think of a way to link his passion for running with a way to make a living.

I have an electrical engineering degree and have been doing technical writing in the computer industry for several years. I have worked for Wang, I-Logix, and Order Trust LCC, where I am now. You can also say I am a computer hobbyist. One of my side businesses is race timing. Kevin Molloy, who was the race director of the Groton, Massachusetts 10K road race, hired me to computerize his finish line. As I was meeting with him and discussing my preparations to work on his road race, I mentioned to him that I was experimenting with the idea of an online running magazine. My idea was to send out disks on a monthly basis with complete race results and calendar information. I built a prototype and showed him.

The next morning I received an email from Kevin saying he liked the idea, but thought it would be better suited for the World Wide Web. Apparently, he was looking at the Web as a mechanism for promoting his event. I think we both independently saw an opportunity to better cover the sport of running than what was available elsewhere. Our philosophy was that all running is local and once we talked we realized the Internet provided the best opportunity to cover the local scene on a national level. Our two ideas meshed nicely and, shortly afterwards, we put together a business plan and formed a company.

Once the formalities of organizing their thoughts were done, Dave and Kevin began building coolrunning.com.

www. coolrunning .com

We began developing the site in May of 1995 and worked on it throughout that summer. Our goal was to have a content-rich site when we publicly announced the site on September 3, 1995.

From the onset, we wanted to be the site for race results and calendar and event promotion information. When we started there were few running sites in existence, and they just linked to each other. No other site had actual content. Cool Running was the first running site to include high-quantity and quality information. The daily news, race reports, training information, forums, kids' page, and other sections were in our original plans, but were developed later as we built our network. Our first posting had only race results, but I'm not sure to which race.

As far as deciding on a name, we bounced several names around, but none of them seemed to fit us. One evening we had a meeting at Kevin's house when his son walked in wearing a T-shirt from a summer running program in which he had participated. The program was called "Cool Running," a take-off on the Jamaican bobsledding movie Cool Runnings. I took one look at his shirt and said, "That's our name!" Kevin agreed. Incidentally, Kevin was the director of the Cool Running summer program, so he gets credit for the name.

When the site was up and running, Dave knew people would find it because it filled a void in the road race community.

We kind of used the "if you build it, they will come" approach to amassing a following. Finding people to view our site was never something that worried us. We felt we had an audience from the first day we went online. Although I admit that the rate of growth has surprised me. We track the amount of hits we get and the number has been climbing steadily to our current level of 2.5 million per month. We usually experience spikes around big events, such as the Boston Marathon.

In terms of readership, only the magazine Runners World can claim a larger audience. However, I would guess that our rate of growth over the last two years would eclipse theirs. Based on our growth over the last three years, we estimate that we'll be over four million hits per month during 2000. Whenever I wear clothing with the Cool Running logo to running events, people approach me to let me know how much they enjoy the site. I've had this happen to me all over the country.

A local runner related a story to me after only our first year of operation that I enjoy telling. It definitely put the power of the Internet in perspective. Apparently, he competed in the Ocean State Marathon in Rhode Island. Because of a prior commitment, after the race he had to leave immediately to get back to his home in New Hampshire. Upon arriving home, he noticed he had a message on his answering machine. The message was from a friend who congratulated him on his run. To this runner's amazement, his friend proceeded to reel off his running time and finishing place. He was amazed and curious as to how his friend obtained the information so quickly. When he called to find out, his friend's reply was Cool Running.

Working on Cool Running has cut into Dave's personal running time.

Personally, I spend about forty to fifty hours per week on the site. Kevin spends an equal amount of time. Our functions entail all the unglamorous jobs associated with running a small growing business. We code, market, sell, and perform just about every function associated with the operation of Cool Running. As far as the distribution of work, we both do a little of everything, but Kevin concentrates more on the technology side and I concentrate a little more on the finances.

It helps that between the two of us we have almost fifty years of experience in the computer industry. Kevin, like myself, has an electrical engineering degree. He has worked on the support side of the computer industry for Digital and Compaq. I've already mentioned my background, which is mainly in technical writing.

Reading and responding to emails also takes time. I would estimate that we get about 500 emails per week. Due to the volume, it is difficult to single out one memorable email; however, the ones that I consider most memorable are the ones that either praise or blast our site. Fortunately, praise is the majority. Most of the other emails ask for information on events or where to find certain information on our site.

As Cool Running's longevity on the Web has increased, so have its revenues.

www. coolrunning .com

In the beginning, we had to overcome two huge hurdles to attract advertisers. First, we were the new kids on the running block. At the time, hardcopy magazines were the predominate source of running information, and the Internet was in its infancy. We did not have a track record, and this was suspect to some people. Also, we were dealing in a new technology that did not have the exposure it enjoys today. Our first break came when we convinced Jon Pearson, director of the Yankee Homecoming Ten-Mile Race in Newburyport, Massachusetts, that this was a cost-effective vehicle for advertising events. Jon, who is one of the most respected race directors in New England, liked the concept. He is also someone who keeps detailed records of his return on advertising investments. Jon's return from his Cool Running advertisement far exceeded his expectations and the return he was getting from his print advertising. This excited him, and he became our biggest advocate.

In the running community, word spread quickly about his experience. We started getting new clients who experienced the same results as Jon. At the same time, we were gaining respect for our timely reporting and as a great source for running information. Things began to solidify quickly. Today, even though Cool Running is well known, we still approach race directors through the traditional means, such as phone and mail. The biggest difference is that many advertisers now come to us unsolicited.

I am amazed at the amount of success many of our clients are experiencing through promoting their businesses or events on our site. My personal expectations were set high and, to my delight, were exceeded by many of our clients. Many of these clients attribute their high growth solely to our site. Many of the events that are advertised with us are abandoning advertising in print media entirely and relying solely on Cool Running. It's nice working in a business that has a ninety-five percent success rate on repeat business.

Overall, it took us two years to become profitable, as we are today. Kevin and I put in a combined investment of a little under $5,000. This included our cash outlay and some equipment purchases. This was nothing compared to our sweat-equity investment, which was huge. Currently, it costs us about $5,000 per month to run the site. Our biggest expense is the cost of renting Web space for our site, which is around $1,000 per month. Ultimately, I'm hoping to turn this into a full-time job.

Keeping the 250 percent annual visitor growth that coolrunning.com has averaged over the last three years requires Dave and Kevin to keep on top of running and technology.

Currently, according to our statistics, the race results section and the race calendar section are tied for the most popular parts of our site. Another popular area is our columnists' portion of Cool Running. We have several running writers who regularly contribute to the site. Finding the first writers was not that difficult, especially because I have been involved in the sport of running and the technical writing business for many years. I knocked on the doors of friends and colleagues who could write and utilized several contacts that Kevin established over the years. Between the two of us, we were able to build a writing team. It was just a matter of persuading them to write for us. Once we gained critical mass, writers began knocking on our door.

Looking forward, I think that technology and trends in the running marketplace will dictate where we go over the next few years. We consistently lead all running sites in innovation. We'll continue to keep our finger on the pulse of technology and running and evolve accordingly.

Most of the specific future enhancements we have in mind will depend on how technology changes. Obviously, online purchasing is coming of age and will offer tremendous opportunities for us. Recently we started offering online race registration via credit card transactions. Although we are not alone in offering this option, clients are coming to us because of our large readership and the exposure we can afford them. I think video is another area where we'll see tremendous growth. However, that will not happen until the bandwidth is increased.

Cool Running will hopefully be Dave's fiscal future; however, even if it is not, it has provided him with some great memories.

I have always been a giant fan of United States Olympic runner and gold medallist Frank Shorter. Through Cool Running, I got the chance to meet and interview Frank. Since then, we have become friends. Frank even visited Massachusetts to be the master of ceremonies when I was inducted into the Greater Lowell Road Runners Hall of Fame. I don't know if this would have been possible if not for Cool Running.

I consider the Internet and my site as the American dream, the new frontier. I feel there are no boundaries to what we can accomplish in this medium. It truly is limitless.

www.
coolrunning
.com

UPMC HEALTH SYSTEM
CITY OF PITTSBURGH
MARATHON
May 7, 2000

Massachusetts Race Results 00

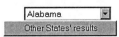 Alabama

Other States' results

January | February | March

March
March 5	Claddagh Pub Classic	Lawrence
March 3	FTC Friday Night Five	Falmouth
March 2	Khoury's Thursday Night 4.13M	E. Somerville

February
February 27	Cape Cod Times 5Mile, 1/2 & Full Marathon	Hyannis
February 27	Cherry Pie Classic	Lawrence
February 27	Jones Town & Country 10-Miler	Amherst
February 26	Hudson Boy's and Girls Club 5.3 Mile	Hudson
February 26	New England High School Championship	Boston
February 26	Snowstorm Classic 5K	Springfield
February 25	FTC Friday Night Five	Falmouth
February 25	Reebok Boston Invitational	Boston
February 24	Khoury's Thursday Night 4.13M	E. Somerville
February 23	MSTCA Girl's Pentathlon Championship Meet	Boston
February 22	MSTCA Boy's Pentathlon Championship	Boston
February 21	MIAA - Auerbach Indoor Championship	Boston
February 20	Foxboro 10 Miler & 5K	Foxboro
February 20	Merrimac Handicap 7 Miler	Merrimac
February 19	Martha's Vineyard 20 Miler	Oak Bluff
February 19	Martha's Vineyard 20 Miler	Oak Bluffs
February 19	Snowstorm Classic 10K	Springfield
February 18	FTC Friday Night Five	Falmouth
February 18	USATF New England Indoor Championship	Boston
February 17	Khoury's Thursday Night 4.13M	E. Somerville
February 13	Alliance Championship Meet - M.A.S.C.A.C. - Little East	Boston
February 13	MIAA Indoor Class A Championship	Boston
February 13	NMC Donnelley's Tavern 5 Mile	Leominster
February 13	Paddy Kelly 5 Miler	Brockton
February 12	CMS 52-Week 5K #6	Worcester
February 12	MIAA Indoor Class B & D Championship	Boston
February 12	Bradford Valentine Road Race	Bradford

**www.roadside
america.com**

**KEN SMITH, DOUG KIRBY,
AND MIKE WILKINS**

**TAKEN AT CARHENGE IN
ALLIANCE, NE**

Off the Beaten Path

About the Site
RoadsideAmerica (www.roadsideamerica.com) provides detailed descriptions of unique tourist attractions across the United States. The site features extensive narrative files, an interactive map, and an attractions hall of fame. The site is based on a very successful book of the same name, which is now in its seventh printing.

It's amazing what three guys can accomplish by talking about their childhood memories of summer vacations with Mom and Dad.

It began with us getting together and realizing that we had a common childhood experience—packing everybody into the van or the station wagon, hitting the road for a couple weeks, and traveling on family vacations. Aside from the beautiful attractions we could see, if we were lucky, we would get to stop at a tourist trap or an offbeat attraction. As adults, it occurred to us that nobody really described these as a separate type of tourism. Thus, our project began.

Roadside America captures the lesser known, the underrated, and the often overlooked aspects of on-the-road travel throughout all fifty states. Based initially on a successful book, roadsideamerica.com uses the Internet

125

and multimedia to bring each trip to life. Doug Kirby, editor of the Web site, explains the story:

There are three authors, Mike is based in California; Ken and I are in New Jersey. Ken is a freelance writer who penned *Raw Deal* and *Ken's Guide to the Bible*. Mike is a fund manager and writer. He recently co-wrote and produced a film: *The Independent*, starring Jerry Stiller. I'm the creative director for ATT.com and a user interface designer for AT&T labs.

Each of us arrived at the project from slightly different directions. I had the classic childhood adventures, shoved in a station wagon with my two brothers and sisters and on the road for a month going to South of the Border, Devil's Tower, Wall Drug, wherever. Ken's experience consisted of what he as a child thought were boring historical attractions to which his parents took him. Therefore, he always wanted to go to these unusual places. In a sense, he's reliving his childhood. Mike also did a lot of travel with his family. He was a big postcard collector. Mike picks the attractions for our whirlwind Boring Tour. It was Mike who put together the original book proposal using a lot of bizarre postcard images of places, though we didn't know if the attractions themselves were still out there.

While most people prefer to drive right by an out-of-the-way tourist attraction advertised on a highway billboard, Mike, Ken, and Doug go to great efforts to seek out these places.

We just went to a great site in Wykoff, Minnesota, Ed's Museum. I think we found it in the state literature. This is a little museum of a guy who lived in the town all of his life. When he died, the people in Wykoff realized that he never threw out anything. So, they turned his house into a museum.

We got there, and it was pretty neat. The guy ran a general store in the town for fifty years. The women of the Wykoff Progress Club made the house presentable. Everything that he had ever owned was organized in boxes—all his pocket planners, calendars, and check stubs. In the basement, there was a box labeled, "Sammy." Sammy turned out to be his cat that died in 1986. They loved this guy in Wykoff. All the townspeople love having this little museum.

Before deciding to launch Roadside America, the three creators explored a range of collaborative projects as side interests.

Early on, we all lived in the New York area and worked together on various humor-related projects. There was a pilot of a magazine called American Bystander, a radio show, and a NYC comedy troupe. Roadside America was one of the projects that we thought: "Oh, this would be a fun thing to do." As things evolved, we realized that we had this amazing common experience. We put the book proposal together and shopped it around.

The first book was pitched with a list of 200 must-sees based on some individual trips we took. With the book, the first reaction was: "Well, the reason nobody's done this kind of thing is because it's not at all easy to do. These places are not well known." As we soon discovered, you can't simply call the state tourism bureau to send you free information on these places. You can't get the Chambers of Commerce to wine and dine you because these aren't necessarily the places they want to promote.

Perseverance and a couple months making the rounds to various publishers eventually produced results. Soon, these unlikely travel writers writing about unlikely travel destinations found themselves with both a contract and an advance.

We hit the road, following tips, combining the tourist mecca, and seeking out those old postcard attractions. After we realized

www.roadside america.com

ALMOST 10mi

NOT QUITE 4mi

that we would have no money left from the advance, we just had fun with it. That's actually something we've kept up; it's still a lot of fun.

Based on their travels to the geographic corners of the nation, Doug, Ken, and Mike put together an unparalleled seven wonders of the roadside America world.

1) Wall Drug, Wall, SD: No one leaves South Dakota alive without stopping at Wall Drug! Since 1931, this classic tourist trap has absorbed most of downtown Wall with souvenir shops, coin operated shows, steak houses, and photo opportunities. Now that founders Ted and Dorothy Hustead have passed away, a third generation Hustead carries on. www.roadsideamerica.com/attract/SDWALdrug.html

2) South of the Border, Dillon, SC: A rare national treasure! This Mexican theme tourist stop features a giant Sombrero Tower that can be spotted for miles. It thrives along I-95 just south of the North Carolina border. Vacationing East Coasters know to stop at South of the Boarder for fireworks, tacky souvenirs, and other surprises. www.roadsideamerica.com/attract/SCDILsob.html

3) House on the Rock, Spring Green, WI: This must-see attraction is at once immense and perplexing. Alex Jordan Jr. built this marvel, which is today expanded to a series of buildings filled with rare treasures: huge sea monsters; automated music machines; and robotic orchestras. Nearly everything is fake. www.roadsideamerica.com/attract/WISPRhouse.html

4) Rock City, Chattanooga, TN: From the bluff on Lookout Mountain you can see seven states. But getting to and from the scenic overlook, known as Rock City, is all the fun. Visitors must brave craggy paths, swaying bridges, and hallucinogenic fairy tale caverns, playfully stalked by teen workers in elf and Humpty Dumpty costumes. www.roadsideamerica.com/attract/GALOOrock.html

5) World of Coca-Cola, Atlanta, GA: Sample the sodas of many lands! Watch Coke spritz through the air! It's the corporation's over-the-top celebration of itself. Any visitor can find more history, videos, and details about a soft drink than they'd ever want to know. World of Coca-Cola West has now opened in Las Vegas. www.road sideamerica.com/attract/GAATLcoke.html

6) Secret Caverns, Cobleskill, NY: A plucky little parasite of an attraction, Secret Caverns feeds off traffic to stately Howe Caverns, a few miles down the road. But Secret Caverns is really the place to go. Strange guides have taken over, painting bizarre billboard enticements and offering funny, offbeat tours. Be very careful whom you're standing next to during the "moment of total darkness." www.roadsideamerica. com/cave

7) Precious Moments Chapel, Carthage, MO: Eye-poppin' scary! Since 1989, Samuel Butcher's Sistine Chapel-inspired creation has drawn millions by the busload. Big-eyed cartoon baby angels grace giant biblical murals and sculptures and, of course, are available for purchase in the endless collectibles gift shops. www.roadsideamerica.com/tour/ 94day5.html#precious

Today, the second book, *The New Roadside America*, is in its seventh printing. The site, meanwhile, receives two million hits per month, or about 300,000 page views. While both formats—the book and the Web site—were extremely successful in building a solid core audience, the pace of publishing on the Internet initially caught the authors a bit by surprise.

www.roadside america.com

While the books grew out of our shared enthusiasm for tourist traps, offbeat roadside attractions, and wacky vacation thrills, when we complete a book manuscript, the attraction reviews are locked into the period of time we submit the manuscript. On the other hand, with the Web site, it's harder for us to get away with leaving up old or stale information. As we've found out from firsthand experience, visitors to the site will start calling us to task on that. We receive mail about a place we've just put up on the Web site: "Perry's Nut House is closed." "Oh no, they're auctioning off all the stuffed animals this weekend, the giant nuts." Of course, we feel obligated to immediately update the write-up on the spot. We'll pull up the Perry's Nut House site and update the information. Then, a few days later: "Now Perry's Nut House is open, but we don't know if the stuffed animals are back."

With a book, places could open and close and reopen and re-close. You don't have to deal with it until you are actually publishing a new edition of the book. However, there is an exciting, yet disturbing continuum about the Web that we haven't quite figured out yet.

We try to report on any news we hear about concerning a place we visited. For instance, Tommy Bartlett died recently. He was one of the founders of the Wisconsin Dells tourism mecca, where you can find Tommy Bartlett's Robot World and Tommy Bartlett's Thrills Show. He was known for slapping bumper stickers on every car in the parking lot so visitors would remember the Wisconsin Dells. That sort of news is timely. We put up a eulogy or obituary pointing to attractions that he brought to life.

Roadside is more about content than flashy technology. Each page has compelling ideas and interesting stories. We try to augment the site with occasional animation and lots of photography or artwork. The material is perfectly suited for the Web. We make sure there is a reward on every page and provide this through our writing style and offbeat approach. While some other sites suffer from that lazy travel-writer syndrome, visitors can tell we've been to these places and that we report honestly on what we see. We also encourage visitors to become virtual guides by contributing tips on new places or updates on known attractions.

Our approach to the travel narrative has always been non-linear. Therefore, our minds are well suited for the world of hyperlinks and the publishing format of the Internet in general.

As an example, we produced a coast-to-coast hyper tour in 1994 for the pre-launch version of Hotwired, which launched us down the Web path. Our weeklong Los Angeles-New York City trip was reported each day online via both AOL and the Web featuring our writing, photos, and videos. We dialed out from a pay phone or pancake house and uploaded to the Hotwired folks in San Francisco. I think they hand-coded the HTML on UNIX workstations. We lugged along a desktop Mac for the video work, and had a couple of souped-up Powerbooks on loan from Apple. We'd drive almost 700 miles each day, visit eight to ten attractions, and then compress the experience in our motel rooms into the wee hours. It was promoted as the first virtual vacation.

The approach we take, which is different from a lot of travel writers, is that we are tourists. We're the ugly Americans traveling in ugly America. These places are built for our entertainment and to convince us to shell out money. So if you approach attractions that way, they're usually more enjoyable than if you go on vacation with the notion that you're going to blend in with the natives, and find the "secluded Eden" where no one else has ever been. That's pretty much a delusion.

These attractions share aspects appealing to our audience and to us. First, there's the sense of personal discovery, which is nearly impossible to feel in the programmed experience of a corporate theme park. Finding an offbeat attraction or interesting tourist site is akin to early pioneers coming over that last mountain range and seeing the Pacific Ocean! In much the same way, a personal tour by the actual creator of a museum or collection is better than having Walt Disney himself walk you around the Enchanted Castle. Then again, an animated Walt would be kind of cool.

I think our readers appreciate the amusing comical aspect of the attractions themselves, the overstuffed gift shop, the dangerously run-down ride, or the cranky owner. Beyond the laughs though, people connect with many of these places as uniquely American, and worthwhile to see. If no one were to visit, many of these attractions would disappear. We get a lot of mail from visitors thanking us for the important work we are doing cataloging and reporting on places around the country. And here we thought we were just having fun.

If you read our Web site, there's a consistency in what we like and what we don't like. So we see it in the same way you would follow a movie reviewer or a book reviewer that you trust. We share some part of our approach with you. You've gone to a place we've recommended, and had a great time there. You're likely to trust some of our other coverage too.

The only things we tell people not to bother with are big water parks and corporate-themed world kind of things. People are going to go to those things anyway. We won't hurt that traffic. We don't usually write anything about National Parks. They're probably happy. They have too many visitors as it is now.

There are a couple of instances where we'll be a little fickle. We might get there on a day where the performance was much better than normal or much worse. The attraction reviews portray our experience and the research we have done.

The trips have ranged from weekend jaunts, twelve to fifteen attractions, one-to-two-week hyper tours or research expeditions seeing fifty to 150 attractions, and even some longer journeys. On one trip, Mike and Ken stayed on the road for two months and traveled 26,000 miles.

Early trips were more like wandering adventures; we didn't know much about what we'd see between a start and an end point. While we'd find exciting and weird attractions, we might also miss places only a block or two out of sight.

www.roadside america.com

After dozens of trips and thousands of miles logged, trip planning is now down to a science.

Our recent travels are more structured, using maps and detailed route plans. We see much more, and still stumble on to the occasional unknown gem. First, we construct a "fantasy route," literally where we would go if we could drive 100 miles per hour and the sun stayed up until midnight. Then we argue over the merits of a detour to the Rocky Taconite statue or the Tuberculin Rabbit shrine. We always call any strange museums or shows to make sure the owner hasn't died or been committed. Finally, we agree on the itinerary and hit the road.

We saw an interesting thing in Madison, Wisconsin. It was in our database: Funeral home with perky animal dioramas. That was all we knew about it. We arrived there to find Sam Sanfillippo, who had taxidermy displays in his basement. The purpose was for individuals who were grieving loved ones to go down in his basement to be cheered up by these scenes of albino squirrels riding on motorcycles and chipmunks on Ferris wheels.

Albino squirrels in Wisconsin, stuffed cats in Minnesota, along with the regular sight of the week and visitor tips, all require tracking and updating myriad bits of information.

We have over 7,000 attractions in the off-line database, which we pull from to feature online. We have enough new material to last for many years. We've written up only about 25 percent of the attractions on the Web site, and we're seeing more places each year.

There are a couple dozen fields in each record. Aside from the basics of address, phone number, directions, hours, and admission fees, we also log visits, contacts, phone calls, details on photos and videos, audio interviews, licensing status, and any souvenirs we bought. There are also fields for attraction category or genre, tour category, map icons, mention of whether or not it has been in any of our books or has appeared as a Site of the Week, URL, and so forth. The description field varies in readiness for publication. Some entries are a jumble of notes, while others are more polished. The humorous angle is already developed.

We currently have 700 pages posted on the Web site. Sometimes we don't know in which direction the site will grow. For example, a single page about Muffler Men in 1996 is now a sprawling hub of 300 sightings with a tracking map, mutation reports, and such. We must reevaluate the architecture of the site to see if it holds up, given our current needs.

Wall Drug

Shimmering ice water oasis.
[Photo courtesy of Wall Drug]

Wall, SD

The name **Wall Drug** strikes a familiar note of horror with anyone who's driven the interstate system west of the Appalachians or east of the Rockies with a back seat full of screaming children. "Mommy, Daddy, lookit the funny signs! Can we stop huh please huh can we just for a minute puh-leeeeeze?" Those who have been denied this experience may still have heard of Wall Drug if they've visited the North or South Poles, for even at the ends of the earth, Wall Drug has posted signs advertising the mileage to itself.

Wall Drug may be the roadside wonder best known to people who've never been to America. Paris Metro riders have seen Wall Drug signs. So have rail commuters in Kenya, bus passengers in London, and visitors to the Taj Mahal. Wall Drug spends thousands each year to maintain some of these signs, but most are the impromptu erections of former Wall Drug visitors. GIs from South Dakota put up signs in Germany, Korea and Vietnam. Every traveller who has stopped at Wall Drug in the past 60-odd years has been given a free Wall Drug sign, so that they might also join the vast Wall Drug self-promotion fraternity.

Wall Drug is a sprawling tourist mall that occupies the majority of downtown Wall, which used to be known by locals as "the geographical center of nowhere." That was before Ted Hustead came along.

The Lure of Ice Water

Wall Drug a half a century ago.

Ted was a Nebraska native who moved to Wall and opened a tiny drug store in 1931. Five years later, it was still a tiny drug store. Dorothy, Ted's wife, thought that the travelers driving past their store must be thirsty, and suggested that Ted put up a sign outside of town advertising free ice water at Wall Drug.

Ted thought it was a silly idea, but he was desperate and put up the sign. By the time he got back, thirsty tourists were already lining up for their free ice water. They've been stopping ever since.

Wall Drug is now managed by Bill Hustead, Ted's son, and under his guiding hand it has grown considerably. "I was embarrassed when I was in high school," Bill remembers. "All those signs, and when you arrived it was just an ordinary small town store. It was my crusade to develop the store into something special." He has. Wall Drug still has a tiny pharmacy (the only one within 500 square miles) but its peripheral amusements have taken over and now extend across several blocks. Wall Drug is the principle industry in Wall. It employs nearly a third of the town's residents. Wall has more public swimming pools per citizen than any other town in the world, thanks to Wall Drug. If every Wall resident decided to rent a motel room in town on the same night, there'd still be over 400 vacancies.

One of the more challenging aspects of managing the site is verifying all the tips that were submitted over the years.

Often, the people who are writing in are not doing research; they're just reacting to something they saw on the road. They might get the town wrong; they might get the highway wrong; they might get the name of the attraction wrong. We receive tips and must follow up on our own research.

The guys at Roadside have a nice, unanticipated side business that produces much of the money now used to pay for some of their travels.

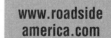

www.roadside america.com

The revenue that the site produces now is mostly a passive sales thing where we get requests for rush licensing of images for various publications. A German magazine needs six photos of Florida tourist attractions that same night. We negotiate a price and the entire transaction takes place electronically. After locating the photos in our database, we upload high-resolution versions and send them instantly to the Internet address provided. The business is nice in terms of income because it helps pay for the expenses of the Web site, travel, and there is still a little extra left. As far as leaving our jobs and sitting on the Roadside dole—we have yet to determine how to accomplish that.

Banner ads are something we may still do. Originally I felt ads would be a betrayal to our fans, but I'm beginning to think to myself: "Hey, we post 700 pages of information and graphics on our site. It's stuff you can't get anywhere else on the Web." Nobody's paying for it. Given this, I guess we're not so troubled by the advertising approach anymore. We have succeeded in creating micro-sites for corporate sponsors. A single sponsor may ultimately be the best strategy for building our Web site to the next level.

CHAPTER 15

TRAVLANG

www.travlang.com

DR. MICHAEL MARTIN

TRAVLANG
Your Travel
& Language
Supersite

A Master of Many Tongues

About the Site

Travlang.com (www.travlang.com) is a site that specializes in translating words from more than sixty languages. The site also provides extensive language and travel link lists, plus bulletin boards, chat areas, and a currency exchange rate calculator. The two primary areas for language translation are the Translating Dictionaries section and the Foreign Language for Travelers pages. The Translating Dictionaries section translates a typed word into any other language. The Foreign Language for Travelers pages provides a list of words in several categories, like numbers or common words, where not only is the translation displayed, but also provides the option of hearing the pronunciation.

For someone with a Ph.D. in Physics, maintaining a Web site about translating languages might seem unusual, but not for Dr. Michael Martin, a twenty-nine-year-old living in San Jose, California.

My interest in languages started when I was twelve years old and my family moved to France for a year. I went right into a regular French school and learned French quickly. Since then, in all my travels, I've found that both a knowledge of another language, or knowing just a handful of useful words and phrases in the specific language of the country you are visiting, makes a large difference in the enjoyment of the visit. People are very friendly when you try to speak a little of their language. Furthermore, I've also found that getting to know a little of another culture really helps make the world a smaller and friendlier place for everyone.

Aside from living in France or the United States, I have lived for shorter periods of time in Stuttgart, Germany; Cambridge, England; and Budapest, Hungary. However,

French is the only language other than English that I claim to have any proficiency speaking. I know a bit of Spanish, but my wife speaks it much better than I do, so she handles most Spanish-speaking occasions.

Michael's world travels for his physics research and his interactions with foreign scientific colleagues gave him an idea.

During 1994, while in graduate school at Stony Brook, New York, I was going to Hungary for a month to do some physics research. I asked a Hungarian colleague to write down a few words and phrases for me to use. I realized then that the brand new World Wide Web would be an excellent place to put a list of words and phrases with sound files. I went to my friends in the physics deparment and got the first ten or so languages that way and posted it on my physics computer account.

My Foreign Languages for Travelers pages started small, but it wasn't too long after the pages were posted that the traffic and size overwhelmed that small server. So I went to a commercial server and started really expanding the Web pages. The Foreign Languages for Travelers pages were entirely reprogrammed to allow translations from any language to any other language. We also added a whole set of Translating Dictionaries, and much more. Currently, the largest translation dictionary, the German/English dictionary, contains over 130,000 words, followed by some of our Dutch dictionaries that include over 50,000 words. Of course, we are constantly adding more languages. We now have over sixty languages, and soon we'll have over seventy.

I knew from the start that my site was successful because I always reviewed the log files showing how many people were viewing the Web pages. In the beginning, I was impressed that people were finding my humble pages and that the numbers consistently grew. It was very gratifying when people started offering their help to translate into yet more languages only a month after I started the pages.

Michael's personal language knowledge is limited, so he has relied on other travlang.com visitors to enhance the content of his site.

One of the greatest things about this site is that it has been a truly worldwide collaboration. People from all over the world offer their help by adding new languages and also through correcting any mistakes that they see. In this manner, we've expanded the pages and have added a lot of sound files with the help of native speakers.

www.
travlang.com

I also enjoy meeting people who, like me, really take pleasure in making something quite useful and providing it free for the Web community. Two of these people have become active participants in Travlang. I provide the Web server space for them, and they continue to make nice programs and content. One is Gerard van Wilgen, the author of our free Ergane dictionary program that translates one language into another. He's really created a nice tool, which we are happy to distribute on the Internet. His data have also allowed us to continually expand our online dictionaries. Another person is Herb Vogel, a retired engineer, who has been learning Web programming. He has made several useful sections for Travlang, including the International Driving Rules pages and holiday calendars for many countries. Plus, he's working on an interactive time zone program.

Most of the other travel information I added to the site can be found in various places on the Web. Travlang has always had many links to other sites that I find useful and well done. I want our users to be able to find additional travel- and language-oriented sites easily.

Although Travlang.com is successful and even profitable, Michael doesn't see it as a full-time job.

We're currently getting over 3.5 million hits per week, and that number continues to grow. We've seen increases in our hit rates mostly when there is a good article about us published somewhere; for example, we've had a couple of articles in the *Los Angeles Times*, in London's *Sunday Times*, and other places. The most popular section of the site is our Foreign Languages for Travelers pages, followed by our Translating Dictionaries. The most looked at languages on our site are Spanish, French, German, English, Italian, Japanese, and Russian, generally in that order. The bulk of our visitors come from the United States, followed by the United Kingdom, Germany, and Japan.

The site does make money in the sense that nothing comes out of my pocket for the Web servers expenses and such, but I am still donating most of my time for programming, answering e-mails, and whatever else needs to be done. Travlang's basic operations, mainly just server-related expenses, cost in the neighborhood of $750 per month. The biggest expense is providing high-speed, redundant Internet access. We currently have five Web servers all connected via multiple T3 connections to ensure fast, reliable throughput. The site covers these costs largely from showing banner ads from our sponsors, but it also gets a small commission from hotel reservations made through the site.

Generating revenue began when the pages moved to a commercial server, and I started accepting advertising to offset the costs of running the site. It worked out nicely when the very first month I rented space on a commercial server for $75 per month, I found an advertiser willing to pay $75 per month for a banner ad. Ever since then, we've always had enough advertisers to pay for all the out-of-pocket expenses. It is also interesting that now advertisers approach us about putting ads on Travlang after seeing the site. We no longer need to approach them. This is especially true of the hotel reservation section of the site. We link to hotels, and they share commissions equivalent to what they give travel agents for booked reservations, and at no extra cost to the consumer.

I probably won't ever make the site a full-time career, as my physics research career continues quite successfully. I do think that we will eventually hire some employees to help Travlang.com continue to grow, but I don't have a specific timetable for this.

Balancing time between his full-time job and the site has been difficult, especially as the popularity of his site grows.

I'm a physicist at Lawrence Berkeley National Laboratory with a Ph.D. in physics, specifically experimental condensed matter physics. I study infrared spectroscopy of many materials from superconductors to new magnetic materials and toxin-eating bacteria. I operate one of the world's brightest sources of infrared light at the Advanced Light Source synchrotron facility in Berkeley, and many scientists come from around the world to do research at my facility. I'm really enjoying working with so many people on a broad array of research. It is full-time, and it is my primary occupation. Travlang.com has grown to become a serious second job over the past few years.

I spend probably about forty hours per week working on the site. Of course, that is in addition to my regular full-time job that I do during the day. Most of my site work entails answering e-mails and making minor updates and changes. I get around sixty e-mails per day, and I try to personally answer everyone who has a real question or comment about Travlang. I do enjoy keeping in touch with users, and I inform users when new items are added, particularly if they requested them. I also work on adding new languages and other features.

I do the entire Web programming myself. I'm comfortable with computers, because I've been exposed to them for a long time, especially since I grew up in Silicon Valley. I first programmed some simple games on a Commodore 64 in 1980. Since then, I've taken a few classes in Basic, Fortran, and Pascal. I have written a number of programs for solving physics problems and running experimental equipment. Currently, most of the site is run via Perl scripts, a language I really prefer.

A personal benefit that Michael's Web site created for him is how people are using the information they find on his site.

Certainly getting to know many different people from all corners of the globe has been great, but it's always fun to hear a story about someone who was able to get on the right bus outside of Rome thanks to a printout of our Web pages. This happened when a tourist was visiting Rome for a conference and was in the outskirts of the city as evening was approaching. He was able to use printouts of our Italian pages to talk to some local people and catch the correct bus to get him back to his hotel. I've also been told a number of

www.
travlang.com

other nice stories. Several people have used our pages to make a foreign exchange student feel welcome upon arrival. A number of visitors have used our pages to get in touch with relatives from other countries. Also, quite a few schoolchildren have used our language pages for class reports on other countries, and teachers have used our pages in helping students learn about other cultures and languages.

Michael has no plans to slow down the development of his site and only sees it getting better.

We certainly plan to continue expanding our site to include more languages, dictionaries, and country-specific information. I have also been making up a list of new words and phrases to more than double the size of our Foreign Languages for Travelers lessons. Into the future, I would like to make CD-ROM versions of our Foreign Languages for Travelers pages to enable people to use them more easily while travelling and to use them off-line.

I'd also like to make the site automatically display links and information about the other material we offer. An example would be if you went to our Dutch dictionaries, you would see links to our Dutch for Travelers pages, the Dutch Guilder exchange rate, holidays in the Netherlands, European driving rules, the time zone, hotels, and other Dutch-related information. This would make the entire site more cohesive and allow everyone to more easily find all the nice extra tools we offer.

I'm also considering the installation of a European mirror site and perhaps an Asian mirror site to help speed access for people from those parts of the world. This, however, is still a ways off in the future.

Michael views Travlang.com in the same way he views the rest of the Internet.

For me, it's primarily loads of good information available instantly. Whether it's looking up a specific part number from some company in Florida, or trying to learn a new language, it's available free and instantly. I can't quite believe how we survived without it for even simple things like looking up directions to a specific store!

www.
travlang.com

CHAPTER 16

FrequentFlier·com

www.frequentflier.com

TIM WINSHIP

Flying for Free

About the Site

FrequentFlier.com (www.frequentflier.com) provides all sorts of information about frequent flyer programs. The site contains sections dealing with news and new airline alliances, in addition to question-and-answer sections about choosing the right program for you. The history of frequent flyer programs is also documented. The site offers a companion newsletter that you can sign up to receive.

Some people take a job because it is available. Others, such as Tim Winship of Los Angeles, age forty-six, find a calling in their chosen career.

I've worked in the travel industry for over twenty years. My interest in frequent flyer programs dates back to the mid-1980s. At the time, I was working in Singapore Airlines' North America marketing department, and frequent flyer programs were beginning to receive recognition as the hot ticket in travel marketing. One of my earliest marketing projects was getting Singapore Air tied up, contract-wise, operations-wise, and marketing-wise with the American Airlines Advantage Program. I've been hooked on frequent flyer programs ever since.

Tim began Theffpsite.org, the precursor to Frequent Flier.com, as a learning experience and nothing more.

My involvement with computers dates back to the Vic-20, if you remember that milestone in personal

frequentflier•com

navigate   [Go to... ▼]

FREQUENT FLYER PROGRAM PROFILES

Following are summaries of the largest frequent flyer programs, including contact information and lists of participating mileage and award partners.

For more complete information, use the Links to the Programs page, which will hyperlink you directly to the frequent flyer program section of the listed airlines' websites.

Frequent Flyer Newsletter

Subscribe!

Important Notes

While every effort is made to keep the following profiles current, bear in mind the following:

- The terms under which partners participate vary considerably. For example, some airlines only give mileage credit for certain routes or fare types.
- The partners themselves change often.
- Even the information shown on the program hosts' web sites may not be completely up-to-date.

So, before doing or deciding anything on the basis of a program's partnerships, call the customer service number (shown beneath the program logo) to confirm the partner's participation, and any restrictions that may be in effect.

AIRLINE PROGRAMS

➤ Alaska Airlines Mileage Plan	➤ Midwest Express Frequent Flyer
➤ American AAdvantage	➤ Northwest WorldPerks
➤ America West FlightFund	➤ TWA Aviators
➤ Continental OnePass	➤ United Mileage Plus
➤ Delta SkyMiles	➤ US Airways Dividend Miles

HOTEL PROGRAMS

➤ Best Western Gold Crown Club	➤ Intercontinental Six Continents
➤ Crowne Plaza Priority Club	➤ Marriott

computing. At that time, I took BASIC programming courses at a local community college, because the only software for the Vic was software you wrote yourself. I was an early adopter of the PC, slaving away at work on an early-model IBM, using the first release of Lotus on a 4.88 MHz processor with a monochrome monitor. I have also been involved with the online community since the early days of Compuserve, back when you used a 1200-baud modem and downloaded text crawled across the screen. For all its limitations, the promise of real-time access to every sort of data imaginable existed.

My interest in the Internet led me to begin Theffpsite.org in 1996 because I wanted to understand the mechanics of Web development. The content, in the beginning, was a secondary consideration. Rather than create a personal site that had pictures of my dog and my car, I focused on frequent flyer programs because I felt I could only make a meaningful contribution in an area where I had significant expertise. I also knew that I would lose momentum if I chose content in which I didn't have an abiding interest. You know what they say, do what you know and what you love.

When I started the site, it was even more graphically challenged than it is now, not that it's particularly slick yet. Nevertheless, it had solid content from the beginning. The only site that surpasses mine content-wise is WebFlyer, the online version of the print publication *InsideFlyer*.

Tim uses his contacts to gather information for keeping his site up-to-date.

Wearing my journalist's hat, I have access to news releases distributed by all the travel provider companies, including airlines, hotels, rental cars, and such. Furthermore, because of my travel industry background, I also have many contacts in the business with whom I maintain communication. Also, I read, read, and read some more. I read every newspaper, trade publication, and online source about frequent flyer programs.

Sometimes airlines help me directly. They usually ask me to update some bit of outdated information, but my relationship with the airlines and other travel providers is somewhat ambiguous. On the one hand, I advocate the use of frequent flyer programs, and serve as a distribution channel for information about the programs—so they love me. On the other hand, I approach the programs very critically and understand my role to be mainly that of a consumer advocate—so they hate me.

www. frequentflier.com

Tim quickly knew that people were reading his site.

I first put up the site on my ISP, Earthlink, using the free server space you get as part of the monthly subscription. Such free Web pages don't include stats, so you have no idea what kind of traffic you're getting, if any. Since moving the site to a commercial hosting company, which provides visitor stats, I have been able to track traffic. The first significant traffic counts came as the result of things like "cool site of the night" awards, and listings in the search engines. I do remember that the first traffic milestone for the site was 1,000 hits per month. At that time, in 1997, that was pretty exciting.

The site has now grown to approximately 30,000 hits per month. The most dramatic traffic increases have been caused by recommendations on other high-profile sites, such as MSNBC, ZD Net, USA Today Online, Business Week Online, and others. Other visitors have come from search engines, the first and foremost being Yahoo!, which is the single most productive source of visitors for the site. You also cannot discount word of mouth, which is the most gratifying to me, especially when it happens in professional circles. I often hear from people at an airline or a loyalty marketing agency who say that they referred the site to a colleague, or they heard about it from a colleague.

I am now beginning to post information regarding the site and newsletter to the various travel newsgroups. This is a sensitive area, because any commercial posts were previously forbidden. The online culture has mellowed somewhat in that regard. Plus, since my site provides information of value to travelers, at no charge, I feel comfortable in posting occasional notices. We await the response.

I receive about fifty to seventy-five e-mails per week. I try to redirect some of these to the forum, so the dialogue can be captured and available to others for learning and responding. The e-mails that always make the greatest impression are those from inexperienced individuals who are trying to make sense of this whole complicated frequent flyer program business and who ask questions about which program they should join, or how many free trips they can expect to earn. Another memorable category of e-mails is from people who were cheated or mistreated by program operators and state that they never received the mileage they were promised. These are the people most in need of assistance, and they're the ones the site was designed to help.

Occasionally I get e-mail from people, often foreigners, who think that I am officially associated with the airlines and their frequent flyer programs. Typically they want me to update their mileage account, or overturn some decision made by the airlines' customer service departments. Of course, I am not in a position to do any of this.

Theffpsite.org was costing Tim a lot of time. He had to make a decision about his future.

It became an either/or situation: Either pursue the Web site and some other independent projects, or remain in the corporate fold. It reached the point where there weren't enough hours in the day to do both, and do both well. I was spending substantial evening and weekend hours on the site, between twenty and twenty-five hours per week. I decided to leave my job with Hilton Hotels Corporation on July 31, 1998, to pursue freelance Web development. Since projects have been scarce so far, I have had more time for the Web site, about forty hours a week or so.

The rough breakdown of my time developing my site is as follows:
- 40 percent—Content development (writing the newsletter, updating Web pages, posting responses to the forum, etc.)
- 10 percent—Maintenance (troubleshooting code and script problems, uploading revised pages, e-mailing the newsletter)
- 10 percent—Promotion (working with the ad rep company, correspondence/proposals regarding sponsorships)
- 40 percent—Surfing (online time spent in search of content, surveillance of competitive sites, seeking prospective sponsor sites)

Once Tim jumped into the Web business full-time, he realized that he needed to make several changes to his site, especially the URL.

I began this site as a nonprofit function with the intention of maintaining the site as a hobby, as an adjunct to my full-time job. Therefore, I had to switch my URL from ".org" to ".com." However, because no one is monitoring and enforcing the conventions associated with the use of .com, .org, and other extensions, I could have kept theffpsite.org. But there's a spirit or ethic associated with the Internet according to which many of us feel responsible for doing the right thing, without being told, because it's good for the Net. I believe if we take care of the Internet ourselves it will evolve into the kind of "place" we want it to be, thus giving less reason for the government to enter the picture and begin imposing its own brand of regulation. Overall, this self-regulation is an interesting area. I see a breakdown in the more traditional Internet ethics as more people come online and dilute the Web's self-policing will. That being said, I wanted to move into the for-profit .com domain.

www.
frequentflier.com

My first choice was frequentflyer.com, but another company had registered it. My second choice, FrequentFlier.com, was also registered by another company; however, they approached me, asking whether I'd be interested in purchasing it. The timing was right, and they were willing to sell for a reasonable price of $500, so I bought it in October of 1998. In addition to being a .com address, FrequentFlier.com is a better name for the duration, because it is easier to remember and punchier than theffpsite.org.

The challenge has been making the change successfully, maintaining my traffic and my position in the search engines and on referring sites without falling off the map. I renewed the theffpsite.org address for another three months, so in the end it will have been up for about six months before I close it down. The reason for this extension with the old URL was largely driven by the failure of the search engines to accurately report site changes. On a number of engines, Theffpsite still shows up, and FrequentFlier.com doesn't show at all. This is in spite of the fact that I registered the new site with all the dominant engines.

Overall, the conversion process is proceeding better than expected, with the exception of the search engines. Yahoo!, which has always been a good traffic-driver, made the change fairly quickly so that traffic was redirected in short order. I sent e-mails to all sites that were sending traffic to the old site, advising them of the new address and thanking them for their past support. Most have made the change already. Also, traffic is building nicely, in spite of the conversion. Page views per month have increased from 10,000 to almost 30,000 over the past several months, and the newsletter subscription list has doubled from 1,000 to 2,000.

Since my recent shift from nonprofit to commercial, I added banners, but I would still like to generate revenue other ways. I plan to cover the costs of maintaining the site through ad banner revenue; sponsorships of my growing e-mail newsletter, The FrequentFlier Crier, which started in April of 1998; and private-labeling the newsletter for use by other travel-related sites. So far, I'm having some limited success with banners and sponsorships of the e-mail newsletter, but to date, I've yet to have a month where the revenues exceeded the costs.

With the name transition completed, Tim wants to continue improving his site.

In general terms, I would like to add more interactivity to the site. Recently, I've added The FrequentFlier Polls, which allows visitors to vote on various travel-related topics and see the results immediately. I've also added a Readers' Rants & Raves section, where readers' e-mail comments and questions that are reprinted in the e-mail newsletter, The FrequentFlier Crier.

In the future, I will have a real-time "You have x days/hours/minutes left before your miles expire" message on the homepage. Other ideas include a mileage calculator and a promotions directory. The mileage calculator will allow you to enter your arrival and departure cities and then will compute the number of miles you will earn for the flight. The promotions directory will permit you to enter the name of the program you participate in and view a list of currently available bonus offers for that program.

Support Our Sponsor

FrequentFlier.com provides frequent flyers
with advice and information
to help them maximize the benefits
of Frequent Flyer Program (FFP) participation.

E-MAIL THAT'S MATCHED TO YOU.

SITE CONTENTS

- How to Choose an FFP
- Links to the Programs
- Program Profiles
- Related Links
- History of FFPs

- How to Enroll
- Maximizing Miles
- Mileage Q-and-A
- Frequent Flyer Marketing
- Site Administration

- Annotated Site Map

FrequentFlier
NEWS

NEWS
For
FREQUENT
FLYERS

www.
frequentflier.com

The Internet has also helped Tim become involved in a software start-up.

I'm working on another business venture with two partners regarding the development of a software product, AirEase, to help frequent flyers manage their miles. The AirEase developers "found" me through the site. We corresponded, met in person, and decided there was a good fit among our various backgrounds and areas of expertise. If it weren't for the Internet, I would not have met them.

Because of my site, I have also been offered consulting jobs, most of which I referred to appropriate individuals or agencies. Until I began doing this full-time, I simply didn't have the time to take on the projects myself. I have also corresponded with many other Webmasters regarding links and sponsorships. It's always nice to hear from people who face the same daily challenges that I do.

Tim is proud of the recognition that Theffpsite.org received. He hopes to continue that tradition under the new name, FrequentFlier.com.

The write-up I received in the print edition of *Business Week* was the biggest vote of confidence, followed by the write-up in the *InsideFlyer* magazine. While neither of these, unfortunately, resulted in any significant traffic increases, validation from the mainstream media was really heartening. As far as Internet recognition is concerned, Business Week Online, USA Today, and Yahoo! would be the most prestigious sites that have mentioned me.

In addition to the recognition the site has gotten, I've had the pleasure of personally meeting a number of people who initially contacted me through the site. Some of these people are: Tony Trujillo, president of Planetfone; Jane Costello, a journalist with *The Wall Street Journal*; and Katherine Wells, producer of the iVillage travel channel. These relationships, whether conducted by e-mail or in person, are one of the unanticipated, and most welcome, byproducts of running the site.

Looking back, Tim might have done things differently, but he feels he is moving in the right direction.

Given that I would now like to have a self-supporting site, I would have chosen a topic of wider interest. Therefore, I could have generated enough revenue to support the site, and perhaps myself as well. I'm hoping to see and be a part of the frequent flyer program information transparency, courtesy of the Internet. I want to prove that if you need information, it's available. If you have a complaint or question, there's a place for both. As a result, there exists a combination of well-informed consumers and accountable product and service providers. I consider my site to be a small step in that direction.

CHAPTER 17

The Astounding B MONSTER

B-MOVIE BUZZ   UPDATED DAILY!

www.
bmonster.com

MARTY
BAUMANN

Addicted to B-Movies

About the Site

Bmonster.com (www.bmonster.com) is an Internet magazine about B-movies from the 1930s, 40s, and 50s. Each monthly issue includes an interview with a star or director of the genre; film reviews; up-to-date news; a mail section; and columns devoted to horror, cult, and sci-fi films of the time.

As a child growing up in suburban Maryland, Marty Baumann's mother once wouldn't allow Marty, an impressionable four-year-old at the time, watch a scary movie on TV. Little did his mother know that this would lead to a lifelong fascination.

My interest in B-movies started in the early 1960s. The "monster culture" that got its start in the late-50s via Late Show-Shock Theater presentations of old movies, horror movie hosts, and science fiction and horror magazines was peaking about the time I was becoming aware of my surroundings in 1962-63. The original *Thing from Another World* was on TV, and my mother refused to let me see it. Nothing could have sparked my imagination more, and that first film I was not allowed to see hooked me.

151

B MONSTER CONFIDENTIAL — PROFILE

MAMIE VAN DOREN "the first authentic sex kitten in cyberspace"

Think you've heard all the Mamie Van Doren stories there are to tell? The flings with Elvis, Eddie Cochran, Warren Beatty and Burt Reynolds; bullet bras, see-through tops and **Playboy** centerfolds? Though she's banked on frankness and flamboyance throughout a near-50-year career, (nipple-printed, autographed photos are available through her recently-launched web site) she never fails to surprise us with an outrage or two that she's held in reserve over the years, even after her sensational autobiography **Playing the Field** (soon to be re-published with passages previously deemed too risque restored) broke new ground among tell-all books. "I want the fans to know that I'm not one of these, so-called ex-glamour queens that's hibernating and is afraid to go out into the world and have anybody see them," she asserts. We're not about to temper the prose of this gracious and outgoing D-cup diva who relishes the opportunity to go on the record. Here's Mamie, only recently named one of **Playboy's 100 Sexiest Women of the Century**, in a straight-up discourse with the B Monster:

THE B MONSTER: You've often described yourself as ahead of your time. I'd say the Mamie Van Doren web site is further proof. How did it come about?

MAMIE: We didn't just hire somebody. My husband and I did the web site together. I've been into computers for a long time. When I wrote my book, **Playing the Field**, in '86 and '87, it was on a little teeny computer.

Q: What's the reaction been like?

MAMIE: There was an item in Liz Smith's column. She gave me a real good plug. **Entertainment Tonight** is going to do a story on me because of it. I asked my publicist, "Why are they doing it?" He said that they saw Liz Smith's column and they checked out the web site. The e-mail is incredible. Don't even ask me how many. God, and I've got to answer them all. I'm surprised that I've only sold about six nipple prints and a couple dozen photographs [through the site]. But I'm not really counting on the site [to make

FILMS FEATURING MAMIE VAN DOREN
Free Ride
1986
The Arizona Kid
1971
Voyage to the Planet of Prehistoric Women
1968
You've Got To Be Smart
1967
Las Vegas Hillbillys
1966
Navy vs. the Night Monsters
1966
The Wild, Wild West
1964
3 Nuts in Search of a Bolt
1964
The Candidate
1964
The Blonde from Buenos Aires
1961
The Private Lives of Adam and Eve
1961
College Confidential
1960
Sex Kittens Go to College
1960
The Beat Generation
1959
The Big Operator
1959
Girls Town
1959
Guns, Girls, and Gangsters
1959
Vice Raid
1959
Teacher's Pet

Marty continued to watch B-movies. Approximately thirty-five years later, he decided to build a Web publication, bmonster.com, devoted to his favorite movie genre.

I was in journalism for about twelve years, six of those at *USA Today* as a designer and graphic artist. When the paper decided to go online, they hired a big shot designer to develop concepts. After paying him a princely sum, they discarded everything he'd done, and conscripted two others and me from in-house to design the site.

I spent a few months learning the rigors of online publishing before I realized that I could create my own publication. While I knew I didn't have tons of capital to publicize the site, I also understood that the overhead is a fraction of the cost for printing a paper magazine. The Internet was leveling the playing field, putting me on equal footing with anybody else who had a good idea and the time to pound that idea into shape. I thought: Why continue laboring for a huge corporation when I could devote my energy to something I really had fun producing? Not only could I turn the spotlight on the unheralded movies that I love, but the B Monster site could act as my portfolio to obtain clients for a Web design business I was considering starting. People could look at bmonster.com and, if they like what they saw, they could then pay me to do the same for them.

Marty's jump into the Web design business happened after bmonster.com was up for only a month.

I ventured out on my own because I was sick of doing the lion's share of the work while some art director took all the credit. I liked designing and needed to eat. As I mentioned, B Monster became my portfolio, and it mushroomed into B Monster Design. Now I make my living designing sites, doing a few print graphics, and writing for several film magazines, all of which came after building my site.

For the most part, all my Web-programming skills are self-taught because I was forced to develop new computer talents with each new job experience. My first computer experience was on a dinky little Mac at a small suburban newspaper. This was before I received a call from *USA Today* asking me if I wanted a job. I worked there for about a

www.
bmonster.com

year and a half. I then left there to become art director for a small chain of newspapers and was later called back to *USA Today* for a second stint. Each job required me to learn more computer skills.

Thus far in my business, I've been lucky. I've yet to chase after a design gig. Most clients have approached me because they like my work, including bmonster.com.

Bmonster.com is Marty's business brochure and enjoyable hobby.

Let me clarify something. The design work for the site is cool and the writing is fun, but B Monster began as an excuse for me to interview the people who made the films I grew up watching. I wasn't looking for a broad audience, and I didn't want my site to deal with any current movies. They get enough attention. There are plenty of slasher and gore magazines to fill that niche. Happily, my site has let me connect with my movie idols who have turned out to be very nice people, with few exceptions. When I first started the site, I picked up the phone on a whim and called director Herbert L. Strock who directed *Teenage Frankenstein*, *The Crawling Hand*, and *How to Make a Monster*. He couldn't have been nicer, and that built my confidence.

When I first designed the site, the .gifs and .jpegs I used were relatively small and few, with absolutely no animation, allowing for quicker downloads. That's always been a concern of mine. Now, modems are a little faster, access is a little easier, so the graphics are a little more elaborate.

Bmonster.com has definitely found a niche on the Web, and people are responding to the content.

On average, I receive approximately 300 e-mails per week. There are also several hundred people on the mailing list. It's important to point out that the cult-film community is relatively small, but intensely loyal. Genre fans discovered B Monster very quickly. The site was only up for a few days when Yahoo! named it their Site of the Day, which also helped generate visitors.

The horror section probably gets the most traffic. People seem to click on the word horror without even thinking about it. The number one keyword people use to find the site is "monster." I hadn't thought about it before I launched the site, but that word really sells. It's difficult to determine when the biggest volume of page views or e-mail occurs, as some issues are more popular than others. The Best & Worst Lists edition that we do at the start of the new year brings a deluge of mail.

The hit count is another Internet intangible that's impossible to determine. What are we counting—images downloaded, page views, individual sessions, click-through rates or unique impressions? I think it's time we settled on one clear way to measure this. *USA Today* used to charge advertisers for every image downloaded. Of course that meant they could claim zillions of hits per day. That didn't last long, and then page views became the standard. The hit reports I get are still a combination of page views, images, visitors, and such; however, on average, I get about 32,000 unique readers per month.

My favorite aspect of the site is that it attracts the right kind of readers. Many directors, producers, screenwriters, authors, and actors have visited the site. I recently interviewed Mamie Van Doren, the quintessential 1950s glamour queen. She already knew who I was and was a regular B Monster reader. That was very exciting. Furthermore, she told me she is deluged with e-mail, but pushed it all aside to answer mine when she saw it was from The B Monster.

Mamie Van Doren is not the only star to "visit" with Marty.

Cult-film director Jack Hill, whose films include *Spider Baby* and *Foxy Brown*, dropped me a line, testily asking why I hadn't written anything about his genre classic *Spider Baby*. He indicated that Quentin Tarantino cited the film as one of his favorites. Another funny note was from character actor Sid Haig who, incidentally, was in Jack Hill's *Spider Baby*, who voted for himself in our "best bad guy" poll.

The awards we've received are nice, as well. Most recently, *Entertainment Weekly* gave us their highest grade, A+, and a flat-out rave review. I can't express how much more gratifying that is than an annual 3 percent raise from some faceless corporation.

Bmonster.com requires time, but luckily Marty has contributors approach him out of common interest to help.

I have obtained contributors by hanging out at film conventions and talking to people about stuff they'd written. Many asked if they could contribute to my site. Regarding the amount of time I spend on my site, there's no consistent yardstick by which I can judge. If I'm juggling several big design projects, then B Monster is a lower priority. If I'm caught up on my contract work, I then have more time to polish B Monster. Some months are busier than others, and if I'm not satisfied with my first pass at designing B Monster, I may go back and redo the whole thing. That's the long way of saying I don't keep track of the time I spend on it.

Marty measures his site profitability not in the traditional terms of revenue versus expenditures, but in exposure.

I do get ad revenue from my site, but it only generates a tiny portion of my income. It's nice to have advertising, because it makes the site look important, but design work is my top priority. However, it seems inevitable that one day, most sites will have a single sponsor to underwrite them, such as "Universal Presents The Astounding B Monster" or "Stouffer's, Makers of the Original French Bread Pizza Presents The Astounding B Monster." It sure makes a lot more sense than nickel-and-diming people with these little blinking .gifs.

Right now, my site is profitable in the sense that it attracts design clients. It has also given me notoriety, which allows me to do some more writing. I didn't do any freelance writing until after B Monster was launched. Since then, I've done reviews, interviews, and set visits for *Sci-Fi Entertainment, Turner Network Television, Sci-Fi Universe, Midnight Marquee, Planet X, Sci-Fi Flix*, and others.

Marty's only plans for bmonster.com include continuing to publish information and demonstrate his design skills. However, if a big sponsor picked up the site and paid him to continue to produce a quality, online, cult movie magazine, he would listen.

Many readers are folks who are just passing through, looking for a fun, quick read about a nostalgic topic. I'm not going to ask them to download sound bites and film clips and Java-scripted goo-gaws. I'll add that other stuff when the Web is fast enough to allow for it.

From the start, the central philosophy behind the site was "keep it simple." No Java or animation, just a slick, simple, quick reading, easily downloadable, film magazine. I have not ventured off in directions that I later regretted. When I started B Monster, people still regarded the Internet as an amateur's playground. Most film-related sites were sloppy attempts to be cutting-edge. In my own humble way, I tried to bring a little legitimacy to the table.

"Zine Scene" critiques the film mags! Convention news and more!

The Astounding B MONSTER™

mamie van doren

MEETS THE B MONSTER

B MONSTER CONFIDENTIAL

exclusive

WHO WAS THE REAL NORMAN BATES?

HORROR • SCI FI • CULT • MAIL

PLUS: REVIEWS — BLURBS — ARCHIVE

Designed and written by Marty Baumann

Senior correspondent Tom Weaver | Special thanks to Mamie Van Doren

the den
DAILY ENTERTAINMENT NETWORK

Hollywood's Worst Nightmare
"Cheerfully Smart-ass!
One of the Top 20 Movie
Sites" - Roger Ebert

BLURBS
HYPERBOLIC GEMS FROM THE BRAZEN B MOVIE POSTERS OF THE PAST

"A helicopter's churning blades whirl inches from your head!" - It Came From Outer S...

"He turned the greatest show on earth into a . . . " - Circus of Horrors

"A Psychedelic trip into the 5th dimension!" - The Curse of the Doll Pe...

ADD YOUR NAME TO OUR E-MAILING LIST   OW!

SEARCH FOR A TITLE, ACTOR OR KEY WORD   EARCH!

ANOTHER B MONSTER SPONSOR

www.hollywoodwebshop...
FOR ALL YOUR HOLLY... NE...

PROFILE | SCI FI | HORROR | CULT | MAIL | ARCHIVE | BULLETIN | REVIEWS | BLURBS

ADVERTISING INFO | WEB DESIGN SERVICES

All contents copyright The Astounding B Monster™ | These pages created by B Monster Design

CHAPTER 18

MARK RAMSEY

Give Me the Juice, the MovieJuice That Is

About the Site

MovieJuice.com (www.moviejuice.com) is a movie review site with a sarcastic tone. The site lists over 200 movies and is growing every week. Once you find the title of the movie you want, you can click on it to see its review. MovieJuice also has an e-mail newsletter, and the site provides some movie parodies via text, video, and audio.

Mark Ramsey is annoyed with the way "movie" people take the movies they make so seriously.

I've always been interested in movies. I suppose my interest began when everyone else's did—as a small kid in that big dark room with dreams spilling over me from the silver screen. It's impossible for anyone to sit through *Jaws* three times and not fall in love with movies.

My site is about more than my interest in movies. It's about my interest in how movies are handled, promoted, analyzed, and discussed. For a long time, I've had this idea about handling movie reviews with a fresh, unique tone. Movies, it seems to me, are taken so seriously by everyone but the folks who go to see them. We have journalists and critics telling us whether or not a movie meets their criteria of quality and "earns stars." Who cares? Movies are entertainment. They are either fun or not fun, good or not good.

159

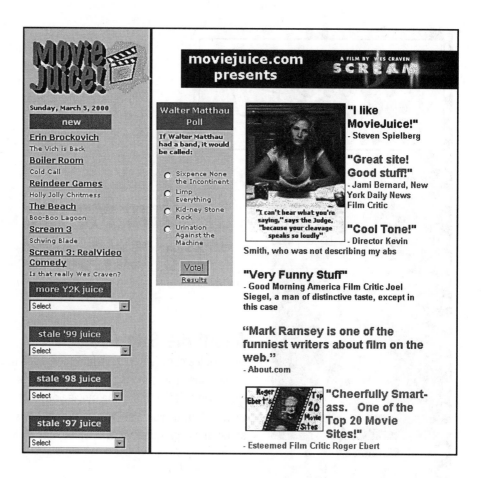

And no amount of analysis paralysis can make even the finest movie more enjoyable if it's a terrible bore. That's why I ignore most of the plot points. That's why I don't have a film degree or a journalistic arrogance. My job is to tell the truth and to speak to people, not at them. My opinion is no more important and no better than yours is. Hollywood is a land of sheep; I'm the black one.

Utilizing his sarcastic wit and computer skills, Mark Ramsey, age thirty-eight, of San Diego, California, doesn't hold back anything as he tells visitors what he thinks of the movies that are in the theater.

I started the site in the spring of 1997. That is seventy years ago in Internet years! I believe the first movie I reviewed was *Shine*, about the Australian concert pianist, which was a horrible choice for MovieJuice, in retrospect. It was too damn highbrow. The presence of British accents is only one step removed from subtitles, as far as I'm concerned, unless the actor's playing a captain with a phaser.

Overall, MovieJuice.com began much as it is now. It was born from the idea of telling people how I feel about the movies, not from trying to think of something to do with my computer. The URL has also always stayed the same. I contemplated MovieSpam, but only Monty Python is allowed to violate that copyright, it seems. Plus, MovieSpam implies that most movies aren't any good, and we know that's not true, right?

The brutal tone of MovieJuice might scare away some people, but it definitely attracts more than just the casual Internet surfer.

Currently, my distribution list contains about 10,000 people, and I get roughly 250,000 hits per month. This is amazing for a publication that updates only weekly with a new page or two. The hit count tends to rise when a hit movie is out and I cover it. I think my *Titanic* page is still getting hits.

I have also had a surprising number of movie industry insiders mention my site, including the famed critic Roger Ebert, who named MovieJuice as "one of the top twenty movie sites." Beyond Roger, there are a number of other film critics, entertainment journalists from places like ABC and Fox—and I'm talking the networks here, not some rinky-dink local affiliates— and studio employees who are regular readers of MovieJuice. My distribution list includes e-mail addresses from places like Miramax, Dreamworks, and other big studios, and those are just the ones who use their work e-mail addresses. Also, MovieJuice seems to strike a chord with young Hollywood, the outsiders working their way into the scenes.

An Oscar winner even mentioned me. A friend once told me he saw Kevin Spacey plug MovieJuice on the independent film channel when asked where he gets his movie information. I was surprised. Wouldn't you be? I expected better of him. Actually, I believe that lots of folks on the A-list read MovieJuice, but they'd rather die than let anybody know, least of all me. That's what I've heard anyway. Did I forget to say thanks, Kevin? Thanks, Kevin!

Just recently, the person in charge of all publicity and distribution for one of the Hollywood studio biggies wrote to me to ask who the heck I am.

Although Mark teases the films he sees, he does take seriously his responsibility to develop a good site.

My reviews are designed to be entertaining first and informative second, but I do not trash movies irresponsibly. In fact, I'll

bet I am more positive than most critics are. However, I do tease every movie, just for the fun of it. That's why my audience visits MovieJuice in the first place. They can get the dry plot details anywhere. Furthermore, I believe you can have fun with a movie, tease a movie, even ridicule a movie, and still promote it and be head-over-heels in love with it.

Before the site, I would see a couple of movies per month, at the most. Now, I view about one or two per week, which is often one or two too many. The fact that a lot of "critics" see movies more than once before delivering their oh-so-important verdict convinces me that movie reviewing is any slob's dream job. Imagine if all you had to do was write one or two newspaper articles per week and go to the movies every day. That's what I call a "rough life."

Besides seeing the movies, which seem to be getting longer and longer nowadays, I spend two to four hours per week on the site, depending on whether I'm writing one piece or two. My time is almost entirely invested in writing, as even a cursory glance at my pathetic, amateurish site design proves. As a computer scientist, I'm a rank amateur. If Microsoft FrontPage didn't exist, I don't know what I'd do.

In the future, I would like to add a way for readers to transmit cash to me in small unmarked bills, or an automated system that reads all the articles aloud in Kurt Russell's voice. Actually, you'll definitely find that more video and some spoofs are in the works.

MovieJuice is currently a hobby that happens to produce some revenue, but Mark views the site's true potential as something outside of the Internet.

I receive revenue from ad banners that are on my site, but Matt Drudge, the Internet journalist, commented on this best: "It pays for cat food." Unfortunately, my fiancée and I have two cats, so we're falling behind with their food. My current revenue plan is to liquidate my expenses before I liquidate myself. It's a long-term plan. In fact, Steven Hawking describes the term as "infinity." Therefore, to make a living, I also work in the radio business doing audience research and marketing.

I would like MovieJuice to be a full-time job, but if it's a full-time job, it must pay a lot better than it does now. Frankly, I'm waiting for the networks to discover that MovieJuice would be a more interesting TV show than anything about the Lincoln White House, anything with Jenny McCarthy, or anything with the words "date" and "line" in the title. This thing will be a hit if it is able to break through into other media. But I can't reveal all my plans to make this possible, since I must invent them first. Until then, it's the satirical Hollywood Web site that all the mucky mucks read, because nobody knows a back-stabber like somebody who works in Hollywood.

Interestingly, companies have approached me to use my site to sell books and movies, even though there are millions of sites tied with booksellers and movie sellers already. Anybody who would rush to MovieJuice to buy the new Bruce Willis flick should have his/her head examined.

I did once make it on the cable TV channel MSNBC, although my memory of the appearance is growing dim, since it was two years ago last summer. A MSNBC line producer called me to participate in a live one-on-one with the anchor one Saturday. What had all the earmarks of an intermittent gig turned rapidly into a one-time nightmare. They wanted to talk about the connection between *Air Force One* and *Conspiracy Theory*, a nutty idea. Naturally the only connection between these movies is that they were opening that weekend. They even provided visual stimuli with scenes from the movies over my ridiculously inane commentary. Any viewer must have thought either that MSNBC was going to the dogs, or that the queen and king of the cosmos were now writing copy. The anchor had an expression of stunned acquiescence when I uttered a remark about Jodie Foster looking bad in a dress, and that was just the beginning.

I'm afraid the media is currently just as afraid of MovieJuice as the readership, but for different reasons. Maybe it's because so many movie critics write whole books critiquing movies and then never say a negative word about a movie in their TV gigs.

Mark's inbox does provide him with e-mail, which displays a range of emotions.

I actually get very few e-mails per week, under a dozen. They range from the predictable "You're brilliant and hilarious." to the equally predictable "You're not funny. You're lousy." You must understand that MovieJuice bites so close to the Hollywood bone that it's widely read without being openly discussed. Even some of the working film critics who are fans would rather I keep that a secret.

The wackiest e-mail I ever received was from someone who wrote: "…if you knew who this was you'd kiss my ass because I've read what you've written about my movies before. The fact that you like something I did makes me sick." My attorney, who's an entertainment lawyer in New York and used to work for some studios, told me that he narrowed down the identity

of the e-mailer to two people, Keri, a sixteen-year-old from Iowa, or Julia Roberts. Personally, I'm betting on Keri.

Don't misunderstand Mark, he does like movies.

One of my favorite movies is *Citizen Kane*, naturally, because I'm a nut for Orson Welles. Not only was he a struggling maverick, but he was so damned proud of it. I also have a soft spot for *It's a Wonderful Life* because I'm an American, plus I absolutely love anything by Cameron Crowe.

Mark understands that it is the Internet that has allowed him to become part of the movie experience.

I've received amazing acceptance among working critics. I have even been invited to join a critics organization with what can only be described as incredibly liberal admission requirements, but it was enough to get me in a room with Jack Nicholson, which means nothing but sounds really impressive. I do also receive some preview passes, but only because they're not quite sure who I am.

Without the Net, I would not have this venue, and the readers of MovieJuice would not have MovieJuice. I would not have the network of industry connections. I would not have the professional opportunities, which are bound to open up for me, thanks to the Net. I would not be writing this now.

Collecting Stuff
& Other Diversions

CHAPTER 19

Find A Grave

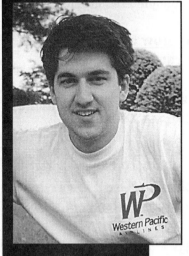

JIM TIPTON

Digging Up the Dead

About the Site

Findagrave.com (www.findagrave.com) lists the grave locations of over 4,000 famous people. Most grave locations include a picture of the gravestone. Each person can be found through several different methods, including searching by name, what made them famous, or even by association, such as all the stars of *The Wizard of Oz*.

Jim Tipton likes to collect stuff, and it doesn't matter what that stuff is as long as it can be collected.

I've always been a collector. In my youth, I couldn't even bring myself to throw away all of my old pencil stubs, so I saved them for years. Then a few years ago, my mother and sister finally had the whole collection framed for me. I now have about sixty pencil stubs all framed and on my wall. My pencil stub collection finally has an appropriate home. Along with my enjoyment of collecting, I've always been the kind of person who likes tangible "tokens" to remember events in my life. So, when I made a pilgrimage to Al Capone's grave during my college years, I wanted to collect something to remember the occasion. Looking around at Al Capone's grave, I didn't see anything "real" that I could take, and I'm not the kind of grave visitor that would chip off a piece of the headstone as they do at James Dean's grave, so collecting some dirt seemed like the obvious choice. There's

Find A Grave

I collect dirt from the graves of noteworthy people...
This is a source for where such people are buried...

→ **Find A Grave T-Shirts are now available!** ←
Now accepting credit card orders!

Search by...
Name
Location
Claim To Fame
Pictures...
Posthumous Reunions...

Links and Accolades...
Bibliography...

no harm done, and I feel there is something symbolic in the actual earth from the person's gravesite.

I collected that first sample of gravesite dirt from Al Capone's grave about five years ago, and the collection has snowballed from there. My favorite sample is from Richard Feynman's grave in Altadena, California. He won a Nobel Prize and is one of my favorite historical figures. I pressed my head against his grave in the hopes for some great transfer of knowledge, but nothing yet. In total, I now have over 430 samples. My collection is possible because unlike many people, I have always liked cemeteries. I call them "parks for introverts" and a nice place where you can go and not worry about someone trying to start a pick-up game of volleyball. I particularly like cemeteries with famous dead folks in them. There is something about being able to be within six feet of Capone, Sinatra, Camus, or Sartre, or at least what's left of them.

Anyway, in my quest for more grave dirt, I painstakingly researched the locations of many notable graves using everything from biographies to obituaries. I also searched the Web for a more focused source of information and found nothing, so I decided to fill the void.

Jim thought someone would be interested in the information he posted, but he had no idea how popular it would be.

I remember when I began posting, I had a counter on my initial iterations of the site. I used to check in every day to see if anyone came to view the pages. Eventually people started coming every day, and then I began checking every couple of hours, and eventually they started to come every hour. Now, I just look at the weekly statistics, because I know that there are people constantly hitting it. That was a fun and thrilling time, when I would wonder who was looking at my page, thinking that maybe it was a sultan in Saudi Arabia, or maybe my neighbor.

Lately, I've been getting an average of 750,000 page views per month. Generating this much traffic is exciting because I never actively promoted my site. It always takes care of itself. When the site went online in February of 1996, it looked quite a bit different than it does now. The overwhelming interest has prompted me to grow my site and make it better. Originally, I listed about 100 graves. Now I have over 4,000 listed on my site. Of those graves, approximately 2,100 have corresponding photos, but the total number of photos is quite a bit higher, around 3,700, due to multiple shots of many of the graves. Also, it was initially and aptly black in color, but I have been intentionally trying to move away from "morbidity" because that is not what this is about, so I switched to the more aesthetically pleasing white background. The site is constantly changing, as is any good site.

The site still resides on the original server. The domain name findagrave.com points to the original URL http://www.orci.com/personal/jim. If I ever wanted to move the site to a server that was under my control, I could do it, but there are a bunch of people that still link to the old address, and I'm lazy. I bought the domain name because the site was getting popular and I foresaw a day when I would change servers and I didn't want to go through the rigamarole of a URL change. It also makes it tremendously easier to publicize the site because I don't have to muck with all of those slashes.

Growing the site requires not only Jim's time, but also the time of his visitors, who add a significant amount of information.

I spend about two to three hours per night working on the site, answering e-mail, adding pictures, and doing what

www.findagrave.com

needs to be done, but I must acknowledge the submissions of hundreds and hundreds of people who have written to me with information and/or pictures. I get hundreds of submissions every month, and I try to verify and post every one of them. Most of the pictures of graves have been contributed directly by visitors. Also, since starting the site, people have introduced me to several books that have helped me tremendously, and are all listed in the bibliography on findagrave.com.

Regarding e-mail, I average about fifteen to twenty-five e-mails per day. The response has been overwhelmingly positive, and I am glad to see the site become such a communal collection of information and images. Furthermore, the many women who write hinting at romantic involvement always shock me. For all they know, I could be some psychotic, death-obsessed, grave-robbing lunatic—none of which are true. I have had quite a few women write and tell me that they would be interested in meeting if I am ever in their city. That seems a little strange to me. For the record, I'm twenty-six, married, and have a six-year-old daughter.

I also get a lot of requests to post graves of viewers' family members, but I have a policy of only posting locations and pictures of graves of famous or noteworthy people. Sometimes the requests to post a grave can be quite unusual. A recent example occurred when I received an e-mail with pictures from a guy who said he loved the site. He said I could keep the pictures and post them after he died. He wasn't famous and the pictures were of him standing in a room in his underwear. Figure out that one!

All this keeps me a busy worker; however, I love the attention that the site gets, so I do get something out of it. Since its inception, I have received quite a bit of press, including articles or mentions in *The Wall Street Journal*, *Los Angeles Times*, *The Washington Post*, *Rocky Mountain News*, and even an interview for the BBC. These media mentions noticeably increased my number of visitors.

Financially, findagrave.com is not a cash windfall for Jim.

Until recently, I received no financial compensation whatsoever and had to actually pay for my site, domain name, and other costs. Technically, it only costs twenty dollars per month, plus a small amount for the prorated rate of the domain name, but it isn't free. The twenty dollars is what the ISP, OnRamp Communications, www.orci.com, run by Ron Cox based in Denver, charges. On their machine, I have about 100 megs of space, but I take up tons of bandwidth. He is a nice guy and I have sent him some good business, so he lets me keep the site going for cheap. For me, my biggest expense is not in dollars, but in time.

The recent addition of banner advertising was added to cover my costs. A few years ago, I used a banner advertising company, but I hated it. I didn't have any control over who would be advertising and although I would rather still do without it, I do need to at least cover my losses. Furthermore, my new banner advertising company gives me control over which advertisers go on and which don't. Now my site is profitable due to the advertisements, but if you compare the time spent versus the income, I am making very little money. Findagrave is really a labor of love. The advertisements are more of a test case and, if they pay well, I'll probably keep them and hopefully start being able to dedicate more time to the site. Another revenue stream I hope to add is a link to Amazon.com from my bibliography page, which is a service I would like to advertise, because many people want to know where they can get the books I reference. By the way, it was Amazon who approached me with this idea.

My real full-time job, which makes ends meet, is computer work, specifically Web application development for the Huntsman Cancer Institute at the University of Utah and the College of Fine Arts at the University of Utah. I graduated from Grinnell College in Iowa, not with a degree in computer science, but as a music major. I went into the computer field as a career because I enjoy it, having played with computers since I was very young. A big part of the reason for my successful transition from music to computers occurred because of my site. Although findagrave did not get me my job, the skills that I acquired while creating the site helped me become employed in the computer world.

Truthfully, I would love, love, love to work on the site full-time. The new advertisement revenue almost allows me to do it half-time, but the future of advertising on the Internet is not really well defined. My guess is that ad banners won't be the primary source of income in five years. So no one knows what will happen. People tell me I should write a book about graves, and I've thought about it, but what good is a reference book anymore? I'm not anti-books, trust me, nothing will replace the tactile sensation of reading a good novel in print, but if there is an error in the information, it can't be fixed until the next edition. If someone famous dies, they can't be listed until the next printing. Findagrave is what I really have loved doing for the past three years. At times, I resent the massive amount of time I must invest to keep up; however, overall, I really love doing it. If I could do it as my only job and make decent money from it, I'd be very, very happy.

There is no single gravestone people are looking to view, but the most viewed gravestone on findagrave.com is actually quite a surprising one.

www.
findagrave.com

Halloween seems to be the most popular "season" of my site, but "big deaths" like the death of Frank Sinatra also cause a marked increase in my traffic. People seem to always enter my site through the home page, not surprisingly. It always gets the most page views. Viewers then seem to go to the alphabetical table of contents/search page. Next appears the most interesting page view reports, which lists the grave picture pages that are most popular. It starts with Lucille Ball, who remains the most viewed gravestone, with the exception of bulge periods like Sinatra's death. The next most popular gravesites are Marilyn Monroe, Jim Morrison, Elvis, Sinatra, Jimi Hendrix, Princess Di, and John Belushi.

Personally, I have no explanation as to why Lucille Ball's gravesite is the most viewed. She was a pop icon, without a doubt, but not really on the level of Elvis or Marilyn. Also, her grave isn't particularly notable, so I guess it is just a testament to her overall popularity.

Jim is looking forward to expanding his site, if he can find the time.

My only wish is that I had more time to dedicate to the site. I still have hundreds more submissions of pictures and information that I haven't had time to add. If the revenues ever start to get substantial, I have many new ideas that I haven't yet implemented. These ideas include adding some sort of a message board where people could help each other find graves that I don't have listed. I'd also like to have a birth/death date search page so people can find whom was born or died on specific dates. I'd like to have e-mail notification for people who are looking for a specific grave. Above the grave shots, I would add biography shots of the person taken while he/she was alive. I have a lot of ideas.

Beyond his own site, Jim is amazed with the infinite capabilities of the Internet.

The instant nature of the Internet is the most thrilling aspect of Web publishing for me. Although I'm usually a month behind with submissions, I occasionally catch up. When someone e-mails me a picture and it gets posted within a day, I still get a thrill. Basically, I update the site constantly, which is something that simply can't happen in the print media, where new editions mean an entire publishing and distribution cycle.

This nearly effortless sharing is amazing to me. The fact that we are in the digital age means that we can represent nearly anything, whether it is music, words, or video. What is really important in the end, of course, is the content. The most incredible thing for me personally about the site is that I am no longer the only person who is responsible for the content of the site. Pictures and information are submitted continuously. In a sense, I have become just the information manager, the guy who is trying to organize it all and get it publicly viewable. The information itself comes from thousands of different people all over the world. At this point, I feel that there is a large community of people creating the site.

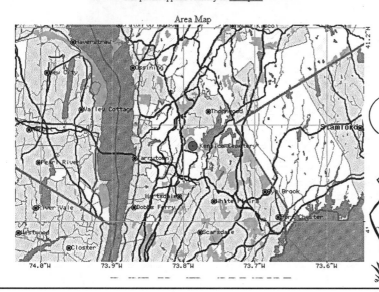

Find A Grave

Search by... Name Location Claim To Fame

Ayn Rand

Writer / Philosohper.
Kensico Cemetery, Valhalla, New York.

This picture appears courtesy of: Jim Tipton

Area Map

www.beaniemom.com

SARA NELSON

Cuddly Collectibles

About the Site

BeanieMom (www.beaniemom.com) provides updated information on new, rare, and existing Beanie Babies, as well as pricing information. Visitors to the site can trade Beanie Babies, participate in auctions and Beanie Baby contests, and find out about nationwide Beanie events.

Sara Nelson, age thirty-nine, is the mother of three. She's also a former accountant who, propelled by the growth of the Web and Beanie Babies, finds herself as the nation's number one Beanie Mom.

I met my first Beanie Baby in June 1996. I had never seen them before they started showing up here in Virgina. I thought they were great, and my kids loved them. I fell in love because it was the type of toy I would have loved as a child. I personally was not big into dolls or Barbie. Something about Beanies tugged at my heart and made me remember my own childhood, in a sense. I enjoyed watching how my three daughters played with them, and I wanted to get them one of each Beanie released to expand what they could do with Beanies. They are simple, but you can do so many different things with them; they are truly

BEANIES FOR SALE!

....ATTENTION COLLECTORS!!! The following BEANIES,
BUDDIES, and TRADING CARDS are for sale!!
FUZZ-ONLY 40.00 EACH-MWMT!!!!!
MILLINIUM ONLY 23.00 EACH !!MWMT!!!
TY SIGNATURE BEAR ONLY 22.00 EACH MWMT!!!
VALENTINA or KICKS-mwmt-22.00 each!!!!!
EGGBERT or SAMMY mwmt 13.00 each!!
HOPE-MWMT-15.00 EACH!!!
HIPPIE-mwmt 15.00 each!!!
EWEY,SCAT,-MWMT ONLY 8.OO EACH!!
BEANIE BUDDIES: MWMT: JAKE, BEAK, QUACKERS, PINKY,
SQUEALER, RIBBIT, PATTI, CHIP--19.00 EACH!
BEANIE BUDDIES-PEANUT OR HUMPHRY-mwmt-40 each!!
CRANBERRY TEDDY BUDDY-mwmt-55 each!!ALL BUDDIES ARE
2ND GEN!
HIPPITY BEANIE BUDDY-MWMT VERY CUTE FOR EASTER-
45EACH!!!!
4.00 each mwmt-nuts,scoop,mel,and currents...
10.00 -each mwmt-valentino,wise...
ERIN BEANIE BABY-MWMT-12.00EACH!
GLORY OR HALO -MWMT-20.00 EACH!!
SCORCH-MWMT-9.00 EACH!!
ATTIC COLLECTABLES-mwmt-strawbunny or esmerlda only 8.00
each.
PLUSH---2ND GEN RUFUS-25.00 SHIPPED!!!!!!!!!!!
TRADING CARDS-blue clear no # squealer-100.00
silver humphry-50.00/silver chilly-35.00, red rookie 1.00each, blue
rookie-2.00each.
blue lizzy-20,red lizzy-10,silver pinky-15,silver glory-10,
red or blue retierd cards 2.00-15.00 please ask for those.
CHRISTMAS SCOOBYS ANTLER 1998 ONLY 10.00 EACH!!
EASTER SCOOBY-35.00/VEGAS SCOOBY-20.00.

magical. It was at this point when my personal hunt began to find other
Beanies in the collection.

I could not find many Beanies locally, so I began searching the Web for
other sources. There were very few Beanie sites at the time. I thought I would
begin my own site and gather information from other collectors. This began
as a hobby for me. It was just supposed to take a couple hours per day and
be something I would dabble around with it. Even though I wasn't expecting
it, this hobby grew as the interest in Beanies grew worldwide.

**In the years since her introduction to Beanies, Sara has had scarcely
a moment to catch her breath. Making the commitment to strike a balance
between her personal responsibilities as a mother and her extensive
involvement as the nation's number one Beanie Mom is not a simple matter.**

My three daughters are in swimming, soccer, and all different types of extracurricular activities. I have to find a balance somewhere. It can really be difficult trying to manage everything. Now, I typically find myself working on the Web page five to six hours during the day when my daughters are at school and another four to five hours in the evenings. I receive approximately 300 e-mails per day and spend time either publishing the page or answering collectors' questions. I have many active sections that require daily posting. I find that there are just not enough hours in the day, given the level of activity and the high level of interest in Beanies.

I recently "met" a Beanie Mom friend who has helped automate some of the more active sections of the page, so I'm able to continue updating them but move through them quickly. I add new sections all the time, although I have trouble keeping up with the sections I already have. With the increasing popularity of the page, and Beanies in general, I find myself spending more time on it.

The public's overwhelming enthusiasm for these tiny, floppy, cuddly, beanbag toys helped bring about a national Beanie movement, which includes conventions, newsletters, clubs, contests, and auctions.

I do not have a page counter on the Web site, but I do know that traffic volume has increased substantially since I first began. The same could be said for the general interest in Beanie Babies as well.

Although Sara didn't initially realize it, this is one hobby that requires a surprising amount of technology. Not many Beanie collectors can say that they maintain a local area network in their home.

www.
beaniemom.com

In the beginning, my system needs were actually pretty minimal. I started out simply using an NT-based server and an ISDN line. Now, I have six computers dedicated specifically for BeanieMom, with a UNIX-based server and a T1 connection. Recently, I had the phone company install another line into the house. I have approximately ten or twelve lines now. I tend to lose count of all the machines we've got running. Although we have eighteen computers in the house, I only rely on six that are dedicated to the BeanieMom site. I can access BeanieMom from just about any room in the house, except the bathroom.

I try to be innovative in terms of saving time. When preparing dinner in the evenings, I think it's the laptop in the kitchen that saves me. I split my time between cooking and answering e-mails. I have three laptops upstairs, and all the network equipment is in the basement. The basement is loaded with equipment, along with a rack to keep everything organized. My latest plan is to move everything from my basement, directly off-site, to the Internet service provider. With three children to raise, we could use the space for other purposes, and BeanieMom needs the extra capacity.

I am self-taught. I was able pick up some basic coding on my own in designing the site. I taught myself a lot about HTML programming, since I didn't know anything about it when I began BeanieMom. I bought a couple books, surfed to some Web resource sites, and gradually learned through trial and error. It also helps that my husband works for an Internet service provider. He's a good resource for advice about the growing technical demands of running the site. Then again, he's always been a techie and interested in all that stuff.

Sara relies on other collectors worldwide to help maintain BeanieMom as an updated resource.

One of the big challenges of BeanieMom is determining and publishing accurate information. That is something on which we pride ourselves. There are so many rumors in the Beanie community that I feel it is necessary to provide accurate information in terms of new releases, rare Beanies, and even forgeries to which to be alerted.

I do have a wonderful group of Beanie Moms who help provide accurate and informative content for the Web page. All of these women have published their own books or are featured in various Beanie magazine publications being distributed worldwide. I also love hearing from collectors around the country who provide a great deal of information about Beanie activity in their specific area.

I do not have all the answers about the Beanie industry, but I've been collecting for several years now and have lived through quite a bit of Beanie history. If I don't personally know an answer, I've met numerous long-time collectors who can help me when necessary. I rarely travel to non-Beanie related Web sites. To be honest, I just don't have the time. Plus, all my friends are Beanie friends now.

The exciting thing for me about being a Beanie collector is that there are always new aspects of the hobby in which people are specifically interested. Collectors are always tossing me questions, many of which are about values of Beanies, oddities, authenticity, how to become a Ty company retailer, and such. (Ty is the company that makes Beanie Babies.) Any anticipated retirement or new release announcements from Ty always increases traffic volume.

Also, any newsworthy items bring traffic to the Web page. I can always expect Ty to continuously introduce and retire Beanie Babies, for new people to enter the market, and for the release of Teenie Beanies. The combination of these factors keeps me very active. It's a very dynamic hobby, never allowing for a dull moment.

Sara currently finds herself on the road quite a bit, routinely traveling to Beanie shows and conferences around the country.

Certainly if I wanted to travel every weekend, I could. For me, this is the best part of all the time and effort I've invested in BeanieMom. I've been able to travel to other parts of the country and meet fellow collectors. I've recently been traveling to California quite a bit, and to Chicago for Beanie World. Last week's trip was a *Beanie World Magazine* show in Pasadena. I have met so many friends online, and it is wonderful to meet with them in person and get a chance to actually talk off-line. I tend to know e-mail addresses more than first names. I spend a lot of time signing autographs and talking to people. It's really strange for me to sign autographs!

www.
beaniemom.com

Most people would be tempted to capitalize on the growth and popularity of a successful hobby; however, the success of BeanieMom.com has not changed Sara's approach to collecting.

All types of individuals for various moneymaking ventures have approached me. I have not pursued many of them, because moneymaking was never my primary focus. I actually keep turning away businesses. It's my own choice. I could make more if I chose. The money has never been my goal. As I mentioned previously, this began as a hobby for me. I'm not interested in marketing the site. In fact, I've never even contacted Ty and have never been contacted by them.

Although I've not worked outside of the home since I had my first child, I did work for several years as an accountant until 1989. That was long before Beanies were introduced and my hobby began.

The interest in my Web page seemed to grow exponentially. It may slow down, but even Cabbage Patch Kids still have a core group of collectors today. It is the same trend as with Barbie dolls. I'll keep maintaining the BeanieMom site and see what the future brings.

CHAPTER 21

HappyToy.com

www.happytoy.com

DAVE SMITH

Fast Food Friends

About the Site

HappyToy (www.happytoy.com) features information and images of Happy Toys available in the United States and in twenty-eight countries around the world. The site includes a trading board, news, and a chat room for collectors. The site is updated regularly with the help of contributors.

Dave Smith, a sales and marketing manager for Corporate Express, a Fortune 500 Company, has been collecting McDonald's Happy Meal toys for many years, initially for his six-year-old daughter Jennifer. Even though his daughter is now twenty, his interest in the collectibles has only increased as a result of his Web site HappyToy.com.

I have been on the Net in one form or another since 1995. I enjoyed cruising the Web and seeing the fun things people were doing on it. It was new for awhile; I visited pages for food, travel, sports, and other topics. They seemed in constant need of replacement by something new each day. Basically, the Internet was losing its newness.

In the meantime, I was looking for something fulfilling to do with my PC besides the basic word processing, spreadsheet work, and database stuff. I can only write so many letters, input so many budgets, and have so many address lists. My dad was a sales representative for IBM and gave me

a keyboard back in the CP/M days, the operating system before MS-DOS, so I felt comfortable just messing around with technology and seeing what I could do on my own.

In 1995, I decided to download a demo of Hot Dog HTML Web Authoring software, and was flabbergasted from the start by what I could do with it. I discovered that through my membership with AOL, I was provided with access to server space. All the pieces were there. It was then when I decided to create my first page on the Web.

Choosing a topic for the site was a difficult decision. Any work I did in terms of a Web site had to be fun and creative at the same time. I also wanted to do something that interested me, but that was also a bit different. I didn't want to be one of many similar sites. I thought of several different ideas, but none really stood out in my mind until I literally began to look around my surroundings. The answer was right in front of me.

My wife and I have two kids—Ben, age eleven, and Jennifer, age twenty. We spend many evenings at McDonald's, more than I would care to admit. When Teenie Beanies arrived at McDonald's, we got into two separate cars and, using our cellular phones to keep in touch, visited eighteen McDonald's in three hours to complete our collection! With Ben's extracurricular activities in the evening and my wife, Mary, often returning late from working out at the club, I can count on visiting the Golden Arches about three times per week. Yes, I do get sick of the burgers at times!

Over the years, Happy Meal toys seemed to pile up in our house as a result of our kids. We often have gone to McDonald's for dinner or during vacation with the kids who inevitably buy Happy Meals that include these small toys along with the burger, fries, and soda. I was impressed with the toys from the time I first saw one, which was the Halloween jack-o-lantern pail that was distributed in 1985. The quality of the toy that McDonald's distributes is really quite good. Plus, they are usually associated with the hottest release in the theaters or the hottest selling toys on the market. The combination of quality and timeliness makes them perfect for collecting. As a kid, I collected Matchbox cars and, therefore, always especially loved the Hot Wheels collections offered annually with Barbie.

It was the explosion of the Web and Dave's ability to create a Happy Toy site that helped to turn searches for routine novelty items into crusades.

Since these collectibles were throughout my home, I actually decided to search the Web for other Happy Meal toys available. Although some listed the toys, none of the sites had any pictures. This was really my exploratory phase. Initially, I spent time just collecting Happy Toy information from the Web. Things got especially interesting once I bought a scanner and immediately realized that I could use it to create images of the McDonald's Happy Meal toys and post them on my

www.
happytoy.com

own site. Posting a picture of the toy was crucial since I had become very frustrated visiting the McDonald's restaurant only to find that they offered the same toy that I already had in my collection. The scanner, in combination with my Web site, provided the answer to all my problems. My idea was to post each week's Happy Meal toy as a service on the Web. By doing this, everyone would know which toy McDonald's was offering on any given day. Hence, the beginning of Deke's Happy Meal Toy of the Week Page. (Deke is my nickname.)

No one, least of all Dave, could have imagined the worldwide interest in this specialized hobby that first emerged as a way to help sell a burger, fries, and Coke.

There is an amazing amount of interest in the United States about Happy Toys that are available overseas and vice-versa. Over the years, I built a good network of worldwide correspondents who e-mail me and help keep all the information on the site as current as possible. My correspondents are my resource, and they tend to stay in touch with me monthly. If not, I e-mail them with pleas for help. With their help, I developed a Toys of the World page in 1997 where I list the current toy in twenty-eight different countries. Some countries are very active, especially the Pacific Rim countries, such as Thailand, Singapore, Japan, Malaysia, and Taiwan. Through my Happy Toy exchanges with people abroad, I have noticed an incredible difference in the philosophy and cultures among different countries and societies.

The worldwide access of the Internet has created a wonderful following. I created a single resource for toy collectors from around the world that is available twenty-four hours per day, free to access, and regularly updated with information from the contributors themselves! Not only do collectors from all over the world visit the site to discover what the current toy in the United States is, but many visit the archives to see an image of the older toys that they want. People always use the Happy Toy archives to help catalog the bags or boxes of Happy Meal toys that they have stored in their attics. They also love to find the toys that match their other collections, such as Barbie or Muppets.

I get the most enjoyment from the many e-mails I receive from collectors and fans of Happy Meal toys. I never imagined all the friendships that I would develop over the years simply based on doing the site. One of my contacts, a Frenchman named Michel-Jacques, even wrote me a recent note of thanks. He met his girlfriend on my Happy Toy's trader board! She visited him in France, and they later became engaged during his visit to the United States! However, the mail that I generally receive deals with

HappyToy Traders Board

[Post Message] [FAQ]

Please Be Civil, Helpful and Above all folks HAVE FUN!

Please help support this board... visit Auction Universe here!

CLICK HERE

Post A Message!

Name:

E-Mail:

Subject:

Message:

Optional Link URL:

Link Title:

Optional Image URL:

[Post Message]   [Reset]

- More toys for sale-McD, BK, KFC - **jeanne** *05:48:44 3/06/2000* (0)

- U-3 'S FROM 1987 TO 1997 FOR SALE - **BRIGID** *04:55:37 3/06/2000* (0)

- TARZAN 2000-MIP#1,3,5,6,7,8 FOR SALE - **brigid** *04:34:27 3/06/2000* (0)

- One time offer! Beanie collection 155.00 shipped - 50 beanies - MWMT, 14 bears included! (3.00 each) - **Laurie** *04:23:15 3/06/2000* (0)

- 26 LOOSE FURBY'S FOR SALE - **brigid** *03:35:34 3/06/2000* (0)

- TWENTY-THREE DIFFERENT SNOOPY WORLD TOUR TOYS 50 CENTS EACH - **David H** *23:34:22 3/05/2000* (1)

  - Website address - **David Harcourt** *23:40:52 3/05/2000* (0)

- Asian Big Buddies Character set - **sita** *23:32:22 3/05/2000* (0)

www. happytoy.com

upcoming promotions or comes from people wanting to know how much money their collections are worth.

One particular woman was a regular visitor to my trader's bulletin board. Her husband had cancer and needed a bone marrow transplant. They had a three-year-old child and had to move from New Jersey to Washington State for seven months for the operation. She asked me if I would help her auction a set of Teenie Beanie Babies. I did, and then established a charity auction page for her husband. Regular visitors to Happy Toy not only started bidding, but also donating other collectibles. We raised nearly a thousand dollars to help the family! I felt really good that my work on the Web was able to make a difference in someone else's life.

While the original motivating factor behind Happy Toy was to learn Web page design and creation, I now find myself interested in helping to provide research for a growing information source. I provide a site to benefit the collectors worldwide, and feel responsible to my following. I really did not expect this. My site and the work I do on it still makes me smile. I feel I have a following or audience that relies on having HappyToy.com up-to-date and available for them to access day after day.

I update the site five times per week or more and work hard to keep all the information up-to-date. The site has several sections with pictures and information about the Happy Toys available in the United States and in some countries overseas. Plus, I always post news about any upcoming releases or discontinued toys. Interestingly, many of my sources are McDonald's managers and employees, and even employees who work at the corporate level. McDonald's has never contacted me directly. One of my correspondents who was a manager for a McDonald's in New Zealand did get reprimanded for informing me of upcoming promo toys before they were introduced. She told me the corporation threatened trouble for me if she continued. Thankfully, nothing ever developed from it and the matter went away.

Interestingly, while keeping the folks at McDonald's relatively content, the site also manages to stay out of the red.

I'm fortunate because, at this point in the operation, I can say that sponsorship covers the bills and a bit more. My banner ad revenue covers my Internet service provider access charges, my Web host charges, and my domain name fees. I make a little bit of profit each month. But it's nothing substantial by any means. I'm really not in this to make a profit. That's not now, nor has it ever been, the underlying factor. Even if I didn't have the sponsorship revenue coming in, I wouldn't stop doing the site. I have a good job working for a Fortune 500 company, and I earn a good salary. The expense of running Happy Toy in comparison to some of my other hobbies—skiing, biking, or golfing—is negligible. My time spent is the real cost for me to consider.

www.toymania.com

ERIC G. MYERS

The Superhero of Action Figure Collecting

About the Site

Toymania.com (www.toymania.com) is the Web site for the Raving Toy Maniac. The site includes news, pictures, and commentary about action figures and the companies that make them. Some of the more unique sections on the site allow toy collectors to interactively talk to each other or look up the existence of a specific toy in the toy archive. The archive catalogs action figures and allows the visitor to find out information, such as a list of every Superman or Spider-Man figure ever made. Additional material posted to the site includes trade show and collecting news. The Raving Toy Maniac doesn't just concentrate on the big companies, but continuously features information about small, independent action figure producers. The site is also built with a sense of humor, providing games and tongue-in-cheek feature columns.

How many specialty action figure collectors live in Columbus, Ohio? A low number is probably a safe bet. However, that is where Eric G. Myers resides, the Webmaster behind the action figure collecting Internet site www.toymania.com.

My interest in action figures was inspired by my lifelong love of superhero comics. Apparently, I'm one of the few people whose parents didn't throw out their comics. Ever since I was old enough to read, I've had comic books. In fact, comics taught me a lot about reading. I was probably the only fourth grader who could use the word "heinous" in a sentence.

Looking for a Specific Advertiser? Try Our Advertiser Index!

Serving the collector community since 1995.

News
Features
Archives
Custom Corner
Buzz Forum
Chat

Toy Toolbox
News Groups
FAQs
Links
Search

RAVING TOY MANIAC
The Magazine for Your Inner Child

Seen by Millions on

Headline CNN NEWS

Try our new Site Map!

INFORMATION FOR Parents

Child Safety & Privacy Policy

AD INFO

Advertiser Information

Awards and Honors

CREDITS

Credits and Thanks

RTM's BEST OF THE WEB

Other Web Resources

GET MOVIES

GetWild.Com

RTM Highlights

Toy Fair 1979!

NEW In celebration of TF99, the Mego Museum looks back at Toy Fair's past through the stunning pages of Mego's Catalogs 1973-80. If you know nothing about Mego, it's action-figure history you should know. If you know everything about Mego, it's history you can't get anywhere else! Click Here!

Famous Covers Uncovered
Guest's columnist **Rob Rooney** takes us through a step by step exploration of the construction of a **Famous Covers** figure. Take part in this toy vivisection and learn exactly what makes these figures tick. If you are a customizer or just a curious fan, you won't want to miss this in depth article on one of today's hottest toy lines. **Click here to find Famous Covers Uncovered!**

TOY FAIR 1999

NEW RTM will be on the scene in New York City gathering up the latest information on this year's lineup of all your favorites. Plus, we'll give you the low-down on what new licenses are planned for the millenium wrap-up. Click Here!

Interview with Famous Covers Designer
We were fortunate enough to grab some time with the **Product Designer** for **Toy Biz's Famous Covers** line, **Tom McCormack**. In this article **Tom** discusses the origin of the line right on through to the line's future. Find out a little bit about what it's like to design one of today's most popular collector lines. **Click here to read an interview with Tom McCormack**

On-Line Guide for Collectors
From the talent of **John Hays** comes the **Beginner's Guide to Collecting Action Figures**. Chock full of great information on nearly every aspect of the hobby from storing your figures to removing those pesky price tags. Even if you are an experienced collector, you'll want to check out this wonderful resource. There is something here for everyone. Just **click here to begin exploring the Beginner's Guide to Collecting Action Figures**

Click the button to tune into the RTM Channel on the PointCast Network!

 &

While growing up, Eric was one of the many children who had small plastic replicas, usually fewer than twelve inches tall, of assorted comic book, television, and movie characters that were manufactured between 1971-1982 by Mego Toys. Now, at age thirty-one, he is buying them again, but not limiting himself to just Mego Toys action figures, although they are his favorite.

I've also always had a soft spot for the Mego Superhero action figures. One of my all time favorites is the plain old Mego Spider-Man, which was the first Mego that I acquired in the 1980s when I began collecting toys. Oddly enough, even though I had many Megos as a kid, I never had Spidey. Unlike my comics, my parents did get rid of my Mego toys.

It wasn't until 1991, when Toy Biz produced a line of action figures based on the X-Men superhero comics that I was hooked on toy collecting again. My collection has expanded since then, but my tastes still gravitate toward superhero items.

Unfortunately, I have had to spend a great deal of time and effort to retrieve the Mego toys I had as a child. I rarely spend over $100 dollars for an individual figure, but with the Megos, you often have to spend considerably more to get a fairly good specimen. I currently have many more Megos than I ever did when I was a child, but that's one of the advantages of being an adult collector.

As with most collectors, I'm not finished collecting because there are so many figures I still want to acquire. I'd love some of the rarer Mego figures, like Zorro or Star Trek Aliens, but the prices are a bit steep for me right now. On the positive side, if I had everything I wanted right now, I'd have nothing to anticipate.

When Eric got on the Internet, he was more interested in finding other collectors and collectibles than building a site for them. As it turned out, he built a top destination for action figure collecting.

I began surfing the Web in 1994 and started a Web site that same year. Then, it was the typical, boring, vanity site about my interests. Toy collecting was a section of that overall site. As things progressed, it became clear to me that to do something really worthwhile on the Web, it was better to focus on a specific area. I considered sites centered around "things I like" to be boring. People were making pages that listed their cassette tapes. Who wants to read that?

www.
toymania.com

I don't think any specific event set me off in this direction. I just looked at my fledgling site one day and thought that it wouldn't really be interesting to anyone but me. So I selected the one aspect of it that I did think had potential, toy collecting. I took down the rest of the site and began solely working on the action figure section. This section was called RTM for Raving Toy Maniac. The name Raving Toy Maniac is taken from another acronym for the Usenet newsgroup rec.toys.misc. It was in this newsgroup that I first found other collectors online that shared my enthusiasm and love of action figures.

At that time, the pinnacle of action figure Web sites was Randy Matthews' Action Figure Web Page. I wanted to do something different but equally useful. So I began accumulating features and content that formed the nucleus of what is now RTM. This original version of RTM included resources for collectors with things like helpful hints for toy hunting and frequently asked questions documents. It also had my own archives on the X-Men and Secret Wars action figures.

In 1997, RTM became a more mature venture with the addition of Jason Geyer, who ran his own Web site focusing on detailed archives of Super Powers, Batman: The Animated Series, and Spider-Man. These archives were the original inspiration for my own X-Men and Secret Wars archives. Together, we revamped nearly everything and expanded the site significantly.

When Jason and I sat down and planned our strategy for expanding the site, we talked about a lot of the other sites in existence and their strong and weak points. We then decided to try to take the good concepts and make them better and attempt to fill the voids we saw. We knew early on that we wouldn't be covering Star Wars in great depth, because there were already so many other sites that did that.

We found that no one was really doing "action figure news." Some sites allowed users to input news, but more often than not the "news" turned out to be false or simply rumors. We also tried to make the site easily navigable. Many sites are so convoluted that you can't get around easily. Later, we noticed that there was a big desire among our readership to interact with each other. Initially, we were reluctant to jump into interactive forums, but eventually we gave in when we were able to do it with a measure of control. We have seen numerous other sites that use interaction of the readers as content; some even rely on it exclusively. We took that concept and made it immediate, with no waiting for a site update, and threaded it, so you could reply directly to another reader and to the general public. Many sites try to subdivide content too finely and succeed in making it more difficult for readers to actually connect.

We also tried to put a bit of the fun back into things. If everything is serious and dry, it really gets boring. We always keep our site playful. There are many games and interactive features that engage the reader. We aspire to the magazine model in a Web-based format. However, simultaneously, we realize that we have some advantages that a print publication will never have. We try to use those advantages to their fullest potential.

Over time, we have taken on various partners to help us expand the content of the site even more. These are mostly people we have gotten to know over the Net, many of whom I have never met face-to-face. We also sought input from our core readership. A lot of our features have been inspired by reader suggestions. Even with all the expansion, RTM has always been about action figures, specifically superhero action figures.

Raving Toy Maniac has not just attracted collectors and other Internet surfers, but paying sponsors are interested, as well.

I wouldn't call it profitable. At this point, it supports itself, and that is a relief because when you add up all the costs, including costs for contacting toy companies, postage, disk space, bandwidth, and so forth, it's probably well over $1,000 per month. Our costs are high because we get an extremely large amount of traffic and have to pay for the bandwidth we use. I wish the site produced enough revenue to support a salary, because it could easily be a full-time job. I think I could make it even better if I could operate it as my sole avocation. Unfortunately, it isn't at that point yet, but we're working toward that goal. We continue to court advertisers to some extent. We are also considering an exclusive action figure offering to help increase the site's revenues.

I'm chief cook and bottle washer when it comes to keeping the ad accounts flowing, and I don't have a lot of time to look for new advertisers. We're in a unique position. If we were a computer-related site, getting the amount of traffic we do, we'd have Microsoft and Compaq advertising on our site. However, we're a toy site and many people view that as a limited audience. Our market research surveys indicate that our core audience consists of twenty-something males with an interest not only in toys, but also in video games, movies, comics, and sci-fi, and they have disposable income to spend on these types of pop-culture-related items. It would seem to be an advertising dream for some markets, but we're in a position where advertising in toy-related print media is pretty inexpensive, compared to other types of magazines, so we have to price ourselves accordingly. Even though our readership is double that of most print magazines on toys, we can't charge nearly the same ad rates. However, the advertisers we have attracted are extremely loyal. Every one of them has renewed. Apparently, it is working for those who take the chance. We serve over half a million ads each month. That's a lot of ads.

Eric works hard to keep the site fresh and updated for his viewers, but wonders how he can get all the toy companies to take his site seriously.

I often do Web site tasks early in the morning, before I go to work, which, until I recently moved to Ohio, was at the M.D. Anderson Cancer Center in California as a project specialist. Currently, I'm looking to move into the Web design field. Anyway, my time on the site is spent writing; scanning photography; doing site maintenance, which is never finished; and developing new ideas for the site. I work on the site between twenty and forty hours per week.

I also spend a lot of time on the phone talking to the various companies with which we keep in contact. You really have to chase down the news. It doesn't come to you, and being a Web-based publication is a drawback sometimes. We have to work twice as hard to get half the respect automatically afforded to any print magazine, and some companies still mistreat us. These companies are not used to dealing with new media. They haven't realized that we have some advantages over the traditional print media. They are used to giving out information and photography and having a one-to-two-month lag in publication. With us, it's virtually immediate. I would imagine that this is a somewhat similar position to the way the print media regarded television years ago.

Eric's mailbox is not only a source of questions, but also a source of information.

Typically, I receive a couple hundred e-mails per day, less on the weekends. Most of them are asking where they can buy a certain item. I used to respond with a form letter, but even that became too time-consuming. Many e-mails inform us of news that people want to share. Whenever possible, we try to credit the source of the information, even if they just are pointing us to another Web site where the information can be located. We find that this encourages people to submit more news items. Of course, we do have a number of industry sources that don't want their names used, and we respect that confidentiality as well.

NEWS

"Extra! Extra! Scalper beat silly in local K-Mart!"

To make this a more enjoyable and easy to navigate page, we have created the RTM Newseum! This set of subpages is where we will archive past news items so that you can always look them up. If you have any news to share, comments to make, or suggestions for future improvements, please contact news@toymania.com .

STAR TREK NEWS | **INDEPENDENT COMPANIES** | **TOY FAIR '99** | **NEWSEUM**

Wanna know what kind of cool stuff **Playmates** is up to now? Then check out the goodies **Scott Gordon** has dug up now! **Click here!**

Jeff Cope takes us on a journey into **RTM's** coverage of **Independent Toy Company** news. From Previews to Antarctic, it's all here! **Click here!**

RTM once again heads to the Big Apple for **Toy Fair '99** Tons of images! **Click here!**

Can't find that news gem from last week? Here's where we archive all past **NEWS** items! Including **SDCC** pics! Better than a hard **punch** in the jaw! **Click here!**

 STAR WARS NEWS For the best and the latest news on the current Star Wars lines, check out **Phillip Wise's Rebelscum.com**, and subscribe to **Adam Pawlus' Newsletter**. You'll be glad you did!

All pictures are the property of Raving Toy Maniac and are not to be used without permission. If you see these on another page, please alert either Jason or Eric. Thank you.

Want to comment on something you see on this page? Head on over to the Toy Buzz or our new live chat forum, The Toy Buzz Live! and share it with the world.

As a central repository for action figure information, Toymania.com connects with a lot of visitors, but it was a parody of a common toy that caused its first big hit increase.

We currently receive between 150,000-200,000 hits per day. The news section is the most popular, with the Interactive Toy Buzz Forum, where people can exchange messages, being the next most-popular page. All this activity translates into about 1.5-2 gigs of Web transfer each day. We've had to switch servers three times this year because of our bandwidth. Each time, I told the server how much traffic we had and I think they thought I was

www. toymania.com

lying or exaggerating or just confused. Then when the site would go up and we'd use all their bandwidth, they realized we weren't kidding. We're finally on a server that understands our traffic and bandwidth needs. We pay more for it, but at least we won't have to move again any time soon.

A few things have increased our hits. The first big bump we got was when I developed a parody called "Traumagotcha," a parody of the virtual pet Tamagotchi. It allows you to pick items like a fork or bat to torture your virtual pet. It pretty much speaks for itself, albeit with tongue firmly planted in cheek. We won a bunch of awards for that, and it opened the site to a larger audience. That was the turning point. Our traffic has increased steadily since then.

Other events that increased our hits include our Toy Fair coverage and the showing of pictures of Kenner's Star Wars Expanded Universe figures before anyone else did. These first pictures scored big hits. Star Wars fans are a wild bunch. You won't find a more dedicated group of fans. However, stuff like this is hit and miss. We've debuted plenty of other things that don't get as much attention or traffic. It's just one of those things you can't predict.

Interestingly, our hits drop about 20 percent during weekends. I assume that most people are busy with activities on the weekends and surf the Net from work during the week.

Eric has gotten some special treatment for being the publisher of Raving Toy Maniac.

We attended Toy Fair this year as press representatives. That would not have been possible two or three years ago for us. We have made connections with most of the major toy companies and have regular contact with them. We hosted the toy events at the 1997 Comic-Con International in San Diego. The Comic-Con is the largest of its kind, and we were invited back to run an expanded set of panels and events this year. We have been covered in magazines and recently on CNN. It is really amazing that all of this developed mostly through word-of-mouth.

If you type "toys" or "action figures" into the search engines, we're lucky if RTM appears within the first ten pages. We've never really tried to promote the site through those means. It just doesn't work. Search engines have become large, unfocused repositories of links. Even if you input our specific name into a search engine, you often end up with links to other sites that have linked to us rather than our site itself. Why waste time, effort, and possibly money to try to get a higher placement in a search engine? Our philosophy has always been that if we do the best job we can, word-of-mouth will bring in the readers. I still believe this, though we have begun forming strategic partnerships with a few select companies that may help to increase our traffic. We recently signed a deal to do a column in the largest free comics newsletter, called Comic Shop News. We feel that efforts like this will introduce us to a whole new audience. Our plan has always been to provide what we think people want, and do it the best way we can. If we accomplish that, the traffic will take care of itself. I think it has.

www.
toymania.com

www.comicbook
resources.com

JONAH WEILAND

The Comic Book King

About the Site

Comicbookresources.com (www.comicbookresources.com) is the resource for comic book fans. Regularly updated comic news, weekly online polls and columns, comic book reviews, Real Audio interviews, contests, TV themes, and a comic book art gallery are all part of this site. It also contains the largest list of comic book sites on the Web, with over 1,400 different comic book links.

Jonah Weiland, a twenty-seven-year-old Los Angeles, California resident, has been reading comic books for thirteen years and collected over 11,000 comics, but it was not his choice to start reading them.

In ninth grade, an English teacher taught us about the evolution of the written word in the twentieth century, and the early history of comics. One of our assignments was to analyze the written structure of comics. To complete this assignment, each student had to go to a comic store to purchase a comic of his/her choice. My first comic was the two-part Alan Moore Superman death story right before John Byrne redid Superman's origin in the mid-1980s. It was an imaginary tale that had Superman dying, with art by Curt Swan, whom many consider to be the best Superman artist. This book showcased good storytelling with wonderful art. After I read it, I was hooked!

As Jonah's interest in comics continued to grow,
he decided to reach out to other comic book readers on the Internet.

Computers have been a hobby of mine since my father introduced them to me when I was a kid. I used them mostly for fun and games; however, once I got on the Internet, I started to self-teach myself about programming and graphic design. I also was using the Internet to surf for information.

When I was looking for a site on the Internet with links to existing comic sites and didn't find one that was any good, I started a single links page. This single page was first posted in early 1995. I called it Jonah Weiland's Comic Book Links Page, and it contained about twenty to thirty links. I knew there was more I could do with my page, so I kept expanding it and then changed the name to Jonah Weiland's Comic Book Resources. It became quite popular. I added graphics, TV themes, an expanded link section, and the like. Recently, I removed my name from it and it is now known as Comic Book Resources, or CBR for short. I removed my name from it because I felt it sounded more professional without it. The site has become more than just another fan site. It has truly become a resource for comic fans, and I wanted to convey the right message about it as such.

Comicbookresources.com has grown so fast that Jonah needed to hire writers.

The site's become much bigger than it was originally. I have continued to add new content constantly and develop new ways to improve the site. Even though the site was always supposed to be just a fan site, I have been forced to start accepting advertising because of the site's own popularity. The site requires a lot of hard drive space and, because of its high activity rate, it takes up a lot of bandwidth—both of which cost a lot of money. I have been careful to make sure that the advertising doesn't distract from the information contained on the site. At the core, CBR is still a site built by fans, created for fans.

www. comicbook resources.com

As the site's popularity grew, my responsibility to the visitors became greater. I wanted to make sure that the return visitor always had something new to see and do. I've had to hire programmers and writers to help with creating new content, so I've very much had to become a manager, as well as a designer. Once I began to accept advertising, all the above became even more important because I wanted to make certain that my advertisers were happy with the results. They seem to be pleased because I still have people advertising at CBR who were with me in the beginning. Meeting the goals of my advertisers is very important, because I currently get all my revenue through advertising.

As the site started producing revenue, I realized that in order to maintain it, the site would have to be updated more often and be more automated—and I could not do all of it alone. That's when I hired part-time help. Some people like to volunteer their time because they are heavy-duty comic fans, but unless you pay them, their production tends to be inconsistent. In this world, we all know money motivates; therefore, I have two people on the "payroll." One does a twice-weekly news column, while the other does a lot of the programming for the site. The great aspect about all the contributors to my site, paid or unpaid, is that they are from all over the world, and each brings a different perspective. There are so many contributors to the site—reviewers, feature writers, new reporters—so some of what you see online is created by them. I have been lucky to find some really great fans who have a real talent for writing.

Even though Jonah has hired people to work on his site, the site does not generate enough money for him to be able to leave his current job.

It would be fun to do Comic Book Resources full-time and I'd love it! If it could pay all my bills, I would commit full-time without hesitation; however, it just isn't capable yet. It does require at least twenty hours of my time per week, so it is almost a full-time job right now.

Currently, I'm a radio producer for a talk show in Los Angeles. My background is in radio. I've worked in the radio industry for twelve years now, since I was fifteen years old. The Internet is just something I happened into. I designed a personal Web page and thought I could do more, so I taught myself how to use graphics programs. The rest is history. My radio background has been beneficial to me in that the two areas very much crossover. At the core of both media is "what's entertaining?" "What grabs the listener or viewer?" "What makes a person come back for more?" Keeping those in mind helped me build CBR into what it is today.

Keeping the site entertaining and informative has produced many loyal readers.

I average about 900,000 to one million pages served per week. Whenever I receive awards like Project Cool and Cool Site of the Day, the site's activity increases significantly for that day and weeks to come. Specifically, winning these two awards were very rewarding for me. These sites highlight some of the best Web sites on the Internet, and it's nice to be included among them. It was also great to win these awards at a time when Comic Book Resources was relatively new. I won the Cool Site of the Day award about a month after my site went live. This was in

October of 1995 when award sites were still heavily trafficked. That really helped to kick-off the site.

Regarding e-mails, I receive about 300 per week. Most people write just to say they enjoy the site and want to know what is forthcoming. I also get a lot of questions, such as "How much is this comic worth?" or "Where can I sell my comics?" The most memorable e-mails were caused by a hoax I put on my site. On April 1, 1998, I ran an April Fool's joke that got people in quite an uproar. When people went to Comic Book Resources on that day, instead of being able to visit the site, they saw a letter from me stating that I was going to remove the site. I informed them that I had to do this because I received a cease-and-desist letter from the copyright holders of the words "comic book." I included the mock cease-and-desist letter from a phony attorney on the page. It was a very official-looking letter, as a lawyer friend of mine wrote it for me.

To say I got responses would be an understatement. In one day, I received 600 e-mails from fans. About 50 percent figured it was a hoax; the other 50 percent believed it and became very active. Some people wrote to the major publishers asking them to support me. Two lawyers even offered their services for free. The most memorable letter, and the one I felt the worst about, was from a fan who actually cried when reading that I was removing the site. I immediately let her in on the joke.

www. comicbook resources.com

Jonah loves the fact that comic book fans like himself enjoy his site, and he's thrilled that comic book insiders also recognize the site's value.

The most important thing to me is the site's popularity with the regular comic-buying public, but many comic book creators have stopped on occasion as well, which has been really exciting. Creators like Kurt Busiek, who has written comics for Marvel; Brian Augustyn, who has written issues of *The Flash*; Erik Larsen, who has created *Savage Dragon* and used to work on *Spider-Man*; and many others have talked to fans on the message boards and even endured some pretty silly comments. That kind of contact for fans with comic professionals would not have been possible if not for the Internet. I have also had several comic book companies contact me, mostly to offer praise or to send press releases or information. A few have advertised on the site. So far, they have never said anything negative.

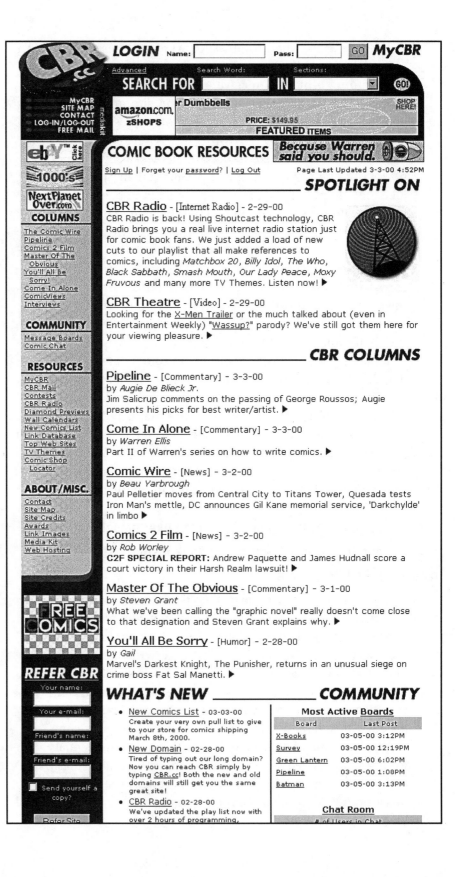

Jonah likes to change his site, but with the size of the site, a total redesign is no longer possible.

I'm the kind of person that gets bored with a style quickly. If the site weren't so huge, I'd probably be redesigning it every week. I'd add new graphic elements, colors, and such. Since its inception, the site has gone through three major redesigns. The redesigns have refocused the energies of the site from a links page to a broader comic book site. Bandwidth, the single largest cost, has also been streamlined. The colors and logo were changed, too. If I started all over today, I'd probably do some of the page layout differently; however, as a whole, I'm pretty happy with the site's navigation and layout.

I would like to have the site be dynamically created. Currently, much, but not all, of the site is static pages, which take a lot more time to develop. Recently, we've upgraded the links section and added a daily review column; both were created dynamically. Other portions of the site are being done that way as well. In the future, I'd also like to add more Real Video clips of the TV shows I have listed in the TV themes area. That's something that just takes a lot of time, but would be really interesting.

www.
comicbook
resources.com

The Internet has allowed Jonah to do something he would have never otherwise been able to do.

Overall, my site has given me an opportunity to take my "fandom" to a new level. I've been able to show my love for comics to the world and give something back to comic fans everywhere.

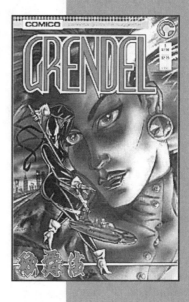

CHAPTER 24

Fish Link Central
Your Guide to Aquarium Resources on the Internet

www.fishlink
central.com

MARK BARNETT

The Fish Man

About the Site

Fishlinkcentral.com (www.fishlinkcentral.com) provides a list of links to any fish or aquarium site on the Web. The site sorts the links according to many categories, including type of fish, habitat, plant, personal home-page, or club. The site also has a bookstore, a photo gallery containing over 500 pictures, a question-and-answer section, and interactive message boards.

Many teachers feel that the most satisfying aspect of their job is watching their students achieve. Molding the minds of young students while influencing and motivating them to succeed is what keeps many in the profession. Although it can be difficult to pinpoint the exact influence a specific teacher has had on someone, in the case of Mark Barnett, it is easy to see what effect his biology teacher has had on him.

"What are the effects of ions and hormones on the pigment cells of fish?" How is that for what started my interest in fish? In ninth grade, I had to do a science fair project, and this was the one my teacher suggested. It entailed putting a scale from a fish in various solutions and watching the pigment cells expand and contract. I began with a twenty-gallon tank at the Junior High with three varieties of fish: platies, swords, and mollies. This was my first fish tank. My biology teacher, Donald Cooper, who was one of Georgia's STAR teachers, a special designation for teachers who made the greatest contribution to a student's scholastic achievement, was able to get me a 110-gallon tank the following year, and my hobby grew from that point.

Currently, I have about twenty tanks. The tanks are all freshwater. They range from ten gallons to my 135-gallon tank built into the wall of my

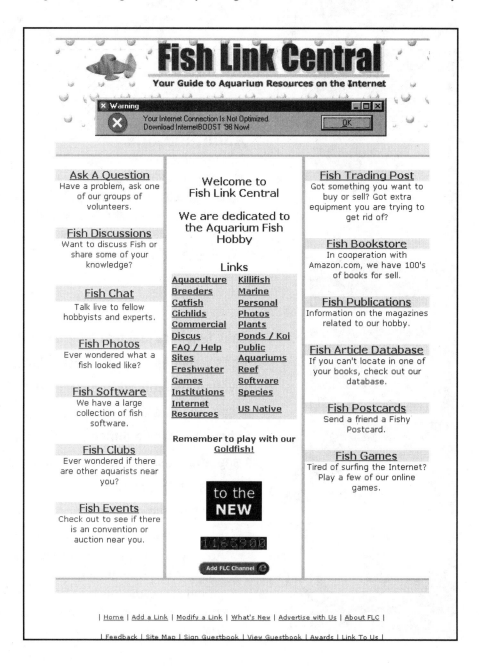

recreation room. Most of the tanks are twenty-nine gallons. In the past, I had a saltwater tank at my office, where I am a cargo sales manager for an airline.

Before building fishlinkcentral.com, a Web site of fish information, Mark, a thirty-four-year-old Atlanta, Georgia resident, became involved in the local aquarium association.

A number of fish clubs have come and gone in Atlanta. I joined one during its last breath. As it died, another member and I decided to start our own club in 1993, which we called the Atlanta Area Aquarium Association. I proposed printing a newsletter for the members, and, I became the editor in May 1993. It slowly grew into a publication that members eagerly anticipated every month. I was doing so well with it, no one else wanted to take over. After a few years, I had to give it up, as I had too many other duties with the club of which I am currently the president. The club now has about 100 members.

When I started the newsletter, I wanted to exchange newsletters with other clubs, so I had to compile a list. I found lists on the Internet, sent out a survey, and discovered that a lot of the information on the Internet was outdated. When I compiled an updated list, I decided to publish it on the Internet for other clubs to use. This was the creation of Fish Club Central. The site grew, and I thought it needed a new name. I changed it from www.mindspring.com/~mbarnett/fishlink.htm to www.fishlinkcentral.com.

Mark's computer skills grew as he continued to improve his site.

Since its inception in June of 1996, the site has changed from just fish club addresses to include more aspects of the hobby, such as links, discussion boards, software, photos, and a bookstore. Like so many other people, my site has changed as my knowledge of HTML has grown. Other than the occasional computer language class at Georgia Institute of Technology, most of my experience has come from playing on the computer. I gained most of my knowledge by finding an already existing site I liked and simply looking at the source code of the site. I have taken many small aspects of various other sites and used them on Fish Link Central. The discussion board script is an example. It was written by someone else and I adapted it to my site. I am always working on a number of new sections or upgrades to the site. The software I currently use most is Microsoft's FrontPage.

www.
fishlinkcentral
.com

The development effort is continuous. I generally spend about seven to ten hours per week on fishlinkcentral.com. The time spent has varied over the past year, depending on if I am adding a new section or simply updating something. The majority of my time is spent looking at sites submitted by viewers and putting them in the correct category. Of course, my personal life, especially the birth of my daughter, has slowed me down some.

Mark knows people like his site based on the number of visitors he receives. One visitor liked his site so much that he wanted to buy it!

In August of 1998, I received 35,000 individual visitors and served over 1,000,000 hits and 15 GB of data. Adding the discussion boards has increased traffic, along with putting advertisements on some of the newsgroups. Most people find fishlinkcentral.com from search engine searches or links from other sites. I also participate in banner exchange programs. Other publicity has happened without me even knowing it. A few of the hobbyist magazines have written about my site. Also, people from around the world have sent me their local newspaper clippings showing where the site was reviewed.

I receive approximately fifty to 100 e-mails per week. The e-mails range from basic questions to people looking for research material. In general, the e-mails are questions about keeping fish as pets. The most memorable e-mail was from someone who wanted to buy the site. I never thought of it as sellable.

When the person who wanted to buy the site e-mailed me, I gave the idea some consideration. After about a week, I told him I was not interested in selling. After a bit more talking, he still wanted me to name a price. I informed him that I would not sell for less than $25,000, thinking he would go away, his reply was: "That is within our budgeted amount." I told him I would think about it some more. Basically, the guy and his brother wanted to use the site to sell their fish and aquarium products. They were developing their own site but thought it might be faster and easier to buy one of the leading sites that already has traffic.

After talking to a number of people, I received various replies from "Hell yeah, I would sell it and start another one," to "It isn't enough for it." I decided that the offer probably wasn't enough. I felt I could develop the site more and make even more than that in the long run.

Mark is using banners and book sales to create a profitable site, but he is not leaving his day job anytime soon.

Fisklinkcentral.com is profitable now. The banners were added to help with the costs. As the traffic has grown, it has become profitable. Unfortunately, I am not becoming a millionaire from it. If I divided the money coming in by the number of hours I have put into it, I wouldn't be making much.

My banners are served by a number of Internet ad agencies. The ad agencies pay me a portion of the revenues for displaying the banners. Currently, the banners can deal with just about anything. In the future, I plan to approach several major aquarium fish-related companies and do the banners myself.

Another revenue source is Amazon.com. I saw their book-selling program on other sites, so I signed up with them, as well. It is very simple. It allows me to have a bookstore portion of my site linked to Amazon.com. By simply adding a search link to Amazon's catalog, you earn 5 percent on every book sold, or you can link to individual books, which you pick, and earn 15 percent. My book section has grown since I expanded the number of books I list. This allows me to get a check from Amazon.com every quarter. Currently, my site sells around 200 books per quarter, and that number is constantly growing. I am working on getting photos of all the books listed, which should help with sales. Also, I just received a letter from a publisher in Germany who wants me to include their fish books and CDs on my site. That is another possibility. Also, through my booklists, I am on several publishers' reviewer lists for their new books. This allows me the benefit of receiving copies of books before they are released. This would not have been possible without the Internet.

It would be great if fishlinkcentral.com could be a full-time job, but I don't see it happening. I am currently trying to decide if I want to simply be a pointer to other resources on the Web, as the site basically is now, or if I want to begin developing content for my site, such as fish information databases or articles. Of course, this would require more of my time. To become a full-time job, I feel I would have to become more of a content developer.

Getting on the publishers' reviewer lists and receiving books before they are released is one benefit Mark has from building his site, but not the greatest one.

The major benefit of my site has been the interaction with other hobbyists, and not just hobbyists in the United States, but all over the world. I am currently working with a public aquarium in southern China. They want advice from me on developing a Web site. I will be helping them contact people in the United States and will be working with them to develop methods to educate their visitors.

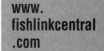

www. fishlinkcentral .com

Your Guide to Aquarium Resources on the Internet

Speed Up Your Internet Connection

Slow ———————————————— Fast

Fish Link Central > Links > Cichlids

Ask A Question

Fish Articles

Fish Bookstore

Fish Chat

Fish Clubs

Fish Discussions

Fish Events

Fish Games

Fish Links

Fish Photos

Fish Postcards

Fish Publications

Fish Software

Fish Trading Post

Sub Sections:	African	Discus
	Angelfish	Oscars
	Apistogramma	South American
	Central American	

Related Sections: **Books on Cichlids**
Breeders & Dealers
Discussion Forum
Personal Homepages
Photos

- CHOP – Cichlid Home Page
- Cichlid Reference Center
- Cichlid Research
- Cichlid Room Home Page
- The Cichlid Tank
- Cichlidés Passion
- Cichlids Cichlids Cichlids
- Devin's Cichlid Homepage
- Don Danko's Cichlid Page
- Fenix's Dwarf Cichlid-World - **Non English**
- Japanese Dwarf Cichlid World
- La Atlantida - **Spanish**
- Real Cichlids Don't Eat Quiche! 0
- RYTIREEFS Dwarf Cichlid Hideout
- The Sydney Cichlid Page
- Webwaves

 World Wide Pet Supply

FishLinkExchange

Mark still feels he can improve his site.

When I started my site, I would have used more scripts to automate more items. Currently, all of the links are being manually added. I am in the process of changing that. All of the links will be put into a database and will be searchable.

The next major addition after that will probably be a chat room. I met a lot of the aquarium "insiders" at various conventions, such as the American Cichlid Association, before my site was created. I hope to use those connections in the future for such things as the chat room or getting them to write for the site. I want to arrange for some of these well-known hobbyists to chat with the group. Another future section will be a list of pet shops and the ability for visitors to rate that pet shop.

After all of this building and planning, Mark has seen one drawback from combining his love for fish and his Web site.

Ironically, with me doing more work on the Web site, I have less time for my own fish.

www.
fishlinkcentral
.com

www.amused.com

CATHIE WALKER

The Mistress of Merriment

About the Site

The Centre for the Easily Amused (www.amused.com) began as a clever idea under the banner C*E*A. C*E*A features cartoons, humor pieces, trivia, chat rooms, games, and even a peeling paint video cam. All this amusement keeps its young audience laughing and telling jokes.

Cathie Walker, with twenty years of experience as an administrative assistant at a local university, created the Centre for the Easily Amused in July of 1995 as a way to teach herself HTML from a how-to manual. Only three years later, an international Web-based gaming company bought her site, and now employs her to run the site full-time.

In 1995, there weren't very many personal Web sites in existence, but I thought, "You know, I could do that. I could have a Web site." I bought a book entitled *Teach Yourself HTML in Seven Days* by Laura LeMay, I started reading in the middle of the book because I learn better randomly, and spent maybe two hours putting together the site.

The site was basically just a list of my bookmarks. I put the whole thing together to challenge myself; I wanted to see if I could do it. There was a picture of Mr. Potato Head as my mascot, a very simple graphic that said C*E*A, Centre

Amusing the world one person at a time - hey, wipe your feet!

Why aren't there ever any GUILTY bystanders?

Cornsilk

www.coolsig.com

☆ Hey boys & girls, just how easily amused are you?
Change background colour with this Amused Coolsig Generator
Hit reload for a new saying and get one for your website here!

Grab cool graphics for linking to us!

You'll find a directory to all of our links pages here

Sites of Dubious Taste ☆ NEW!
Amusing Sites for Kids
Cartoon Hot Picks
Sites That Do Stuff
Sites That Do Stuff: Games
Random Silliness
RS2: Son of Silliness
CONKI/C*E*A Site of the Day
Short Attention-Span Site of the Week
Previous SASS Winners
Other People's Hotlists
Music & Magazines
Movies & TV
Friends of C*E*A

Amused News - sign up to get it by e-mail!
Coolsig - cool sigs for your e-mail! ☆ NEW!
Dear God Nooooo! ☆ NEW!
Nick's Chocolate-covered Musings ☆ NEW!

♥ It's not too late to send Valentine Activegrams!☆ NEW!

♥ Valentine Amusements!☆ NEW!

♥ Win prizes by writing a Love Poem to us!☆ NEW!

☆ What's New and Nifty around here

Not a Step - humour on life in your 20s

Cathie's Corner looks at men's underwear ☆ NEW!

Read our exclusive daily jokes from Joke A Day☆ NEW!

The amazing new Time-Wasting Calculator! ☆ NEW!

New Trivia Game - The Game of Love ☆ NEW!

Backstreet & South Park Amuse-o-Matics! ☆ NEW!

More Chocolate-Covered Musings from Nick☆ NEW!

More unbelievable sites at Dear God Nooooo!

Life's Little Annoyances - add your own! ☆ UPDATED!

3-Pronged Poll - a quiz with attitude!

Free Toons & Coolsig Generator for your web site!

for The Easily Amused, a brief introduction, "presented by Cathie Walker, who is rushing right out to get a life," and my favorite links under different headings. I tried to make it a genuine reflection of my personality, entertaining and personable. Initially, my ex-boyfriend's name was on the site as well, but we parted ways shortly after the site's creation.

Working at a university, I had access to the Web. I've always been interested in technology, and was hooked from the moment I saw Mosaic in action and saw the ability of a hypertext document. At that point, I was already accessing files from other computers using Gopher and FTP, but I had never seen a site with both graphics and text formatted together. I was really flabbergasted by the ability to be able to hyperlink through space. The things I could do amazed me. Then the launch of Netscape 1.1 changed everything.

This all occurred in the earlier days of the Internet, and the Web was a lot smaller at that time. After I finished my site, I submitted it to the few search engines and awards sites that existed back then. Since there were mostly academic sites online, mine was a refreshing change. All were taking themselves so seriously on the Net at the time.

The C*E*A is pure entertainment and features chat rooms, humorous interactive features, thousands of links, and a variety of games. It's the online equivalent of taking a comic book into the bathroom at work, to get a couple minutes of stolen time to yourself and have a laugh or two. From the outset, I knew intuitively that the site would be popular, but I never imagined that it would be this big. It started as a hobby, and working full-time online was not my original goal. I started adding original material to the site approximately two years ago.

Before long, the traffic started picking up, and the accolades began. The C*E*A, as I called it (I added the asterisks because they were pretty), was picked up by Netscape's What's New, boosting the site's traffic so much that my Internet service provider had to upgrade their servers.

After that, the growth snowballed.

I believe that the most successful Web sites let the personality of its particular owner shine. In this day and age of faceless Web sites, those who appear approachable will be remembered. As for design, I believe in keeping it simple and fast-loading, and in making your site accessible to all, not just those with large monitors, fast connections, and the latest processor.

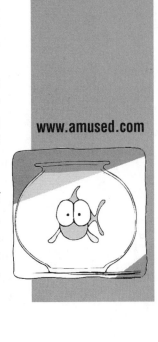

www.amused.com

My original goal was to create a central resource directory for humor and entertainment sites. After a couple of years, I had enough traffic to start selling ads through an online agency, which proved very successful for my advertisers due to my demographics. One advertiser thought so highly of the results that they decided to buy the site to have as much ad space as they wanted, and to resell the ad space to others that needed similarly strong results. In order to maintain the sense of community, they hired me full-time to keep people coming back.

I sold the site in March of 1998 and am now employed full-time to manage it by E-Pub Services, whose headquarters is in Budapest. Uproar is their flagship site, and the company has really grown in the time that I've known them. Uproar is an online gaming and entertainment site that includes puzzles, online game shows, trivia contests, and diverse member services, such as free homepages. According to NetGravity, the leading provider of online advertising management and direct marketing software solutions, Uproar is the largest online gaming site in terms of page views and unique visitors. The C*E*A is managed and reported separately, but is still part of the Uproar family.

My traffic has increased two and a half times in total page views since I took over full-time. I get about three million page views per month, which is pretty good for a one-person site. Plus, as a result of C*E*A's popularity and press, I have become a featured speaker and radio guest.

Although she never intended to focus her site on one audience in particular, Cathie has become the Pied Piper of teenagers.

I recently compiled 40,000 surveys from my users. Many were in the thirteen to seventeen year-old age range. The next highest segment fell between the ages of eighteen and twenty-four, and the age thirty-five and up visitors to C*E*A reflect about 20 percent of my overall audience. When I first compiled this data, I was a little disappointed, assuming that advertisers weren't going to want to advertise to kids. However, evidently, it's the best demographic to have, because these kids have the most money to spend in terms of disposable income. And they're so opinionated about all the money that's spent on them by the advertisers. I don't have any children, but I'm the perceived leader of a whole bunch of teens.

I can tell what content will be a good fit and only outsource some of the technical work. This is one of the reasons that the site is successful financially. By having one person who can do it all in a reasonable amount of time, not all the revenues are paid out to employees. It also gives the site its unique personality. I'm at the point where I need some help with daily operations, and I'll have to choose my future direction carefully so that the personality of the site doesn't get diluted.

I've always been creative and project-oriented. I designed my own needlework and sewing projects. That design experience actually helped me to create eye-pleasing features online. At one point, I was designing teddy bears, teaching classes, wholesaling them to stores, and sometimes even selling them out of my car. I've never been one to just sit around and watch TV. Because I designed my own projects, I was able to use that creative knowledge and my ability to put things together into a cohesive unit to transfer that onto the Web. I have no formal design experience, but just intuitively know what works, especially when it comes to my Web audience.

Although Cathie now works at home with her cat seated on her lap and coffee brewing nearby, she approaches her work online with all the professionalism of any office environment.

I get up at 8:30 each morning now, which is quite a change from before. When I was working at the university, I would get up at six o'clock, work for two hours at home, go into the office all day, and then come home and work for another few hours at night, plus several hours each weekend. I really had no life outside of the Web site, but I was determined to make it a success and not lose momentum.

Now, the first thing I do each morning is check my e-mail and respond to the most pressing issues. I have a cable modem and maintain a communication link with the staff in New York via the ICQ real-time communication program, and I speak regularly on the phone with the staff there. I'm working between eight and ten hours per day during the week, and several hours on the weekends. Because I have chat rooms and other interactive pages that require monitoring, I can't go far from the computer. Each day I add new links, edit the pen pal page, or redesign certain pages. It's a work-in-progress. A lot of time is also spent surfing site submissions; I get up to a hundred per day with most being people's humor and cartoon Web sites. It's easy to get behind. It's an honor to be listed on my site, and I'm very selective about what gets added.

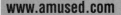

www.amused.com

As well as new features and links being constantly added, I try to maintain a high profile. By going into the chat rooms and making my presence known, I am able to ensure that certain standards of behavior are followed. I also tailor the site to the opinions of my demographic by listening to their feedback and keeping a close eye on my statistics. When I give my visitors a chance to have their opinions shape the C*E*A's future, they feel like they are part of the process. I try to answer all my fan mail and check out every site submission. I receive a lot of e-mail from teens with HTML and graphics questions, and I try to help them. Parents know that my site is family-friendly, and that I keep an eye open for bad behavior. Troublemakers in the chat rooms are banned and unable to return. Some offenders may be placed on chat probation and required to conform to the rules under threat of being banned permanently. Several of these chatters have turned into what I refer to as the chat monitors, letting me know of potential problems, and it's rewarding to see their behavior improve after being given a second chance.

I have an e-mail newsletter, Amused News, that I send every two weeks to about 10,000 people. Every issue contains jokes, trivia, a puzzle, and news about the site as well as site reviews. There have always been many things happening within the C*E*A community, and my newsletter is a way to make people feel that they are involved with real human beings. Some sites have no personality; they show their awards and that is all. In Amused News, I also talk about the media appearances, my travel, and meeting online friends in person. People actually think that it's a real office, and I often receive resumes, which always gives me a laugh.

Cathie has a lot of loyal fans, and is inundated with daily mail asking for advice, suggestions, and even personal information.

I receive about 400 e-mail messages per day. They are a combination of general mail, questions, fan mail, and site submissions. I get a lot of messages from teenage boys wanting to know my stats, how old I am and whether or not I'm single. I inform them that I'm a little old for them! Sometimes they ask for me for advice about their cyber relationships.

One couple had a cyber wedding in the chat room. They wanted me to be the bridesmaid, but I declined. There are a lot of cyber relationships occurring in my chat room, both good and bad. I don't really understand how these people can meet online and think they know each other so well. Then again, I'm an extrovert and can't see spending eight hours each day in the chat room. I try to keep myself removed enough so that when I do go into the chat room, I am respected.

Although occasionally surprised by it all, Cathie regularly finds herself in a Manhattan boardroom giving advice and commentary about the direction of online content production.

I travel to New York from my home in British Columbia every two months for a week. While there, I work and attend meetings with the Uproar team to obtain feedback, see how I fit in with their projects, and to keep the momentum going. It's a chance to congregate with people that are involved. I've also met with affiliate partners and a lot of people that

I've only previously met online. Uproar had a large media event during a recent trip, and it was exciting to meet people in the industry. I love New York, but it's very noisy compared to Victoria. I wouldn't want to live there, but it's an exciting place to visit for just a week. I have an expense account, something I've never had before. At the university, the budget was so tight that I wasn't even letting people have new pens and pencils.

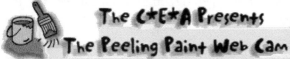

The C*E*A Presents
The Peeling Paint Web Cam

Welcome to the discretely amusing **Peeling Paint WebCam.** Through the wonder of the world wide web, digital imaging and quirky homemade software you can now actually watch paint peel **LIVE** from the comfort of your home or office.

Hours of fun for the easily amused!

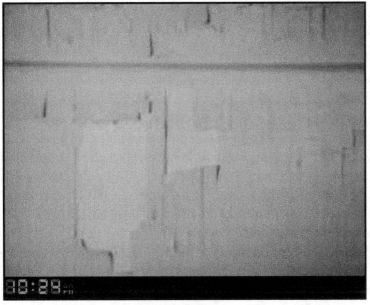

Image updates every 60 seconds.

** NEW **

Can't wait for the paint to peel? Get the latest 30 day time-lapse video **HERE!**

www.amused.com

Building on her success with C*E*A, Cathie is creating complementary sites with other Webmasters and always looking to the future.

I'm working on another site with two friends that focuses on design and marketing, as well as teaching the fundamentals of what makes some sites successful while others fail. We offer a unique way for our visitors to show Webmasters what bothers them about their sites. We invented the fork-o-gram to send to those sites we think need some help. The Forkinthehead.com site has bite and attitude, and we're getting some great feedback on it, thanks in part to a mention in *The New York Times* during our first week online.

Before the trips to New York, the media events, the expense accounts, and answering hundreds of e-mails each day from teenagers around the world, Cathie had a fairly routine life.

I worked at the University of Victoria for twenty years. I was assistant to the director of the School and Child Youth Care, administering the office, handling the budget, and other managerial duties. I'm on leave now, since I felt that I couldn't just walk away from years of seniority. I still keep in touch with the people at the university and the people I worked with over the years. I miss the people; I don't miss the job.

Now that C*E*A has arrived on the scene in such a big way, it's time to get the recognition the site deserves.

I always wanted to be recognized as the Cool Site of the Day. That was the ultimate award to me, and I never got it. I sent them an e-mail awhile back saying, "You think my life is pretty good because I quit my day job and I've got 50,000 visitors each day, but you guys have never acknowledged me." Two days later, I was Cool Site of the Day. Then I received an e-mail stating that they wanted to hire me to redesign their site. I declined, saying that I was sorry, but I just didn't have the time, otherwise I would love to do it.

If the Internet blows up, and I don't have a career anymore, I can go back to the university, but I'd rather work at the Dairy Queen than go back there. It would be a huge step backward to return, and am looking forward to my future working in new media. The Internet is my dream come true. Everybody wants to be paid for doing what they love and to be appreciated. It sure beats filling out forms all day. I'm working at home, the cat is on my lap, I'm listening to nice music—I really feel very spoiled now. I'm incredibly happy. I've met new friends online, many of whom I've met in person, and I have traveled, and, basically, changed my life! Thanks to the Web site, I was able to quit my day job to do what I love. Cool, eh?

CHAPTER 26

Kissthisguy.com

The Online Archive of MISHEARD LYRICS

www.kissthisguy.com

SCOT HACKER

Putting Words to Music

About the Site

KissThisGuy.com (www.kissthisguy.com), featuring The Archive of Misheard Lyrics, is a collection of misheard song lyrics organized by specific song or artist. Visitors can search among 1,700 different lyrics in the database to find out which words were misheard, the actual lyric, and when the realization took place.

The creator of the archive, Scot Hacker, age thirty-two, launched his site on the Web in 1995. A long-time fan of Jimi Hendrix, Scot decided to use a misheard Hendrix lyric as The Archive's address on the Web. From the outset, the site has helped bring thousands of visitors together around a surprisingly common experience.

The mother of a close friend of mine inspired the concept for The Archive of Misheard Lyrics. In 1995, she confessed that, as a young girl, she thought that the old church hymn "A Little Walk with Jesus" was called "A Little Chocolate Jesus." In fact, until she was almost forty-five years old, she assumed the song was really about a chocolate Jesus. For more than three decades, she went along, humming these same lyrics. The amazing thing is that the longer we've been working on our site, the more it seems that just about everyone has a story very similar to hers.

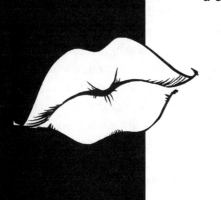

221

The archive identifies closely with something that, at one point or another, has happened to each of us. We've been thinking that these bizarre song lyrics, first heard as an eight-year-old or some time, were the actual words to a real song. Suddenly, at age thirty-four, someone realizes, "Oh my God, for twenty-six years I thought that song was this..." People get a lot of enjoyment from the site. Kissthisguy.com serves as a sort of encyclopedia of misheard lyrics. It is a bit of nostalgia to which everyone can truly relate.

There are also other kinds of memories that the site seems to trigger. I get a lot of mail associated with the site's Web address, KissThisGuy, which is really a play on the words of a well-known Jimi Hendrix song, Purple Haze, from the late sixties. While the exact lyrics are "'scuse me while I kiss this sky," a lot of old-timers who saw Hendrix in concert have let me know they were there in the audience when he himself realized people were mishearing the song as "kiss this guy." He started vamping on the same theme, and he actually did start singing it that way. He would go over to the drummer, Noel Redding, and kiss him on the cheek, singing, " 'scuse me, while I kiss this guy." In effect, it's like a double irony. That misheard lyric is not really misheard if you saw one of those concerts, since he really did sing it that way.

The site draws a very broad audience and contains more than 1,700 misheard lyrics, indexed by individual song and specific artist. The archive works by allowing people to submit their misheard lyrics of well-known songs, which are then filed alongside the real lyrics by Scot. Since the content of the site is completely user-driven, contributors to the site feel like they're very much a part of the overall process. Each posted submission is presented in a small user profile that includes the embarrassing moment of revelation, the age they were when they realized just how wrong they had been, and even whether or not they believe their misheard version is better than the original. Since just about everyone can think back to a set of song lyrics that always seemed kind of weird but were repeated for years anyway, the site pulls in e-mail filled with personal stories and memories of growing up.

www.
kissthisguy.com

I rely on a tremendous amount of feedback from visitors to the site. I get a lot of mail saying, "I haven't laughed this hard in a long time." I think people laugh largely because things are familiar to them in a strange way. Certainly they remember being eight years old and singing some song in a bizarre way. I've even had some memorable letters from people who have suddenly been shaken out of their depression. They took this piece of nostalgia for granted, as anyone would, and didn't think of it as strange when they were young. They never even questioned it as time progressed. Now, seeing the actual lyrics in context, it has an almost cathartic value for them.

Each submission to the archive carries a bit of personal history and nostalgia with it. However, as Scot discovered, not every misheard lyric is necessarily appropriate for the archive.

I continuously have to explain to people why I didn't post their submissions, which is really difficult. First of all, it's tough because it's difficult to reject anyone without hurting feelings. It isn't easy to say: "I want to keep the quality of the site high, so I'm very selective." No matter how you phrase it, feelings get hurt. The vast majority of the time, I'm not able to associate the name of the person querying me with any particular submission because I receive about 1,000 submissions per week. I just don't have time to sift through the database and make those kinds of connections. A lot of people get really testy, and seem to think I'm at their beck and call. It gets frustrating sometimes. Many seem to think I owe them something. On the other hand, there are a lot of really nice people out there. Visitors to the site often write to say, "I know you get a lot of submissions and you're very busy, but I just want to thank you for making my day. I've been laughing for hours." Those kinds of letters make it all worthwhile.

Of course, when dealing with tens of thousands of different visitors over the course of a year or so, and with direct editing responsibilities, some people will inevitably write to complain. The occasional negative response is similar to: "Hey, I sent you a submission two months ago, and you never posted it." So, a lot of people seem to think that I will post anything that is misheard, regardless of whether it's funny or not. Actually, if you could see these submissions, it's inconceivable that I could post everything. People will submit things like, "I misheard "Goodbye Yellow Brick Road" as "Goodbye Yellow Brick Kroad." Isn't that hilarious?" Well, no, it isn't hilarious at all. And then there are the misspellings I regularly receive. I mean, not just a letter out of place here and there, but stuff that's barely even readable. You just have to shake your head and wonder sometimes what's going on in this country's schools. In the end, I usually post about one sixth of what is submitted. It has actually been an eye-opening lesson about the state of American education.

Scot never expected to tap into what has proven to be a widely shared, and now highly publicized, individual experience.

The traffic level and popularity of the site is far beyond my wildest expectations. The site actually began as a single page on The Birdhouse Arts Collective, Birdhouse.org, in September of 1995. Birdhouse is an arts collective I began in late 1994 to showcase some images and writings that my friends and I have done. One day I posted a page chronicling several misheard lyrics I had heard floating around, and invited other people to submit their own to this page on Birdhouse. Over the course of a few months, the archive grew to seven pages for a total of about 100 entries. When I moved it to a separate domain and began databasing the lyrics, the media caught on right away. There was actually a period of a couple of months when it was just relentless. It was out of control. First the site was featured in *The New York Times*, then the site appeared on Netscape's What's Cool? section, then Yahoo! started highlighting it. National Public Radio and MTV did stories about misheard lyrics, and both talked about my site. Voice of America picked up the story, and the pace kept going like this for several months.

I was amazed at how the media goes on these frenzies, all copying each other, picking up each other's stories. Anyway, much to my enjoyment, the traffic was phenomenal as a result. I also really enjoyed the advertising revenues during this spike in the site's popularity. While I'm by no means disappointed, my current fifty to 100,000 hits per day translate into 25,000-50,000 daily visitors. I guess I really can't complain since advertising revenue from the site almost, but not quite, pays the rent.

As the popularity of the archive continues to grow, there is the issue of scalability, which can present quite a challenge. Although I wasn't expecting this to be the case, I have more submissions to read and far more lyrics than I can feature now. As the site gets bigger, it gets more and more difficult to organize it. I currently have about 2,000 pages featuring new artists each week, as well as a short profile of the person who made the submission. It becomes a real problem to present that amount of information sorted by various fields within a single interface. The whole thing became really unwieldy, really fast.

Scot not only has created a site that helps put a roof over his head, he's also quickly built a solid professional track record working with Internet media and is now an author as well.

Until recently, I worked as a managing editor at ZDNet, but I left the company to work as a freelance journalist. My main focus and motivation is BeOS, a radical new desktop operating system for Macs and PCs from a company called Be. All you have to do is think about the Linux operating system without the chaos, and with a much better ease-of-use factor. I write on BeOS and its applications for various industry publications, and have just finished writing a book on BeOS for Peachpit Press, *The BeOS Bible*.

www.
kissthisguy.com

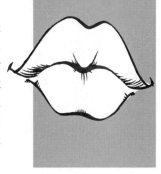

Before taking up the freelance writing, I was a manager of a team of six people at ZDNet. We ran the Internet channel there. I managed the Internet channel for three years. I'm no longer doing that, since I basically got burnt out on corporate life. They were grooming me to climb, and I was not really interested in climbing. I find writing JavaScript and CGI scripts to be much more interesting. I knew I wanted to focus my energies in writing and code development instead of devoting my time to building corporate-supported Web sites through aggregation. Now, of course, I also have the freedom to work until four o'clock in the morning and get up at noon the next day if I want to. That's essentially what I'm doing now, and I love it.

With regards to publishing the archive online, I've moved through several solutions based on the very dependable and time-honored process of trial and error. My publishing method is a very nice, one-click solution by storing everything in an Access database. Then I use a tool called GDIdb, which I found one evening doing a Web search for "+database +html." I sort and organize the database in Access, then extract the data into HTML pages via a collection of inter-linked scripts. With this system, I can generate the entire 2,000-page site in less than five minutes, upload the whole thing as a single compressed archive, and telnet in to decompress the new archive onto the server. This last step overwrites the old content. It's really very elegant, though there was a lot of development time involved in getting it to where it is now.

I must add that while this system is ideal from a technical standpoint, it doesn't help with the editing process of information that is submitted. All the work on the front-end takes several hours of reading and editing before ever going into the Access database. In addition, the sheer volume and nature of submissions prevents me from being able to shorten that process. There are some things, such as editing for quality, that computers just don't make any easier.

In the short span of a few years, Scot himself has seen the transformation of the Web from a resource for the technically savvy to a genuine entertainment medium for the general public's direct use.

I think that what was known as the Web culture a couple of years ago is really starting to change, because the Web has become so normalized. In other words, when I was getting into the Web four years ago, having specific coding skills was really rare; it was really something special. Today, anyone who has a computer can at least figure out how to make a basic Web page. If they spend a little bit more time and energy, they can do some pretty killer stuff, making the site much more dynamic with DHTML, JavaScript, Perl, or any of the other popular Web programming solutions.

Having basic Web skills now is no more special than having any random job skill, but as Web sites evolve to become more like distributed applications, the onus is on Web developers to evolve their programming skills or be drowned in the flood.

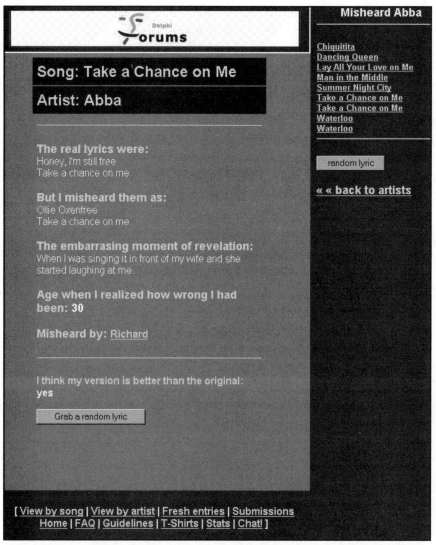

Delphi Forums

Song: Take a Chance on Me

Artist: Abba

The real lyrics were:
Honey, I'm still free
Take a chance on me

But I misheard them as:
Ollie Oxenfree
Take a chance on me

The embarrasing moment of revelation:
When I was singing it in front of my wife and she started laughing at me

Age when I realized how wrong I had been: 30

Misheard by: Richard

I think my version is better than the original:
yes

Grab a random lyric

Misheard Abba

Chiquitita
Dancing Queen
Lay All Your Love on Me
Man in the Middle
Summer Night City
Take a Chance on Me
Take a Chance on Me
Waterloo
Waterloo

random lyric

« « back to artists

[View by song | View by artist | Fresh entries | Submissions
Home | FAQ | Guidelines | T-Shirts | Stats | Chat!]

As Scot notes, the continued mainstreaming of the Internet can also begin to work against it over time.

Some of the culture that surrounded the Web initially had to do with its alternative status. I think some of the people that were involved in the beginning with the Internet are starting to say, "Sure, you can publish your own zine. But you can go down to the neighborhood Kinko's and publish your own zine that way too.

www.
kissthisguy.com

What's the big deal?" Now that the Web no longer has that alternative status, it's just one more stream in the cultural river. I still enjoy being a part of it, though. Most importantly, it's really nice to be able to see that all of my labor has finally paid off for me. There aren't many non-porn, non-commerce sites run by individuals that actually make a living for their progenitors. I'm selling ad space on pure content pages alone, and doing well with it. That, in itself, is very satisfying.

Looking back, there is nothing that I wish I did differently, because that's the wonderful thing about the Web. It never assumes a static or fixed format. You can always change anything after the fact. So I've corrected my mistakes on the fly, changed publishing systems several times, changed the design, and changed the way I handle and process submissions. I'm not stuck with any particular aspect of the site that was started three years ago. In my experience, it has been a process of constant evolution.

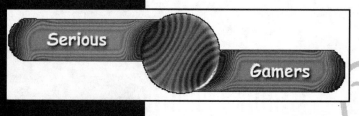

www.serious
gamers.com

**TERRY PETERS AND HIS
FIANCÉE, CORA FEHR**

A Lifelong Gamer

About the Site

Seriousgamers.com (www.seriousgamers.com) allows you to click on a list of over twenty game titles to find additional Web sites about those specific games. Seriousgamers.com prides itself on having only high-quality, existent sites listed. Other Serious Gamer sections include gaming news, game strategy information, message boards, game reviews, and a contest area for free gaming products.

Who says computer games are just for kids? Definitely not Terry Peters, a thirty-one-year-old elementary school teacher from Fisher Branch, Manitoba, Canada.

I first became interested in computer gaming in my early teens. At the time, I was playing games like Missile Command and Adventure on my Atari 2600 console. I then went on to own a Commodore 64, Vectrex, Sega Genesis, Sega CD, and, ultimately, my IBM PC, which is currently my gaming platform of choice. Although I always enjoyed playing the games, I was just a casual computer gamer through my teens and into early adulthood. I did not get the serious computer gaming "bug" until I entered my early twenties and started playing games on my PC. The first game I played on my PC was Doom. After playing that something in me changed, though I am not quite sure what. Shortly thereafter, I played Dune II and knew from that moment on that I was hooked.

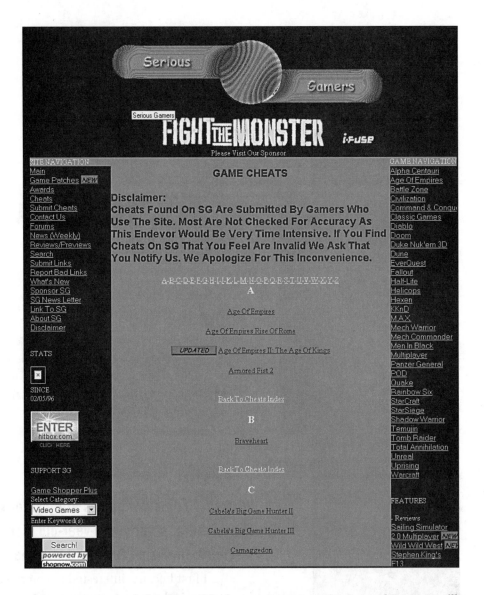

In case you aren't familiar with these two games, Doom and Dune II, I'll explain. Doom is a game played from the first-person perspective in a virtual 3D world. The player is a space marine who must face an array of monster-type enemies to successfully complete each level and episode. Each episode consists of various levels and the game is comprised of several episodes. Dune II is a real-time strategy game that takes place on the planet Dune. The player commands an army of forces against two other factions and the forces of the Emperor for control of the planet. The action takes place in real-time. While the player is planning and making movements and attacks, the enemy factions are doing the same simultaneously. The great thing about real-time strategy games is the player does not have to wait for enemy factions to move and attack before they can move and attack with their force again.

Once these games captured me, my game sessions lengthened. In my teens, gaming would have been limited to a few hours per week. At the present time, however, a short gaming session lasts for several hours, and I have been known to be prone to marathon gaming sessions in which all available hours, except those spent at my regular job and eating, are spent in game play. Note the lack of hours allotted to sleep. I once went three days with no sleep during a marathon gaming session.

Terry enjoyed playing so much that he turned to the Internet to find more gaming information. Unfortunately, he couldn't find what he wanted, so he decided to start his own resource on the Web.

I started www.seriousgamers.com because I was tired of searching the Internet for game sites and finding instead, "404—file does not exist errors," rather than information on games and gaming. I decided it would be nice to have a site where all the searching for the best game sites was done for you. Also, I thought it would be even better if someone was willing to keep broken links to a minimum. This was the beginning of Serious Gamers.

I did the first posting of Serious Gamers on the Internet in late 1995. Originally, the site had a bright red background and was a single page with only five to six game categories. Some of the first games I listed were Doom, Dune II, and Hexen 2. I picked the links that I would profile for these games based on certain criteria, including that the site contained only game-related content, was well presented, easy to navigate through, and regularly updated. In the early days of Serious Gamers, I looked only at sites relating to real-time strategy games, such as Dune II, and first-person shooter type games, such as Doom.

When I was thinking about what information my site was going to contain, the vast majority of game sites already on the Internet, at that time, covered a single or sometimes a few games. For awhile, I considered going this path myself but decided that I wanted to hopefully build longevity into Serious Gamers by covering a wide variety of games and gaming interests. In the short term, dealing with a single title might have been more rewarding, given that I wouldn't have had to put in as much time to make the site popular compared to the time needed to deal with several games, but I was in this for the long haul. Looking back, I'm glad I chose to profile multiple games, even though concentrating on one or a very few games was a tempting option at the time.

www.serious
gamers.com

After the site was running for only five months, other gamers started to respond to Terry.

I first realized people were really viewing Serious Gamers seriously when I began receiving e-mail from readers asking for help with everything from installing games to strategies to use in games covered on Serious Gamers. Today, the site averages about 7,000 visitors per week, with the areas devoted to game cheat codes and to the different game link sections, especially the link section for Age of Empires, a real-time strategy title from Microsoft, getting the most visitor interest. On average, I receive between 400 and 600 e-mails per week. Some are very memorable. The most memorable e-mails are those from game companies and from readers of Serious Gamers asking for assistance with games or commenting on the site. Perhaps the most memorable e-mail I have ever received was from a fan saying that he trusted the reviews on Serious Gamers and checked them faithfully before he purchased a game.

Other notable e-mails received were those asking me, because I was the administrator of Serious Gamers, to contribute game reviews to the AllGames Guide Web site, www.allgame.com, which is a site that is attempting to compile a review of every computer game in existence. Another exciting e-mail notified me that I was accepted as an affiliate to the GameStats News Network, www.gamestats.com, which is a respected gaming news site and a central repository of game sites that accepts only quality sites into their affiliate program. I approached them with the proposal that Serious Gamers join the GameStats network. They accepted Serious Gamers readily. Finally, the e-mail asking me to be in this book was also very memorable.

Terry feels his site is successful because of the time he takes in making sure the other gaming sites that he provides as links meet his high standards.

The link sections for various games are the most popular part of Serious Gamers. I feel people like the links section because very few sites have a comprehensive set of game links organized by category. There are many news sites dedicated to a particular game or game genre, but Serious Gamers is much more than that. I am very careful to include only the highest quality sites on Serious Gamers. Only about 20 percent of links submitted for inclusion on Serious Gamers are accepted for inclusion on my site.

Ensuring that high-quality links and other aspects of the site are well done makes my site a very time-intensive responsibility, and although the time I spend working on Serious Gamers varies, on average it is about twenty to thirty hours per week. Maintaining the site involves many things, including reporting news from the game industry, expanding the number of games that

I cover, adding new links to existing game sections, checking existing links to make sure they are still viable, posting cheat codes for games, monitoring the message boards, reviewing games, and running contests and giveaways.

Terry's hobby has turned profitable, although not profitable enough for him to leave his "day job."

Yes, Serious Gamers is a profitable site, generating revenue through banner advertising. However, the site is a totally free resource for my visitors. One day, Serious Gamers may become my full-time job, but for the last two years, I have been an elementary school teacher, having previously taught junior high and high school science. I hold bachelor degrees in science and education. I am also a partner in a company called Web Wonders—Internet Site Creation Services, www.escape.ca/~wonders/, which specializes in Web site design.

I have been lucky enough to have interest in Serious Gamers from advertisers, so I have not needed to approach companies for advertisements. They have approached me. I have also been equally lucky by not having to directly handle the ads displayed on my site. All banner ads on Serious Gamers are handled and distributed to Serious Gamers by the GameStats News Network.

Another type of advertisement, which is not handled by the GameStats News Network but is displayed on my site, is a price shopper agent that does generate revenue for Serious Gamers on the basis of the number of searches done. I was approached in early 1998 by the Bottom Dollar Network to use their price-searching agent on Serious Gamers. You can search not only for prices of games but also for prices on CDs, books, and other items.

Getting revenue from advertising is not the only fiscal benefit Terry earns from running his site. He also doesn't have to buy new games.

I have developed a number of contacts with game companies from the very small to the very large. I regularly receive two to three game products per month from companies for review, and I have been involved in the play testing for a number of game titles. I even was a play tester for the groundbreaking title Uprising from Cyclone Studios and the 3DO Company. Uprising was the first PC game title to successfully combine first person shooter game elements with real-time strategy game elements.

www.serious
gamers.com

I believe that my contact with these game companies is very positive for Serious Gamers, as it allows me to deliver new content to my readers on emerging titles in a cost-effective manner. I remain objective about any and all products I review, because I believe in keeping the integrity of the site and its content intact. This is what readers of the site have come to expect.

This close association with the companies that make the games has allowed Terry to add a contest to his site that has increased readership.

The Lost Link Contest sponsored by Serious Gamers and various game companies usually results in an increase in traffic. The Lost Link Contest requires the viewer to find some lost links on different Web sites and then enter a drawing for free software. Usually, game companies wishing to sponsor the contest and give away software approach me. However, I have publicized the contest in newsgroups, as well as issuing press releases relating to the contest. Also, as an affiliate of GameStats, I have a cross promotion agreement with them. So they promote the contests and features from Serious Gamers, and I do the same for them.

Terry plans to keep adding games to his site, as there seems to be no end to the amount of games that companies are producing or the influence the Internet is having on the industry.

Presently, I am scheduling several new game sections to be added to Serious Gamers. Some of the possible games are Fallout, Rainbow Six, Shogo, Half-Life, and Mech Commander. When I'm deciding which games get included on the site, I accept suggestions from visitors, take into account my personal preference, and determine the overall popularity of a game. Later, I hope Serious Gamers will eventually be a site that deals with hundreds of games. To make this a reality, of course, Serious Gamers would need to employ a staff of several dedicated gamers.

Even with a large staff to help, I never envision running out of material, because new games are always being produced. In the next few years, I see the real-time strategy genre continuing to dominate computer gaming. You just can't argue with the continuing appeal of the flood of great real-time strategy games that are available on the market today. The Internet has also opened up a whole new facet to computer gaming by allowing the public to game against one another over great distances. Today, a game without multi-player, Internet capability will have a difficult time becoming successful.

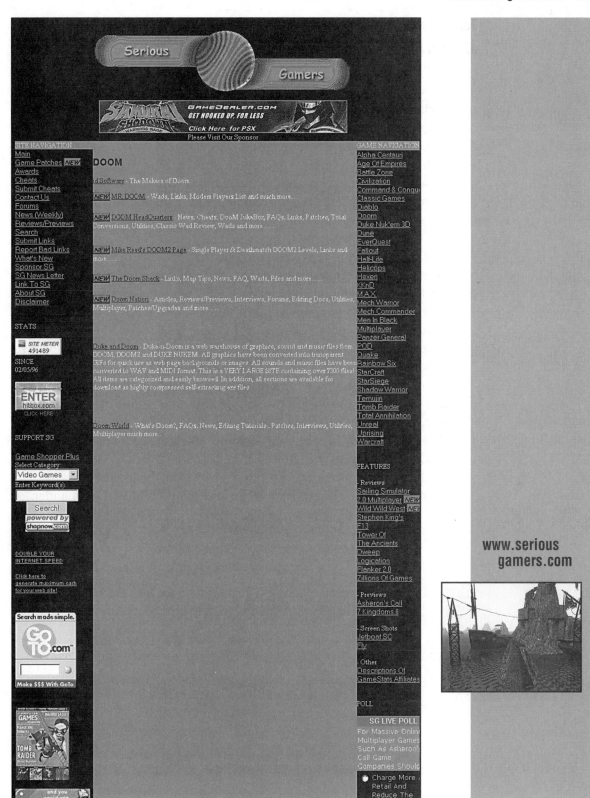

Terry is truly happy with what the Internet and his Web site have allowed him to accomplish.

I met some great people in the gaming industry and also many serious game players like myself because of Serious Gamers. Some of these people include John Hoskin, the head of GameStats; many media relations employees from various game companies; and dozens of other people who run game fan sites on the Web.

I think Serious Gamers and other game sites let readers know which games on the market are worth the purchase price. This influences game companies to strive to produce high-quality titles that will pass the test of the serious gamers that run game Web sites.

My site has given me the opportunity to indulge in my love for computer games by giving my passion a presence, a voice on the Internet. The Internet is simply the single greatest information-serving vehicle ever created. If it weren't for the Internet, I wouldn't have met my fiancée. I met her as a result of the nickname I use on the Web, which is of course Serious Gamer or just Gamer. I was in an Internet Relay Chat room looking for other gamers when we started a conversation because of our respective nicknames in the chat room. She was identified as Doe Eyes. We continued talking and I asked her if she had big brown eyes, as her nickname implied, and if she had a picture to prove it. She sent me a picture over the Internet and, indeed, she had the brown eyes. We continued to talk, discovering that we had much in common, although, in reality she is not a gamer at all. In October of 1998, she moved here to Fisher Branch, Manitoba, from Medicine Hat, Alberta. So, you can see why I like the Internet.

By the way, one of my personal favorite games is Mech Commander.

The Written Word
& Journalistic
Endeavors

www.riotgrrl.com

NIKKI DOUGLAS

Grrl Power

About the Site

The Grrl Web world consists of a trio of sites. RiotGrrl.com (www.riot grrl.com) is an edgy woman's zine with columns and articles about celebrities, supermodels, sex, music, television, and movies. GrrlGamer. com (www.grrlgamer.com) is a zine dedicated to female computer game players. The site includes game reviews, editorials, news, and an area to buy games. TeenGrrl.com (www.teengrrl.com) is an attitude-laden zine aimed at teenage girls, with information about celebrities, art, activism, sports, music, and entertainment. All three sites feature bulletin boards and chat rooms.

Nikki Douglas loves books and writing.

Since I was about eight years old, I wanted to be a writer. I just knew that was my calling, like the way you know about a good melon. I was inspired by voraciously reading science fiction in my youth, especially Ray Bradbury, Issac Asimov, Philip K. Dick, and Harlan Ellison. I also loved science fiction television and movies, like *Star Trek*, the original series; all the *Star Wars* films; and *Blade Runner*, which inspired me on many levels, mostly having to do with the human condition and the process of imagination. My love of sci-fi led me to other books and a love of literature. To this day, I read at least one book every day.

After graduating from the University of Akron in 1990 with degrees in English and theatre, I moved to Key West, Florida, and worked for several local papers in many different capacities, including creative director, advertising sales, graphic design, and features editor. I also did a lot of freelance writing, mostly in game and computer magazines like *Electronic Gaming Monthly*, *US Official Playstation*, *Games Business*, *The Net*, and others.

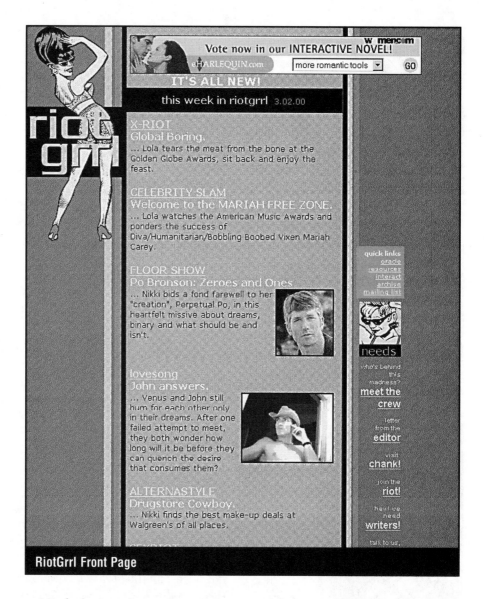

RiotGrrl Front Page

My desire to write, under my own terms, led me to begin thinking about publishing on the Web. I wanted to really make a difference with my writing, to venture out on my own and get my message to the world. The Web was built for this, so I took advantage.

In August of 1996, Nikki became a Web publisher by starting RiotGrrl.com, a female-oriented technology zine, updated monthly.

My background in journalism and feature writing was excellent to take into Web publishing. The only hurdles I foresaw were the actual design and technical work. Fortunately, I had a background in graphic design and had gotten into computers about five years earlier, so I didn't feel overwhelmed.

I always had a knack for electronics, too, as I was the kind of kid who took apart her radio to find out how it worked.

Originally I saw RiotGrrl as the female-oriented version of Wired, but I soon realized that not every woman was as interested in cyberpunk, technology, and rampant idealism as I was. This was apparent, because they didn't read those articles and features in RiotGrrl that discussed the technology aspect as much as they logged on to the entertainment features like Feed the Supermodel, which was an entertainment celebrity-focused column. The audience also always seemed to respond more vocally to features that focused on entertainment and media. Women just didn't seem to take the tech articles and stuff about the Web to heart.

As I realized what my audience wanted, I began to tailor RiotGrrl to a more personal voice. The readers of the site loved the little peeks into our writers' psyches, as well as the more humorous celebrity-based articles. One of our most popular features was a daily diary that one of our writers, Venus, wrote about her exciting and sexy adventures. However, the advertisers weren't prepared to deal with a very vocal and sexually liberated woman. We had to kill the feature, even though it was tremendously popular. It made too many people nervous. It was always going in a direction that could have been dangerous for the rest of the site. On the Web, there is a fine line between art and porn.

The change in the focus of RiotGrrl to a more personal voice happened almost three years ago. I think today my viewers would be more responsive to my original technological focus of the zine. I still have a vision of making RiotGrrl a much harder enterprise. I see it getting deeper into computers and technology and the changing concerns of women as we venture deeper into this new sphere of knowledge.

Nikki didn't stop with RiotGrrl, but continued her quest to build the power of the Grrl brand by launching another zine in December of 1997 titled GrrlGamer.

GrrlGamer is a natural evolution of RiotGrrl. I saw that women were underrepresented in the computer gaming market and, because I love gaming (it's a personal passion of mine), I wanted to write about it. I liked many types of games, including the so-called "guy games," which were first-person shooters and action and adventure. Online, I found a lot of women who felt the same way, and we had no voice in the medium. GrrlGamer is that voice.

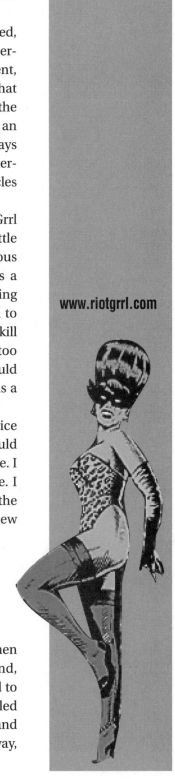

www.riotgrrl.com

GrrlGamer is still relatively new, and the design will probably look the same for a while longer, but GrrlGamer has changed its content over the past year. We've added many more reviews, resources, and guides, all geared toward women who are just starting out in gaming, or who want to get the most out of their gaming experiences.

Even though GrrlGamer is geared towards women, men make up about half of our audience. Visitors seem to like it because it's not overly technical and it explains things very clearly. Also, the game review section has a lot of personality, which people enjoy. Furthermore, a lot of the women who write for GrrlGamer work in the industry and really know their stuff. They have become gaming celebrities, like our news hound Wesley Hall, who writes the GrrlGamer News section, and our Quake Grrl Alana Gilbert, who writes the insanely popular Quake Grrl column.

In June of 1998, Nikki added TeenGrrl.com to her growing list of sites. As each site was built, she learned more about the Web publishing world.

TeenGrrl was developed for the younger readers of RiotGrrl so they could have a place entirely of their own. It is still being developed but looks as promising as GrrlGamer and RiotGrrl.

Through my sites, I have mostly learned what not to do with a Web site! There were so many mistakes I made with the start of RiotGrrl, especially later on when I ventured into some very courageous content, the kind of envelope-pushing stuff that earned RiotGrrl a reputation as being very controversial. When we decided to put advertising on the site through chickclick.com, an advertising network, we had to temper some of our more racy features to fit our advertisers. While these changes did not directly affect the level of content quality on RiotGrrl, it made me much more aware of what we could get away with if we did not take money making into account. While in some ways this was limiting, it was also liberating when it came to the other two sites, GrrlGamer and TeenGrrl, because from the start I faced the challenge of creating sites that would fit comfortably into a broader market.

As far as the look and feel of the sites, RiotGrrl appears very different from when it started, whereas GrrlGamer and TeenGrrl have a more consistent edge. It only took one try to get GrrlGamer where I wanted it to be. It's more directed, less open-ended. We write about games and gaming, period. TeenGrrl is different, too, because it depends on the content generated from the young women that it's aimed at pleasing.

Nikki is kept very busy running three sites, but she does get help from some readers who have become contributors.

Because I have a limited staff—only me—I do spend considerable time on the sites. It takes about seven hours to update each site, and I usually update three times per week, but it's the administration and public relations that really is time consuming. I spend countless hours on the phone, hours answering my seventy to 100 e-mails per day, and a lot of time editing, designing, and researching. According to my Internet service provider, I spend about 300 hours per month online. It's not just an adventure; it's a job!

Other people contribute columns and articles to my sites. I have never paid anyone to write for any of the Web sites, although at GrrlGamer there are a few perks, like free games, which our writers seem to like. Most of the people who write for the sites do it because they have something to say, and the sites afford them a well-known avenue to get their opinions and thoughts heard. Many of our writers go on to successful freelance writing careers at other magazines and Web sites. It's a great way to become involved in the industry and to build a portfolio of work.

My main focus right now is on GrrlGamer, but I still keep the other sites active. It does stretch me very thin, and recently I had to take an extended break after almost three years of working non-stop on the sites. I have to be careful that I don't get fried because it's only me running these sites. Recharging is absolutely necessary, as well as working on other creative endeavors, such as the freelance writing of my novel and the RiotGrrl book.

It's also important to really live life, to get out there in the real world and taste it all. You can't get the real thing from behind a computer screen. Sometimes people can get lost in their virtual lives. I make sure that I don't.

www.riotgrrl.com

Spending all this time and effort on her sites has provided Nikki with many rewards, and soon she will be receiving financial rewards as well.

One of the most popular and groundbreaking sections on RiotGrrl is the SexRiot column. It was the first column on the Web written by a real sexually liberated woman, Venus D. Wyld. Many other columns on bigger Web sites started after Venus', but she really has made her mark, and her work is consistently the favorite of most people to RiotGrrl. Feed the Supermodel and Supermodel Wrestling are also very popular on RiotGrrl, as is the ongoing real-life online love story between John Halcyon Styn and Venus called "lovesong." On GrrlGamer, the reviews are the most popular feature, followed by the Frag 'em area where we comment on any new creations in the gaming industry that really bother us. The communities also do very well, we have Sound Off on GrrlGamer, RiotGrrl has Interact, and TeenGrrl has the TeenGrrl Board. Our mailing lists on each site are also very large.

RiotGrrl is the best known and oldest of the three sites and generates the most revenue, but in a short time GrrlGamer has achieved nearly as much revenue, and the potential seems to be much more promising. GrrlGamer is a very innovative and original property, and advertisers are drawn to that.

For the first time in two years, the sites are profitable, and I'm looking forward to considerable revenue in the future. Although I still write freelance articles about computer gaming, my sites are a full-time job for me now, something I only dreamed of happening. While I may never make Yahoo! money off of it, the sites have succeeded where many other Web sites and Webzines have failed.

One way I generate revenue is through advertising. I still approach some advertisers, but many are approaching us now, which is very exciting. I also started with Chickclick for ad placement in February 1998, and it has been extremely advantageous for us. We also sell games via a sponsor and get a portion of those monies. We will be doing more of that in the future. Eventually, books that tie-in with the sites will help generate revenue, as well. I also plan to expand the sites in the future, particularly GrrlGamer, and I would like to see GrrlGamer get into game development, too. You can make a living doing this if you have the perseverance and a good product.

My biggest expenses are hardware and keeping up with technology. Fortunately, I get a lot of good deals through companies that sponsor my sites, but I would say that since I started the sites I've probably invested about $20,000. In the first year with advertisers, I nearly broke even. As I mentioned before, this year I will turn a profit.

I am also fortunate to have an exclusive deal with my hosting service through the New Dream Network. It's not expensive, and they have the best and most scalable hosting on the planet. I've been with them for almost two years. They are my technical geniuses and help to administer the sites. I could work with no one else the way I work with them.

My sites have also led to my first book deal, *RiotGrrl Guide to Webcraft*. I've been working on the book for two years, and it should be published soon. I approached the original publisher of the book myself through their Web site. That first deal ended up being amended, and then I made some serious changes to the book. It has taken a long time and a lot of rewrites to keep the book fairly current, but when it's released I think people will really enjoy it. It's quite different from the typical computer book. It's irreverent and humorous, but also contains great tips and an interesting story.

expect the
unexpected

teengrrl

archives   main menu   messages   forums

login: new user ||
interact back online
sign up or login

forums

messages

grrl politic
seat of
powah

grrl activists by jessica bopp

Many girls avoid political discussions like the plague. Personally, I know I often do. There are many reasons for this, anywhere from your opponent's ignorance to your own. For my part, often I don't feel like discussing something I can't do anything about. I feel helpless about the problems that face our world today, and I don't know what to do about it.

It reminds me of my favorite poem, *The Love Song of J. Alfred Prufrock* by T.S. Eliot. Prufrock is the kind of guy who goes around lamenting his lack of involvement in life, noting that it's probably too late for him to say anything. He's afraid of being looked down on for his ideas, so he chooses not to voice them at all. He prefers to sit quietly in a corner, like "a pair of ragged claws, scuttling across the ocean floor." He doesn't dare

"He prefers to sit quietly in a corner, like "a pair of ragged claws, scuttling across the ocean floor." He doesn't dare to shake things up, because he's too afraid."

A stop at the House of Representatives web site will give you information on the individual US representatives as well as their committees, media galleries, and that ever-popular Independent Council report.

If you want information on particular government officials, I'd strongly suggest going to Vote Smart Web. They have a TON of information, and it's a great place to stop if any of you are 18 and ready to cast your ballots this November.

www.riotgrrl.com

TeenGrrl Front Page

Nikki plans to continue all three sites, and keeping them fresh is her main goal.

I'm interested in building the communities of all three sites and in adding more information and resources to them. I think people are looking to the Net for information, connection, and entertainment. We want to be able to fulfill the needs of our audience as their needs change. You have to be willing to knock it all down and build it all over again every once in a while just to keep it fresh. We want our audience to feel that what they get from our sites, they can get nowhere else. Accomplishing this goal requires us to stay one step ahead of everyone else. Basically, I look at what other people do and then try to do something different. Otherwise, it's too much sameness, no individuality, and the audience feels stifled, hammered down by the entire so-called original content. I've got to give them more, make them think that every time they come to the site there will be something new and different. It's not hard to do this; you just have to stay aware of everything that is transpiring.

I also know that it has to be kept fun, with only measured doses of more serious content. I don't want to overwhelm the audience. There are already too many mediums of entertainment that do this. I don't ever want my sites to be like that. Too many sites out there, many of the more personal storytelling variety, concentrate on these heavy messages, which I think neither enrich their audience nor are particularly entertaining, unless you are interested in being a voyeur to someone else's misery. If these sentiments of tragedy are what you are looking for, then you are better off watching the news on TV.

Nikki feels the Internet has been very empowering, especially as a woman interested in technology.

The Internet means freedom to me. My first book, *RiotGrrl Guide to Webcraft*, would not have been possible without the Internet, nor GrrlGamer, both of which mean so much to me. GrrlGamer is the first project I've worked on that really does what it set out to do, which is empower women and break through barriers. Before GrrlGamer, the notion that women even played hardcore games was like a phantom. We brought it into the light and are currently changing the way games are developed and marketed. To me, that is truly exciting. GrrlGamer is a twenty-first century Web site, and I am thrilled to be heading her into the new media age. RiotGrrl will always be special to me though, because it gave me a place to cause a riot. That's what I've done, what we've done, all of the grrls who contributed—and this has paved the way for a site like GrrlGamer to appeal to both men and women and give us a landmark in this daring new medium.

www.fray.com

Photo by Carter Dow

DEREK POWAZEK

The Leading Storyteller

About the Site

The Fray (www.fray.com) is a storytelling site that features a new, unique-ly designed personal story each month. At the end of each story, a question is posed to the readers. A story about moving across the country might be followed by "Who have you left?" Readers are then asked to post their own personal stories, completing the storytelling cycle. The correct title of the site is {fray}.

Derek Powazek, age twenty-five, always had an interest in publishing, but it wasn't until he discovered that he could use his college's darkroom for free that things began to fall into place.

I've always been interested in writing and publishing. When I was a kid and had to do book reports for school, I'd format them like magazines. Beyond the writing, I have also always enjoyed photography. When I was in college at the University of California at Santa Cruz, I learned that if you shot photos for the campus newspaper, you could access the darkroom free of charge. So I joined the newspaper staff and began submitting pictures to be published. By the end of the year, I decided to do an individual major in photo-journalism instead of becoming a music major as originally planned. The following year, I became the editor of an alter-native newspaper and began to do design work. During this time, I also bought my first Mac and learned PageMaker. In 1994, I discovered the Web and was hooked.

When Derek graduated from college, he realized the type of job he wanted would combine his love for publishing and the Internet. Unfortunately, the job he found at one of the most famous online and print magazines dedicated to cyberculture wasn't all he hoped it would be.

It was in 1996 that I got my first real job out of college at HotWired. It seemed like the perfect job. Admittedly, I was also very idealistic at the time. I wanted to be involved in everything from writing and designing to coding. I wanted to be doing the same thing I'd been doing with the newspapers in college, and I thought I would. But it became clear that I wouldn't be able to do all those things at this job. In the end, I was doing only production work, basically just writing HTML. Eventually, I did a little bit of design, but not much. Mostly, I was an HTML grub.

My frustration led me to begin working on my own projects while at HotWired. I started with a site called Tweak.com. Tweak was my first Web-based magazine venture. I founded it with some of the people with whom I used to work on newspapers in college. It was an alternative, attitude-laden Webzine, and I loved it. Unfortunately, I felt many of the people I was working with were never really able to break out of their newspaper mindsets.

I left Tweak after about six months due to frustration. The whole experience taught me a lot about how not to work collaboratively. I learned to never work with friends unless you have a clear set of roles and responsibilities and to never let a project mean more to you than a friend.

Although his first attempt to start a Web magazine was not all he hoped it would be, Derek never wavered in his desire to start a successful online project. This time he decided to attempt it alone.

Traditional print media is about the publishing cycle. You prepare, you write, you edit, you publish, you take a day off at the end of it all. The Web destroys all that because you can publish anytime, and revise at anytime. No more cycle. It is a constant stream of work that never stops. Because of the immediacy of Web publishing, the audience expects immediate interactivity and response. That is a good thing. But the newspaper people were totally unprepared for it. They like having their readers somewhere "out there." Not in their face, telling them they're wrong. However, that is why I love the Net. I enjoy the interactivity and online community involvement.

Approximately six months after I left the Tweak project, I started fray.com. I've always been interested in personal storytelling, so the concept for {fray} seemed very natural. I wanted a place for personal stories, artfully presented, but with an interactive twist.

I feel what the Web brings to the equation of publishing is the ability for anyone, anywhere to get involved in the storytelling. So, I added a simple guest book script to the end of each story and asked a question at the top of it. People then post their own personal stories based on the question after reading the original personal story that was posted. That is the formula we've used to this day, and it works.

{fray}'s popularity has grown significantly since Derek first posted it on the Web in September of 1996, but, unlike many sites, he has not needed to make any significant changes over the life of the site.

Surprisingly, {fray} has changed little since it was started. I'm incorporating more new technology to tell the stories now. A little DHTML here, a little more JavaScript there, but only where it makes

hope

www.fray.com

criminal

sense. Other than that, the basic format and design hasn't changed in two years. A change has not been necessary.

I receive hundreds of e-mails each week, possibly more than 500 per week. It is insane. I'm getting very bad at replying to all of them. Currently, the site serves 15,000 to 30,000 pages per week. That rate is higher when a new personal story is posted or when a prominent link, such as Netscape's What's Cool or Cool Site of the Day, publicizes the site.

To determine which story has been the most popular on the site is difficult. Every story is very popular when it first appears. Some get more posts than others do, which is a measure of how much the story and the question impressed people.

In the recent past, Janelle Brown's story, entitled "Strange Beds," http://fray.com/hope/strange/, has gotten an amazing amount of response. The story is about her memories of the beds she has slept in, and what those beds said about their owners, her lovers, and her. It's amazingly touching. And the question at the end, "Whose bed do you remember?" has elicited some interesting stories.

I received an amazing piece of mail the other day. It was from a random Microsoft employee who wrote to me because he identified with one of my stories so much. The story was about my experience at HotWired, the crash of my idealism, and the rebirth of my hope. It is titled "Stoked," http://fray.com/work/stoked/. He said he was experiencing something similar. That e-mail meant a lot to me because that is what the Web is about for me. No matter what kind of freaky thing you're going through, you can bet that someone out there is going through it, too. The Web is the ultimate proof that we are not ever as alone as we think we are.

{fray} survives as a free forum for the Internet community.

No one pays for the site. Someone who believes in what we're doing donates the server space, and I donate my time and energy to keep it going. The stories come from contributors, who receive a T-shirt in return. It is completely a volunteer effort. I never want to confuse the issues. I never want to make anyone doubt the sincerity of the words they are reading. I'm trying to create a place that is very personal, revealing, and intimate. I'm trying to get people to talk about personal things, to tell their stories to the world. I strongly believe that flashing ad banners would destroy that atmosphere.

As a result, {fray} is a labor of love for me. Sometimes I spend ten hours per week working on the site; sometimes I spend fifty. It all depends on my freelance Web design workload. As the primary designer for my site, I design all the stories. I work with writers to help them edit their stories to get ready for publication. I watch the posting areas on the site, making sure people are using them appropriately. Basically, I do it all.

Through Derek's diligent work on {fray}, more than just regular visitors to the site notice his efforts—the Web industry as a whole has taken notice.

I received the *ID Magazine* Interactive Media Design Review Silver Award, which was really special to me. It's a yearly competition held by *ID Magazine,* with awards given based on excellence in design. This award is great because it covers "interactive media," so I was competing against CD-ROMs and kiosks, as well as Web sites. They really understood what {fray} is all about. They called it a "community collector." That is right on target.

Beyond awards, {fray} has also given me the chance to be a featured speaker at several conferences. I was the speaker for two consecutive years at the South by Southwest Interactive conference on Web design and was on panels at Mactivity Web, Web97, and Web98. At Web98, I moderated a panel on personal storytelling on the Web, which was fun.

Derek's creation fray.com has also changed the direction of his career.

I no longer work at HotWired. I was actually "downsized" in December of 1996. After that, I went to work for Electric Minds, a site that attempted to blur the line between community and content in a way that had never been done before. Five months later, that company ran out of money and went out of business. Following all that, I decided that being self-employed would actually be more stable. Therefore, I now earn my living by doing freelance Web design and consulting. I've been hired to do assignments for everyone from Netscape to Nike and, I won't lie, {fray} has led directly to most of these jobs. People come to me with design jobs because of {fray}. I don't know where I'd be if I had not started the site. That's what {fray} gives to me.

Derek will not cease in creating sites until he can design one that provides him with a decent living, and even then, he will probably still develop more.

I wish I could develop a site to provide me with full-time income. There's nothing that would make me happier. Unfortunately, I

www.fray.com

strongly believe that putting ads on {fray} would compromise its integrity to the point that the site would no longer be meaningful to anyone. So, I'll never do it. Hence, I "work" for a living instead.

Another site I created is Kvetch.com, which is the flip side of {fray}. Both sites are about soliciting user feedback; however, {fray} is meant to be deep and personal, while kvetch is intended to be light and funny. I thought that the world would be a better place if we had more safe places to vent our nasty sides. And what could be safer than griping anonymously in a randomly generated posting forum? There is no way it could cause any hurt feelings or harm, there is no way to bookmark it, so let loose! Then smile the rest of the day. It's a fun project, and I do take ads in Kvetch, but the advertising interest has been tepid. I think advertisers are scared of appearing near that much bile.

Other sites that I personally develop include powazek.com, which houses my professional site and displays my resume and portfolio. Its primary function is to link all my projects; therefore, I redesign it all the time. San Francisco Stories, sfstories.com, is a site that I recently launched. It is a personal space for me to tell my tales of living in the city.

I have also launched a companion site to fray.com called fray.org, which is the real-life version of fray.com, bringing the storytelling out from behind the glass. I wanted to see what would happen if we took the idea of {fray} into the real world. Fray.org accomplished this by publicizing fray.com's second birthday party, which was a really special moment for me—150 people in a warehouse, telling stories and drinking wine, all because of a Web site. After two years of connecting virtually, it was such a pleasure to connect in reality. The party featured an open mic, the real-life equivalent of the {fray} posting area. In many ways, it was like coming full circle for me because I started and emceed an open mic in college.

Derek doesn't know what the future holds for {fray}, but he is happy about where it has gotten him.

I'd like to give the readers more ways to become writers. I'd like for visitors to be able to tell stories outside of the context of the big {fray} story. However, all that takes time and technology, and I don't have much of either.

Doing {fray} has changed my life; there's no doubt about that. Because of {fray}, I can work at home as a professional Web designer and consultant; I have a circle of friends I made through the site; I've met some of the most amazing, talented people I've ever known; and, well, I get to have "conversations" like these.

Not bad for a collection of HTML documents and a few .gifs, huh?

For the Record

**DANIEL GREEN, EDITOR;
BARBARA GLAUBER,
    DESIGNER;
BEVERLY JOEL, DESIGNER;
WILLIAM BASTONE, EDITOR;
MIKE ESSL, TECHNICAL
    DIRECTOR.**

About the Site

The Smoking Gun (www.thesmokinggun.com) is devoted to posting original documents ranging from crime to politics to popular culture. The site includes first-hand copies of police reports, government files, and assorted official documents concerning well-known personalities from the past and present. The Smoking Gun often reveals information that government officials, politicians, business executives, and public figures would prefer not to see disclosed.

If you have ever read a news or current events article hoping to find "just the facts," then William Bastone and Daniel Green's approach to journalism may be just what you've been wanting.

All who work on The Smoking Gun come from journalism backgrounds. While Bill is a staff writer at the *Village Voice*, I've worked for monthlies and freelanced for a variety of publications. Bill is probably one of the best investigative reporters in New York. He has broken countless stories on politics and organized crime. However, as a freelance writer, I constantly need to sell myself and find editors, publishers, and others to notice me. I've done some investigative reporting, but not nearly at the level Bill has.

A couple of years ago, Bill and I thought of a way in which the documents that we obtain through our work as investigative journalists could serve more purpose. These documents weren't necessarily worthy of a whole feature story. The fact that Lou Costello, according to an FBI report, had

Don't be a dork!
COMPUTER GEEKS

Dressed only in a nightgown and bunny slippers, Athena Marie Rolando recently decided to stop by Brad Pitt's Los Angeles home. Though the actor wasn't there--and the 19-year-old woman wasn't invited--Rolando decided to break into Pitt's home, rummage around, and try on some of the hunk's clothing. The teenager was arrested and Pitt has filed for a restraining order against his lovesick stalker. Here are some of the legal documents filed in late-January in Los Angeles Superior Court:

Pages 1-5: Petition for injunction.

Page 6: Brad Pitt declaration.

Page 7: Text of Rolando letter.

Pages 8-10 LAPD arrest report.

Food, Glorious Food?

Visit the Boutique.

---

1   **ATTACHMENT "A"**

2   Although Plaintiff William Bradley Pitt ("Pitt") is an actor

3   and film star, he is entitled, like any citizen, to his privacy

4   and to be free of intrusion, harassment and stalking.

5   Pitt does not know Defendant Athena Marie Rolando

6   ("Rolando"), has never spoken with Rolando nor initiated personal

7   contact of any type with Rolando. Pitt has never invited Rolando

8   to his property nor into his home (Pitt Decl., ¶3).

9   Rolando has committed repeated acts of harassment and

10   stalking against Pitt and has admitted to visiting his residence

11   at least three times in the last two years. As evidenced by her

12   recent break-in, the nature of her conduct has become much more

13   alarming and her motivation and admitted obsession have become

14   more ominous and intrusive.

15   As set forth in the Declarations of Richard Malchar, William

16   Bradley Pitt, John H. Lavely, Esq., as well as the statements and

17   admissions of Rolando herself, Rolando has committed the

18   following wrongful acts of harassment and stalking against Pitt

19   and made the following statements indicating that unless

20   restrained the conduct is very likely to continue:

21   1.   In September of 1996 Rolando began what was to become a

22   series of harassing and stalking conduct. At that time, as

23   stated in the Police Report, Rolando left the first of many

24   menacing and bizarre letters for Pitt at the front gate of Pitt's

25   residence (Lavely Decl., Exhibit "C").

26   2.   On a second occasion, approximately one year ago, at

27   about 2:00 a.m., Rolando was found lurking outside the front gate

28   of Pitt's property. Rolando was wearing a bathrobe and slippers.

4

one of Hollywood's largest collections of pornography, or that George Bush, before he was President, was real gung-ho about doing surveillance on the Jewish Defense League, was not really newsworthy in 1998. However, we thought it was sort of interesting. And we thought, "How can we share these documents with other people who might find them interesting?"

We decided on a few different ways, but none were really ideal. Around that time, the Net was starting to be in the newspaper on a daily basis. We began thinking that the Net could be the perfect place in which to disseminate and showcase these documents. Based on his years of investigative reporting, Bill had a real treasure trove of documents about organized crime, politics, and other issues he covered for the *Voice*. These and other documents we found each week were both topically and historically interesting. They could provide a new angle on a current story that was in the news, or just describe a particularly strange crime.

Accustomed to the print media and its publishing cycle, William and Daniel knew they would have to learn all they could about the Internet by meeting people directly involved with it.

For approximately ten months, we took to lunch those people who were involved with the Internet. We dined with a wide range of individuals: executives at Time-Warner Inc., new-media professors at NYU, and even twenty-two-year-old programmers with nose rings and flannel shirts. We wanted to learn every aspect of how online publishing worked.

We tried to get everyone's opinion, allowing a year's time, if needed, to turn this idea into a reality. We did not want to start it, have it become somewhat popular, and then realize, "Wait a second; we didn't think of this. We need to shut down the site or change the way we're going to operate it."

We didn't know how often we needed to update things, whether it was every day or once per month. Therefore, we went through four or five different ways of putting up documents. We had no idea how the Net really worked in terms of its pace. To us, it was sort of like dog years, with every year counting as seven years, as with dogs. We didn't know what the proper equivalent was on the Internet. Through research, we discovered that things were greatly quickened, and you can't have a

www.
thesmokinggun
.com

monthly for what we were doing. Changing things just once per month wasn't going to work. Probably changing things once per week wasn't going to be enough!

We realized the importance of changing content to get return visitors. For example, a fan of *Vanity Fair* will go to a newsstand and look at the cover of *Vanity Fair*. After finding Ronald Reagan on its cover, this person recognizes that he/she has already seen this issue. Without a second thought, this person looks for another magazine and returns to *Vanity Fair* again in a few days. With the Internet, if people go back two or three times and they see the same material, they get frustrated and maybe don't return. They get frustrated in a way that they would not get frustrated at a magazine stand.

Currently, we are doing updates twice per week. We would like to eventually go to three times per week, or even five times per week. However, for the amount of time we can invest right now, we can only provide updates twice per week. We also do a special every three weeks or so, which is a big collection of ten or more documents about a particular theme or individual.

Daniel and William rely on the expertise of others for the site's production work.

We hired Barbara Glauber to design the site. She is the president of a company called Heavy Meta. She also does the scanning work. Barbara does a great job. She gives the site its particular look, its file folder, and the motif. Basically, she designed how the site would be organized from the start.

We also work with Mike Essl, who co-owns a company called The Chopping Block. He is very savvy about the Internet. When we need to show a potential business partner that we really know what we're talking about with the Internet, we bring Mike along. He gives us some credibility.

The site debuted in April of 1997 and was nominated for a coveted Kodak GTE Cool Site of the Year award that October.

I'm sure we were the newest of all the sites that were nominated in our category. This award is one of the most prestigious Web awards. It came from Cool Site of the Day, the original Cool Site rating service. Since then, there have been dozens, if not hundreds, of other ones that do similar things. I think there's a Cool Site of the Hour. There may even be Cool Site of the Minute, but I can't remember. This was a very prestigious award. We traveled to the awards ceremony in San Francisco. We lost to another site, but it was still very interesting for us.

There are a lot of awards on the Internet; for some, we haven't a clue of their meaning. Nearly every site has a little top percent Web sites symbol. We avoid putting those on our site. You have no idea what is actually legitimate and what is not. An icon for some stupid ratings top 5 percent category looks the same as winning the Nobel Peace Prize. You can't really tell the difference. We avoid doing that type of self-congratulatory stuff on the front page or anywhere on the site.

While we were attending the awards ceremony in San Francisco, we spent an extra day going to the courthouse. Whenever we travel, we try to set time aside for visiting the courthouse and going through the computer to see if any documents might be available. In San Francisco, we looked up everybody we could think of, from Jerry Brown to Joe DiMaggio to John Fogarty to Robin Williams. We finally came up with some interesting Don Johnson sexual harassment cases that we posted on the site.

To encourage return visits to the site, The Smoking Gun holds a regular contest based upon specific documents that are featured.

We're getting more mail than we used to, probably because our contest is becoming very popular. We post a document with some information extracted from it. The reader must guess what bit of information is missing, e.g., a criminal's name, an instrument that was used for a murder, or something of that nature. We posted a monthly expense report from an Academy Award-winning actor. I opened e-mails twenty-five times each day. The e-mail headlines read "contest answer." The replies say: "I know it's Jim Carrey." "I know it's Bruce Willis." I think to myself: "Don't these people know that those guys didn't win Oscars?" It says a lot about people following directions.

People write us regularly and say: "Are you guys for real? Is this all legitimate?" I usually reply with a nice note, saying, "Yes, everything we do is 100 percent authentic." Most of our e-mails are from people who really enjoy what we do. We received one e-mail from someone who said that if we ever stopped putting up documents, he would "go into a hole and eat just lettuce." This actually sounds kind of good to me. I wouldn't mind doing that every couple of months. He was a big fan, I assume.

We receive occasional letters from journalists telling us how much they like our site. They mention what a big hit it is in the

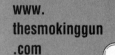

www.
thesmokinggun
.com

newsroom. I think it probably saves those lazy reporters some time when trying to find documents. They can go right to our site without having to do any research.

We got a very interesting e-mail from a guy who said he was in a witness protection program. I think he had turned state's evidence on some guys in the mob. He saw some organized crime documents and wrote to us saying something like, "The FBI had it wrong! You know, Franky Legs didn't whack Johnny Bones. It was Johnny Eggs who did that!" I think we kept up our correspondence with him for a while.

Each set of new documents seems to trigger a new reaction from readers.

We posted a really good set of *Titanic* documents during the time of the movie frenzy, around the week it won all the Academy Awards. Hence, we got e-mails from confused people who thought we were the official Leonardo DiCaprio site. They told us how much they loved us and wanted to meet us. We declined on that. Somebody else told us that we were her favorite singers and that "My Heart Will Go On" was her favorite song.

To increase viewer traffic, the site recently signed a cooperative marketing agreement with Playboy magazine.

Playboy saw our site and was interested in adding to their content and doing more with their Web page. They are mirroring what we put on our site. When we put something up, *Playboy* adds the material on their site as well, in a section called *Playboy* Presents the Smoking Gun. We then share in their advertising revenue from those pages. It is a good deal, since *Playboy* is one of the most well-known sites in the world.

In terms of the business arrangement, *Playboy* approached us to discuss the deal. They knew of us and thought the site would be a good match with the magazine. I guess they visited The Smoking Gun and felt that we would appeal to the people who go to the *Playboy* site. They thought that we would provide some interesting content for *Playboy's* visitors.

Daniel and William don't plan on making major changes to their current approach, which has already proven quite successful.

We've seen a nice increase in the number of people coming to our site since we first started. It has been steadily building. There was an article about us in *The New York Times'* cyber, online edition. That was pretty exciting. Also, I was quoted in *The Washington Post*. That impressed my family a good deal, and helped with site publicity. Our site has been online for awhile now. We feel like an old Wall Street firm, compared to some of the other sites that exist.

www.
thesmokinggun
.com

CHAPTER 31

TOR HYAMS

DAVID SCHARFF

www.fierce.com

Publishing with Attitude

About the Site

Fierce (www.fierce.com) is a zine that specializes in reviews and commentary about sites on the Web. Each new issue features letters to Fontaine, the son of a real psychologist; specific site reviews, and recommended sites to visit. Also, the site includes Fierce products and licensed gifts for sale.

While many musicians might work a second job to help make ends meet, choosing to launch an online zine would not be a typical choice for extra income. However, it is an option if you're Tor Hyams, composer, freelance writer, and Webmaster.

I have been working on the Web since 1993, doing business development and marketing in New York. The problem was that my training and background is in music. It was only around the beginning of 1998 that I switched from the Web business to being a full-time composer and musician. Until then, I had done each full-time and had very little sleep.

I moved to Los Angeles to try to get my music career started. New York was dead for composers and I wanted to build on the solo performances I had already done in the states and abroad. I wanted to score films and television, and produce my own CD. Though I didn't really have prospects of

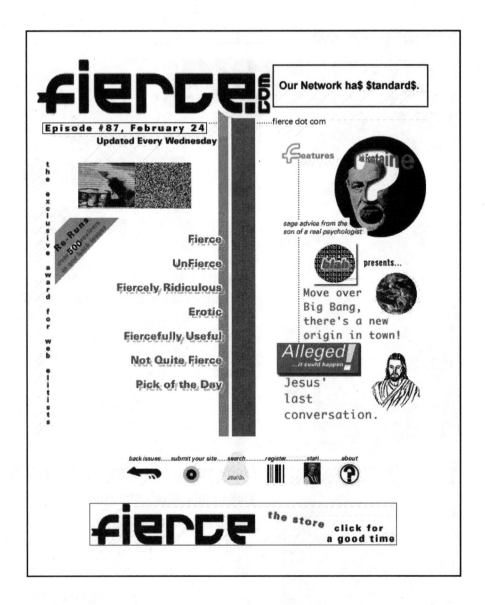

earning my income through music at the time, I proceeded with the switch. It was important for me to take the plunge, because life is too short to play it safe, and I rarely play anything safe.

For Tor, doing the traditional nine-to-five job in a cubicle was not going to be an option.

I have always had traditional office jobs that I hated. I felt like every time I entered the office environment, my soul started to shrivel. It was like the seventh circle of Hell. I just wasn't cut out for the nine-to-five, the bending to authority, and the complete absolution of devoting each day to what was considered worthy pursuits. I was struggling to be a working musician and simultaneously make some money. This existence wasn't exactly easy or fun. So I left that scene in favor of devoting my life to music full-time. Getting out of the transition phase, a kind of purgatory, was a great idea, except that I was living off my mother's money and getting deeper and deeper into debt.

My debt became outrageous, and my mother's continuous loan to me was about to diminish. I no longer had options. I had to get a job. So I picked up the paper and began the search. It was really horrible. Not only were very few particularly interesting jobs available, but I had a nagging pit at the bottom of my stomach that told me a traditional job was all wrong. I would never attain the freedom and creative outlet I so strongly wanted from working in an office. Then, flipping through the want ads in what I thought was another effort spent in vain, I saw an ad that caught my eye: Seeking Publicist/Assistant Editor for New Online Media Publication.

"Online," I thought to myself. What the hell was that? I really had no clue what that meant. I had never been technically inclined. I replied to the ad anyway. I followed up by faxing a resume, and I managed to get the interview. The position was with Sonicnet. They were in the process of transitioning from a bulletin board system to a Web site. Though I felt like the interview went great, and I loved the cool atmosphere of their New York Tribeca loft office, I didn't get the job.

Though he wasn't offered the publicist job, Tor persisted and talked his way into an entry-level position as an online marketing representative. Rather than risk the real possibility of defaulting on a loan, especially one from his mother, Tor concentrated on learning all he could about the Web. Along with his cousin, David Scharff, who was also living in New York, they spent the next year surfing to every known corner of cyberspace.

After about a year of figuring out the Web and working as an online marketing representative, I realized that the awards sites were getting a lot of attention. Since acquiring traditional press for Web projects seemed nearly impossible, the grass-roots awards sites were having a field day, driving traffic to sites and directly helping to raise advertising revenue. However, most of the award sites were "picks of the day" kind of sites, like Spider's Picks and Cool Site of the Day. Though these sites were great resources for the cool and weird sites out there, no one was really doing reviews. Ranking and

www.fierce.com

assigning numbers was fine, but we thought that we could provide a lot more interesting information about the sites themselves.

At the time, one of the clients at the company where I worked was a Web development company. I was supposed to develop some content for their network that would attract visitors. Thinking back to the experience David and I had visiting thousands of different sites, I thought about the award site. However, I also knew that it had already been done and I was not interested in doing it again.

By gaining a real understanding of what was driving the interest in and the reputation of Web award sites at the time, Tor and David decided to try a unique approach. The launch of Fierce.com would be a review site with a definite attitude. Tor and David were committed to setting the Web culture straight. With thousands of awards being given for no reason, Fierce reviews would give the reader a different kind of insight about the Web, not just another rubber stamp award.

The whole process was organic. David and I would be up late at night, basically from one to five o'clock in the morning, calling each other when we found a Web page that was either completely inane, horrible, or both. We were glued to the Web. We talked during all hours of the night, sharing our amazement of it all. "What the hell is this? Have you seen this site?"

We would chat on the phone while surfing to the same sites and berating them. That was how Fierce really got started, basically out of arrogance. We felt that everyone else should hear what we had to say, if only because we found it so hilarious ourselves that we figured others would too.

All the stuff we discovered on the Web had to be noted. We found sites that made no sense, sites that were simply wacky, and plenty of sites that appeared as if the person who created them spent no more than five minutes on the job, in total. The more of this we found, the less were we able to keep our dialog between only the two of us. Currently, we have a book in the works, so I guess the whole process may never end.

This project began just for fun. It was never intended to be a revenue source for us. However, we are now generating revenue through advertising, not enough to provide a full year's income for either of us, though.

David is the vision behind Fierce.

We both lived in New York for quite a long time. David was heavily involved in the subculture of the 1970s and 1980s. He was in a punk band called the Student Teachers that got several deal offers. They played in New York between 1978 and 1980 at Max's Kansas City, CBGB's, and other clubs

of the era. The Student Teachers opened for bands like Blondie, The Ramones, The Dead Boys, and Richard Hell and the Voidoids. Then, as typical in the business, drugs and egos ended the band before they were actually signed. David took a spiritual career path to a Buddhist retreat, where he now lives in northern California. Today, he is a serious student of Buddhism, following in the path his Lama has provided for him, and studying to become a Lama himself. David's really the guy who has seen it all and has given Fierce its basic attitude.

Once David and Tor's intense surfing and bashing of sites became its own art form, the explosion of the Internet and Web authoring tools made setting up Fierce very easy.

David already tried to build a print magazine, but it was a big headache, so he wasn't about to try again. As anyone who has tried it knows, one magazine a lifetime is enough. My problem was that I never had the inclination to write at all. With the Web, however, it was easy. We had little, if any costs—no overhead, no printing expenses, nothing. It was just us, our thoughts, and a couple of computers. We also figured no one would ever read our stupid articles, so we could say anything we wanted. Indeed, we proceeded with full force.

Fierce is something we predominately do for fun. The only thing that separates us from the thousands of other home publishers is that we write exactly how we feel. We don't curb our language or our politics for anyone or anything. We do it because we want people to understand our point of view. We also want the positive reputation. At the same time, we don't mind if people say what jerks we are.

What you read is almost exactly what is in our heads as we write. Our whole thing is that we don't have ethics. We don't have objectives, not even a little smidgen of them. The articles and reviews are pure and honest. This doesn't mean each issue is always good or at all literary or credible, but it's honest. Also, the folks who visit our site love being able to be obnoxious vicariously through others.

When I work on Fierce, I am gripped by another personality altogether. It's almost like being taken over by the snobbish, pseudo-intellectual, obnoxious side of my personality.

When you are not looking at someone face-to-face or even speaking to them on the phone, your subconscious is set free. For me it is the, "On the Web, you can be a lesbian" mentality that sort of changes my persona from its normal, sensitive offline Tor, the quiet musician, to the obnoxious and quasi-intellectual Tor, the in-your-face attitude guy, online.

Through my writing online, I have been able to get out a significant amount of frustration and angst, which would have otherwise probably required therapy if I had done so in real life. In that sense, the Web and my site, Fierce, have provided me with a voice to vent issues that are important or annoying to me. The Web is the ultimate playground for the nonconformist. In normal life, it is much more difficult to find a venue for this, short of standing on a soapbox in a park and having everyone think you are crazy.

It is not that it's easier to establish a market by being obnoxious. It has worked for us and, in radio media, it worked quite well for a guy like Howard Stern. However, it was never our intention to be that way. It just simply came to be. So, yes, it is a part of me that is genuine, but that is constantly evolving.

By working relentlessly to carve out a unique position on the Net and delivering irreverent reviews, humor, and off-the-wall advice, Fierce has developed a loyal following.

We are getting about 250,000 page views per month and that figure is growing exponentially. If there is anything I can rely on, it's that our visitation is completely random. The only trend I have noticed is when I think an issue is lousy, the public loves it, and when I think we have a really good episode up, no one cares.

We receive about 100 e-mails per week, including letters, sites that want to be reviewed, and the usual comments. I actually got a scoring job out of it. A movie producer in Australia read my bio and requested some of my music. I sent it to her and she offered me a composing job. I thought that was pretty cool.

Our most popular category is questions for Fontaine, the son of a real psychologist. People write in with questions about how to improve their love life, how to get more friends, how to confront some issue. Fontaine has heard it all. We also get our share of fan mail. A couple of the more fantastic mails have been from a group of guys in San Francisco who want to start a Tor fan club. One of them claims to have erected a shrine to me in his house. There have also been a few from women who want to see me naked and have offered naked pictures of themselves in return.

fierce dot com

the exclusive award for web elitists

Fierce Site of the Week

APHICADELIC, baby

Fierce

UnFierce

Fiercely Ridiculous

Erotic

Fiercefully Useful

Not Quite Fierce

Pick of the Day

K10k

 Tor is on a mission this week. I'm not sure what it is - I've read his columns very carefully (more than once and I still can't figure out exactly what he's saying, but that's ok...whenever someone is on a mission there is a chance of them melting down and becoming coherent only to themselves).

Maybe I'm just describing myself. OK, *I'm* on a mission this week, and just like the missions established to help relieve the suffering of the homeless in big cities, my mission is to relieve suffering on the web - but I'm NOT HANDING OUT SOUP!

KALIBER10000 IT'S SO TYPOGRAPHICADELIC, BABY

Table of Contents

 What I am giving away for free is advice of a very high calibre - in fact it's KALIBER 10000 (k10k). K10k is a design zine! Can ya stand it? I'm so happy I'm feeling a little moist-eyed. It just makes me so happy when people put together a zine to highlight what they consider to be good design work.

And I quote :

"It's a design forum done by designers, and aimed primarily at other designers, or people in general who are fed up with the multitude of crap which can be found on the net."

Do I have to say anything more? These guys are singing my song. They're giving out the soup here baby, and it's 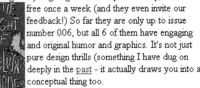 free once a week (and they even invite our feedback!) So far they are only up to issue number 006, but all 6 of them have engaging and original humor and graphics. It's not just pure design thrills (something I have dug on deeply in the past - it actually draws you into a conceptual thing too.

This weeks issue, "The Night of Mr. Melvyn's Murder" is an html comic mystery (that keeps me clicking away to find out what happens) populated with creepy cartoon characters, and what they were doing on the night of Mr. Melvyn's Murder.

Since its debut, Fierce has evolved with its own style and approach as the Web itself has changed.

If you read Fierce from the first issue until the present, you will see that our attitude has changed significantly. The writing has become a bit softer, but, at the same time, more focused. We are able to make our points now, but hopefully in a more positive and proactive way. In the beginning, we were harsh for the sake of being harsh. Hey, we all learn over time.

I loved the challenge when I first got online. I actually still love the challenge of trying to figure out this incredibly dynamic medium. It is not just how it works, and the text stuff, but more of figuring out how the world is connected by the Net that is so fascinating. So far, the Web is our best medium to give the whole thing some context.

A long way from the seventh circle of Hell, Tor can now see just how far Fierce has come.

We have been approached with a couple of offers to buy our site, content, and trademark, but so far haven't felt the offers were substantial enough. Since a site like ours could easily be made into other products like a television show and movies, it's really worth something more than just five hundred pages on the Web. We don't want to sell it, to be done with it, and walk away. We want to sell it and at least keep up the demeanor of Fierce, to a certain point. We are married to the obnoxious attitude and reputation that has grown around it. We want to remain true to the voice. I feel the complete sell is worth a good chunk of money, and so far no one has been prepared to make that kind of financial commitment.

Recently, Tor has gotten advertising for the site and signed a deal with Flycast, which bundles and resells the advertising for larger network buys. Meanwhile, Tor is waiting for the right offer to buy the site outright or for one company to sponsor the entire site.

For me, success is being able to be proud of what you have accomplished, whether it was for money or not. If you are going to do it, do it because you enjoy it. For us, the virtual page is an amazing opportunity, where we continue to learn and have a lot of fun.

CHAPTER 32

This is True®

RANDY CASSINGHAM

"...Bit by bit, Darwin is being proved right."

Stories You Won't Believe

About the Site

This is true (www.thisistrue.com) provides subscription information about a syndicated column focusing on offbeat or bizarre news stories in the national press. The site also features sample news stories, samples of the column for visitors, press coverage of This Is True, and a list of the author's upcoming speaking engagements.

Randy Cassingham, creator of This Is True, and a former software engineer with NASA, writes for a global audience. While building a following worldwide with his weekly column, he eschewed traditional business alliances. He was even offered a contract to write for the same syndicate as Ann Landers, but rejected the offer. Randy already had plenty of readers.

I have over 150,000 subscribers in 164 countries. Some of the countries where my e-mail newsletter is read include: the United States; Canada; Singapore; South Africa; Netherlands; England; Denmark; Sweden; Australia; Slovakia; France; Japan; Belgium; New Zealand; Germany; Ireland; India; Malaysia; Finland; Korea; Austria; Iceland; Norway; Italy; Croatia; Kuwait; Estonia; Spain; Poland; Israel; Hungary; Thailand; Switzerland; Venezuela; Mexico; Greece; Bermuda; Tunisia; Czech Republic; Slovenia; Turkey; Taiwan; Zimbabwe; Indonesia; Hong Kong; Namibia;

This is True®

This is True...

So, What Are You Wearing? Steve Toncheff, 34, a 911 operator in Daytona Beach, Fla., has been suspended after authorities found he was using his position to get dates. "He said he knew it was inappropriate and said he had never done this before, but would I like to go out sometime," said a woman who had called 911 to report a burglary. She dated Toncheff for three weeks. An investigation showed he used sheriff's office systems to gather personal information about women, including their names, phone numbers, and ages. (AP) ...*Who do you call to report something like that?*

Click here for **more story samples** or
here to continue or
Enter your e-mail here to join ***This is True***'s Free Distribution List
(Or you can join by sending *any* e-mail message to join-this-is-true@lyris.net.)

Your e-mail address: [_____]

*Enter your complete Internet e-mail address. Example: bob@somewhere.com
Then press the "Save" button below to subscribe.*

[Save]

Note: You must "confirm" your subscription request by e-mail before it will become active. See our Privacy Policy if you're concerned about your e-mail security (we do **not** release your e-mail address to advertisers or third-parties!)

This is True is a weekly syndicated newspaper column by Colorado humorist Randy Cassingham. *True* is a commentary on the news, and reports on bizarre-but-*true* news items from "legitimate" printed news sources from around the world. Each story is punctuated with commentary by Randy -- a tagline which is humorous, ironic or opinionated -- with luck, some combination, or even all three. It has been publishing weekly since **June, 1994**, and

Ecuador; Costa Rica; Guatemala; Chile; Jamaica; Philippines; Russia; Pakistan; Fiji; Latvia; Peru; Colombia; Egypt; Romania; Morocco; Argentina; Uzbekistan; Luxembourg; Botswana; China; Saudi Arabia; Guine-Bissau; Panama; Mozambique; Rwanda; Malta; Monaco; Kazakhstan; Sri Lanka; Lebanon; Kenya; Jordan; United Arab Emirates; Barbados; Dominican Republic; Mauritius; Belize; Uganda; El Salvador; Vietnam; Uruguay; Zambia; Nepal; Lithuania; Moldova; Haiti; Macedonia; Bolivia; Iran; Guyana; Ethiopia; Bangladesh; Bahamas; Belarus; Cuba; Tonga; Cambodia; Nigeria; Qatar; Oman; Tanzania; Azerbaijan; Mali; Turkmenistan; Paraguay; Liechtenstein; Ivory Coast; Maldives; Mongolia; Papua New Guinea; Lesotho; Armenia; and Yemen.

While eagerly read on computer screens around the world, this story had an unlikely beginning. Working in Los Angeles, Randy Cassingham was looking for an opportunity to leave the engineering and aeronautics field, establish a meaningful outlet for his creative interests, and earn a

decent living at the same time. **This new business also needed to include a one-way ticket out of Los Angeles.**

This Is True went online in July 1994. I estimated that it would be two years before I could be making enough money to quit my day job and leave Los Angeles. That was one of my goals. I spent three years wondering, "How am I going to get out of Los Angeles?" because I couldn't stand it anymore. I lived there for ten years. Once I had my This Is True business plan in place, I figured it would take me two years before I could do it full-time. Almost exactly two years later, I moved to Colorado, arriving on the Fourth of July. Independence Day; I thought that was rather symbolic. I haven't regretted my decision a bit. Now my purpose is to make enough money so I never have to get another job again.

I've been online continuously since 1982, and I've always had an interest in the online culture—I do believe there is a distinct online culture. It wasn't until the early 1990s, however, that the Net attained a critical mass that made me realize that I had to immerse myself in it. That enabled me to do some of the things I wanted to do, not the least of which was getting out of the industrial aerospace field.

During his ten-year aerospace career, one of Randy's hobbies was posting news clippings on the office bulletin board to help others get through the day-to-day work at NASA's Jet Propulsion Laboratory (JPL) in Los Angeles. It was these news stories and accompanying commentary that would later form the basis of This Is True.

The bulletin board was located right outside my office. It started with just little clips from the newspaper—cartoons and things like that. Over time, it got more specialized, highlighting weird news and strange news stories. When I purposely started looking for these stories, I would find them everywhere I looked. I would routinely have twenty stories a week posted.

By glancing through the newspaper every day, Randy was never faced with a shortage of material to post. At the end of each story, he attached his signature comments.

The following are examples of Randy's postings:
Diana LaPorta, running for a seat on the Volusia County (Florida) school board, insists that she has a bachelor's degree, even though a

www.
thisistrue.com

...About as
hard as
being the
ideal
man..."

local newspaper has revealed she earned it at Hamburger University, a training program for employees of the McDonald's hamburger chain.

If she gets on the school board, Hamburger University may be the only university for which the kids in that school will be eligible.

Joshua Nkomo, the vice president of Zimbabwe, is rearing more than 100 goats at his official residence. Neighbors have complained, saying it's against city regulations. Meanwhile, police in Brasilia are investigating the death of a goat running for mayor of Pilar, where it had been leading in the polls. The animal's political supporters have suggested that a political rival assassinated "Frederico." "He had a lot of foam in his mouth," his owner said.

Foaming at the mouth? Typical politician.

I wasn't content with just posting stories on the office bulletin board. To put them really into perspective, I started jotting little comments in the margins. I did that for quite a while, and continue it to this day.

Some of my friends from JPL moved to other places, but we kept in contact. I would enclose some of my bulletin board postings in with my letters to them. However, this quickly got out of control because there were too many people with whom I was corresponding. I was copying, handwriting, and highlighting all these pieces. About that time, e-mail started getting to be more ubiquitous.

Two critical pieces of the puzzle about how to launch Randy's new career were coming into focus.

As e-mail was starting to become more widespread for the end-user, I hesitated and thought before I proceeded. While lying in bed, unable to sleep because of the heat, I had a flash of inspiration as to how this whole thing could work. The whole idea instantly fell into place. I got out of bed and wrote it down, because I didn't want to forget any of it. The next day, I spoke with a couple of my friends and sketched out my idea for them. I explained that I could send out the stories to thousands, even millions of people, by e-mail. A lot of people would sign up for it because it would be free, and everyone likes these kinds of stories.

None of my friends understood this concept. They didn't grasp the technical aspect. They assumed it would be difficult for someone working from home to send as many e-mails as I knew I would be sending, and they didn't understand the business part of it. They didn't understand how sending out these stories for free would make any money.

Typically, I would hear, "Well, I don't see how that's going to work." And I would say, "Well, I do." I would take the notes I wrote when I got out of bed that hot night and expand them into a business plan so they could see it more clearly. Hence, I wrote a business plan even though part of the beauty of the business is that it didn't need any funding, which is the classic reason to write one.

Randy's business plan covered the specific format and style that This Is True would take, the distribution by e-mail, and the underlying fact that, for the subscriber, the newsletter would be completely free. Advertising on each e-mail would cover Randy's costs. Once This Is True had attained a critical mass of subscribers, the business plan detailed how yearly book compilations would be sold online, while the content would itself be marketed as a newspaper column with worldwide recognition.

There is no one aspect that, by itself, would ensure that I could make a decent living. But when you consider ad sales, book sales, newspaper syndication, premium subscriptions, and other sales, it actually works out nicely.

The Internet has been incredibly powerful for launching and growing This Is True in a very short period of time. The Internet not only lets me publish directly to a huge worldwide audience, it also has enabled me to decline an offer from a large newspaper syndicate who wanted to market my column to regular newspapers. Why decline? Because I could syndicate my column to newspapers without them! And in fact, This Is True is syndicated to newspapers in three countries. Naturally, I deliver the text to them every week by e-mail.

As long as you can read English, there's something to entertain you in This Is True, even if you miss the subtlety of the commentary. If nothing else, people like the stories themselves, all of which are completely true, and which come from all over the world. That universal appeal has translated to readers in more than 164 countries.

The Web site gets 75,000-80,000 hits per month, and the e-mail version goes to about 156,000 e-mail recipients per week. I receive between 200-300 e-mails per day. I answer all the mail that asks a specific question within reason or that contains a thoughtful comment, even if it is criticism.

Despite having a Web site with more details than anyone could possibly want regarding how to subscribe and unsubscribe, and despite including the basics of that information in every issue that is sent out, readers still come to me asking for information. It is absolutely impossible for me to personally handle the e-mail address maintenance needs of 156,000 people—and the list keeps growing! Basically, a lot of the e-mail I answer is to decline in helping. It's significantly easier for

www. thisistrue.com

...That's the secret to his success: he never opens his mouth..."

a reader to unsubscribe than it is for me to change their address, especially considering the time it would take to do this for fifty to sixty people per week.

I often get questions, such as: "Have you seen the story about such-and-such yet? It's a good story that you may want for your column." The answer is usually yes. Being online makes it very easy for readers to reply to authors. The feedback you get from readers can really help put things in perspective. The comments and opinions are of a wide range, from "Your column is the only reason I'm staying online," or "Great stuff," to the occasional "You're an idiot."

The ability to provide people with a chance to enjoy a laugh and lift their spirits is an awesome gift that Randy has. One woman's note to him is an example.

I was quite honored to get a copy of the new Breast Cancer Resource Guide of Massachusetts, which lists This Is True as a leading humor resource for victims of breast cancer. The resource guide is an excellent compendium of information and pointers toward more details about this killer disease, against which progress is being made.

Another woman wrote and said, "Randy, I just wanted to say 'thanks' for helping make the beginning of my day a very special one. I'm recovering from breast cancer, and laughing is one of the best 'healers' I can think of to help get through. Please keep up the wonderful work you're doing. Much love and many hugs. Patti."

I was very speechless when I got this, and that is pretty unusual for me! I received a nearly identical message about two years before; it was my pleasure to put the two women in touch with each other. They live on opposite coasts of the United States. Is there any other medium that could have helped these two women find each other? The Net is very, very powerful.

Recognizing the potential to impact so many lives, the first part of building a genuine online presence is knowing your audience and establishing a realistic timeframe for developing your site and steadily building traffic. Online culture is something you figure out over time. Most people scoff at the idea of an online culture. Those are the people who aren't making any money. The only way to make money online is to have a sustained effort. During my first year, I lost three thousand dollars. That loss bothered me so little, I had to look it up at year's end. The next year I made money. It wasn't quite double the year after that. Two years after that, I quit my aerospace job, along with its $50,000 salary.

I'm not rich by any means, but if things keep growing the way they have, after five years I'm going to be doing pretty well. That is part of the culture, too. You just can't expect to make a million dollars overnight. However, it has been my sole source of income for two years now.

This is True®
by Randy Cassingham

"Cassingham is a humorist for the Information Age, an Internet-savvy satirist and social commentator. The Jay Leno of Cyberspace."
--Los Angeles Times

Sample *This is True* Stories

Navigation:

Home
Main
Selections

Sample
Stories
Source Info
Submit Stories

Subscriptions

Premium
Upgrade
Change Yours

Country List
Your Privacy

True Books

Press
Coverage
RC
Appearances
Your
Comments

Placing Ads
Linking To Us

Online
Orders

Copyright
FAQ

**Other
Pages:**

Spam Primer

Would You Like Fries With That? Diana LaPorta, running for a seat on the Volusia County (Fla.) School Board, insists she has a bachelor's degree even though a local newspaper has revealed she earned it at "Hamburger University", a training program for employees of the McDonald's hamburger chain. When asked to clarify her education, LaPorta said "it does say on my diploma that it is a 'degree of bachelor'." (Reuters) ...*If she gets on the school board, that may be the only university the kids will be eligible for.*

And a Chocolate Shake: Pembroke Pines, Fla., Police Detective Earl Feugill was working undercover at a Checkers fast-food drive-through, waiting to spot the suspects in a rash of restaurant robberies. After waiting 90 minutes dressed as a bush outside the door, Feugill got his quarry -- one adult and three juveniles, armed and wearing masks, as they tried to sneak in a back door. Feugill jumped up with a shotgun, taking the robbers by surprise. "Scottish gamekeepers used these suits to cull their game herds," Feugill said of his camouflage suit. (AP) ...*Florida? Maybe that is the one other thing that the kids could do with their LaPorta-defined public educations.*

Oh... My... God!!
Man Goes Berserk in Car Saleroom, Many Volvos Hurt
Reuters headline

Get Your Goat: Joshua Nkomo, the vice president of Zimbabwe, is rearing more than 100 goats at his official residence. Neighbors have complained, saying it's against city regulations. Meanwhile, police in Brasilia are investigating the death of a goat running for mayor of Pilar -- where it had been leading in the polls. The animal's political supporters have suggested that "Frederico" was assassinated by a political rival. "He had a lot of foam in his mouth," his owner said. (Reuters) ...*Foaming at the mouth? Typical politician.*

If It's For Me, I'm Not In: Zach Williams, 18, was robbed in Chattanooga, Tenn. He tried to run away and was shot to death. One of the things the robbers stole: his pager. Police, upon learning about the beeper, figured "why not?" and sent it a page. When the murderers returned the cops' call, it was traced to George Morgan, 19, and his cousin Antonio Morgan, 18, who were arrested and charged with murder. (AP) ...*Bit by bit, Darwin is being proved right.*

Plain Brown Wrapper: British postal carrier Michael Hales, 38 -- and, Reuters was careful to point out, a bachelor -- was convicted and sentenced to a year in jail for stealing some of the mail he was supposed to deliver. Apparently, he learned to recognize the distinctive wrappers used by companies to ship sex toys -- vibrators, condoms, and pornography -- well enough to collect eight mail sacks full. "He has suffered a great deal of embarrassment and shame," his lawyer said. (Reuters) ...*Probably not until he got caught.*

...She also apparently had a hand in planning her wedding night..."

Central to Randy's eventual success was understanding the role of technology and computers.

I've been using computers since 1971, so I have a wide range of experience that has greatly helped my success. I view computers as tools, not as an end in themselves. The same holds true for the Net. It's what you do with those tools that is important. I don't need help with my core functions, since computers do most of the time-consuming work. That's exactly what they're intended to do. As things grow, I'll probably outsource some of the non-creative work.

Rather than depend on software and computer tools as a matter of faith, Randy has overcome the challenges of managing a growing business by acquiring more skills and knowledge about the online industry.

If the latest developments in technology don't solve real world problems, they're useless toys. If I have a problem that needs to be solved, I'll see what solutions are available and learn about them in my quest to solve the problem. For instance, I used to publish by e-mail, using software called Majordomo, but This Is True grew so much I outstripped its capabilities. Through much research, I was able to find a new software package that could not only handle the level to which I had grown, but also was capable of handling significantly more growth.

I'm actually waiting for technology to catch up to my needs. For instance, I'm awaiting the day a truly universal "micro-payments" mechanism is in place on the Net. It would be great to have a way that people could pay pennies, for instance, to search for a "This Is True" story on a particular subject. Right now, it costs significantly more than pennies to collect money from people, so such a system is not yet feasible. It will be someday. Hopefully, that day will come soon.

In the meantime, I've had some people and companies come to me wanting to join forces, but virtually none of them had anything to offer. I'm already making money; I'm already selling advertising; I'm already worldwide; I already get good press; I already syndicate This Is True to newspapers and magazines and own the syndicate myself; I already sell book compilations; and I own the book publisher myself. The bottom line is that there are few people who are already successful online, and they're off being successes, not trying to leech off others' success. So I really have no reason to partner with anyone at this point.

That's not to say that I don't cooperate with others. As I said, there are a few sites here and there on the Net that are successful. More importantly, the people who run those sites really grasp how a successful Web business operates. I sometimes will work with them for some cross-promotion. For example, I will give them an unsold ad spot, and they will provide me with one of theirs. It helps us both grow, and no money changes hands.

Randy focuses on publishing This Is True weekly, rather than spending time constantly updating his Web site. Randy's formula recognizes how the Web, specifically his site, can best serve his needs.

The Web is a great place for reference material. I do have a Web site, of course. It explains the contents of my column, displays a number of example stories, tells you how to subscribe, tells you how to buy book compilations, and has pages to answer all sorts of questions so people don't have to e-mail me. However, you cannot get the full text of This Is True there every week. Web publishers expect people to come back week after week to see what is new. Do people do that? No! And that is why few Web sites make money.

Look at it this way: If you subscribe to *Newsweek*, do you have to call their 800 number every week and say "Yo! Send me my copy!"? Of course not! That would be ridiculous. Instead, my copy of *Newsweek* shows up in my mailbox every week, whether I think of it or not. Similarly, This Is True shows up in subscribers' e-mail week after week, whether or not they think about it. For periodic publications, I think that e-mail is clearly the method of choice.

Today, if you visit Randy's site, you can see his picture from a live CNN feed as well as accolades from over sixty different media sources covering both news and entertainment. Randy frequently speaks around the country to business and technology audiences. By any measure of success, Randy Cassingham not only accomplished his central mission, but also managed to write his book.

The purpose was to create a new career for me. That was successful. I was able to quit my day job almost exactly two years after launch, which was the timetable in my business plan. The Internet literally enabled my new career.

www.
thisistrue.com

"Foaming at the mouth? Typical politician."

CHAPTER 33

Joke A Day

www.jokeaday.com

RAY OWENS

A Good Laugh Every Day of the Year

About the Site

Jokeaday (www.jokeaday.com) offers visitors the opportunity to subscribe to an e-mail list that goes out daily. Readers are able to receive a standard Joke a Day subscription, which can be emailed to them at no cost, and a premium Joke a Day that features no advertisements, but is only available by paid subscription. The site also features cartoons, greeting cards, and crossword puzzles.

People have trouble taking Ray Owens seriously.

It always amazes me when people ask what I do for a living. I tell them, "I run a daily joke list." Their eyes light up and right away they ask the inevitable—for me to tell them a joke. I usually shrug my shoulders and tell them that I really don't know any off the top of my head. It is moments like those when I just can't think of one.

For someone who earns his living telling jokes on the Web, this is saying a lot.

I was a trainer for a California-based computer software company. I live in Columbus, Ohio, and was able to work from my home most of the time. The job fit well with my personality. I love to get in front of people and just talk. I've never had a fear of a crowd or an audience. If I'm relatively sure that I know more about my subject than my audience does, then I'm as confident as possible.

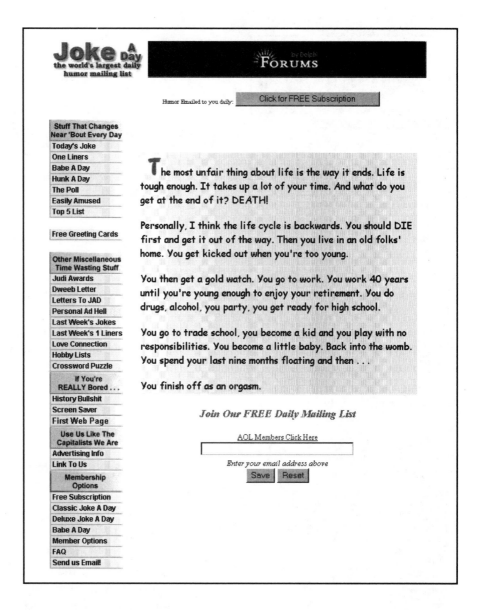

It was my responsibility to bring my company into the twentieth century. That meant learning how to do HTML and the like. As I experimented with making a Web page for my company, I started toying with the idea of creating a business for myself. At the start, I was seeing the process as a commercial thing. I decided to give it a year. If it did not prove successful within one year, I was going to walk away from it. That was my timeframe. When I started Joke a Day, the company I worked for had just been sold to another large corporation. I had some stock options that put a little jingle in my pocket. I thought, "Ah heck, let's see how far we can take this."

Based on those stock options, I knew I could fund Joke a Day for a year. Whether or not I could make any money was undetermined, but I knew I could cover my expenses. At the end of the year, I would reevaluate; if was making something, I would stick with it, if I wasn't making anything, I would pull the plug on it. Like every other humor-listing site, the goal was to share a laugh with other folks. Now, I'm all for sharing laughs, but I've also got a business mind. The difference between my site and others is that I treated this operation like a business.

I'm a bit surprised, but happy to say that my site turned into a real cash cow. When I started it, I would have been happy just to break even. With the hundred bucks or so per month I was spending at the time, I would have been thrilled just for that. However, it translated into being a lot more lucrative than I ever expected it to be.

In 1996, I started working with the Internet only. Prior to that, I thought the height of getting online was my Genie account. I thought Compuserve was the ugliest thing I'd ever seen, and difficult to use. I was really a latecomer to the Net as everybody knows it now. I've not been around since the Stone Age, i.e., pre-Mosaic, as some of the other folks who run sites like mine.

January 1, 1997 was the debut date of Joke a Day. Since I already had a Pentium 266, I bought the credit card machine, registered the domain name, and started telling jokes on the Net. At this point, it was my plan to simply send one joke out via e-mail, and not bother people any further. I'd keep the "chatter" to a minimum. Who wants to get a ten-page e-mail every day to go through? Make a funny, and be done with it.

Ray never imagined that his jokes would actually become important to his readers.

A funny thing started to occur to me: People started telling me how important it was that someone, somewhere actually cared enough to send them an e-mail every day with absolutely no need to do anything in return. Joke a Day started to become important to people. I don't expect people to think about me the rest of the day. But they do! The few times that I didn't get one of the daily jokes out (due to technical reasons), I got deluged with e-mail: "Did you drop me off the list?" "What happened?" "Is there a problem?" "Are you sick?" Folks, it's really just a joke. But unfortunately, some people really live for it. And that really worries me. Maybe I can claim them on my 1040 next year. Imagine me having 100,000 dependants!

By just "talking" with my readers, it is amazing the feedback that I receive. Telling them a joke isn't that important. My readers respond when I'm really speaking to them, saying, "Listen to me. I need to tell you this." It can be about anything. I talk about my family a lot, my

www.
jokeaday.com

daughters, traveling. Everyone always wants to hear about the horror stories of traveling when I return from a destination. Also, I receive a lot of e-mail from older folks, people in nursing homes. They tell me, "The first thing I do in the morning is go down to the computer, before anybody gets to it, check the joke, and go tell everybody."

For the average subscriber, it's free. Ninety nine percent of the money I make is from advertising. My prices reflect the Taco Bell theory. I want to be available for the little businessperson, the fellow who doesn't have $10,000 in his advertising budget. For my advertisers, a couple hundred bucks will get you an audience of tens of thousands of people. Heck, if you're really serious about your business, you can scrape together $200!

But the $200 is for the Cadillac-level ads, too. In addition to the regular ads, I decided to do something with my archives of jokes—to just go ahead and make money off of them, too. I started another listing called Joke a Day Classic. It's only about a tenth of the size of my regular listing, but I'm accepting advertising for it. I simply took a page from Nickelodeon's playbook. People want to see reruns.

In addition to the free joke service, I also run a deluxe service. It carries no advertisements. It's like buying cable. It costs $20 per year. They receive four jokes instead of two, and they get no advertisements. A number of people went from the free version to the deluxe version. Then they write me almost sheepishly and ask, "Can I remain on the free version, too? I miss all the little goofy things you say in the standard version that you don't say in the deluxe version." I put them on the listing again, and advise them to "get a life." I figured that folks would want just the "meat and potatoes," i.e., the humor, and they are coming back for the "human touch."

One subscriber wrote to say that he was the boss at his office, which employed about a dozen people. He said that he took one of the jokes and put it on the office bulletin board. (He explained that because he was the boss he could do that.) After that, about half of the people wanted to sign up for the service. They even asked him how to subscribe. He also stated that those six individuals who subscribe actually get more work done; they are much more productive. We are all in the rat race together, but anything that can help lighten the load makes it a whole lot easier to get work completed. This person claimed that I increased the productivity of his company just by providing my service. That was great feedback.

Without a doubt, I realized the impact I had on people's lives on April 1, 1998. Some months earlier, an angry lawyer wrote to me about unsubscribing. He wanted me to unsubscribe for him. I told him to follow the directions like everyone else. He made threats and sent angry letters, which I ignored. I used that situation to craft an April Fool's event. I sent an e-mail to all of my subscribers, telling them that this lawyer decided to bring a five-million-dollar lawsuit against me for "pain and suffering." I told everyone that since I didn't have five million dollars, my lawyer, Lirpa Sloof (spell it backwards), was advising me to shut down my site. I received over 2,500 pieces of mail from folks simply outraged that this kind of thing would happen. I received phone calls from *The Wall Street Journal*, my own brother, and four of my closest friends asking me if all was all right. Those hundreds of mails were simply aghast that they were losing Joke a Day, and claimed how empty their lives were going to be. It was very humbling.

With a worldwide audience comes the great likelihood that someone, somewhere will eventually be offended by a particular joke; therefore, Ray is usually prepared for anything.

I tend to pick on the stupid people, the folks who have absolutely no business near a computer at all. I made a shrine to these people in the form of a Judi Award. In June 1997, a woman got upset over a couple of jokes about blondes that I sent. (If I'm not making someone mad every day, I'm probably not telling the jokes right.) The woman's name was Judi. She was a blonde who proved herself quite the fool, although I may not have fared better. She sent me complaints about being offended, and I responded. Before long, one thing led to another and a small, insignificant issue had become one giant mess. People who are stupid enough to get into a fight with the moderator of a group are a few fries short of a Happy Meal, anyway.

I thought the whole thing was funny and a bit bizarre. I took the entire e-mail exchange and posted it in one of Joke a Day's mailings. My only criteria for having something show up in Joke a Day is that it has to make me laugh. This woman's antics surely did. This exchange got such a tremendous response; over 400 people wrote in my support, and nine in opposition. I decided to make a Judi Award in honor of the first person to get a public spanking from me. Since then, several other people have disagreed with me, and they were awarded Judi Awards, also.

Who are the people running down to their computers or boosting company productivity as a result of Joke a Day? Ray indicates that there is not a specific demographic that visits the site.

I've got subscribers in 137 countries, eighteen to eighty years old, black, white, blue, and green. The only commonness of Joke a Day subscribers is a sense of humor. It attracts a general audience. Plus, for my site to be attractive to potential advertisers, it is necessary to

www.
jokeaday.com

make the readership so big that even though it never gets above a 1, or 1.5 percent response rate, that is still a lot of viewers coming to a site.

Joke a Day has been built almost completely by electronic word of mouth. The increase from eight subscribers on my mailing list on January 1, 1997 to over 120,000 today, is due to people passing along e-mails that I've sent. This has helped make it the biggest list of its kind in the world.

My personality is reflected in the e-mail. I compare it to a Top 40 radio station. If a listener has five Top 40 radio stations in a town, and Top 40 is his/her style of choice, which one would he/she listen to? The listener will chose the station with the best personality, the one with the DJs who make you laugh. The music is the same, but everything else that is done better, sets it apart. The same is true with Joke a Day. There are no new jokes. I rarely come up with anything original. These jokes have been circulating for years. It's my personal belief that there are only new audiences for jokes. I make the difference. My little asides keep people returning. I get a lot of mail telling me, "Your jokes suck. But, I appreciate it when you 'talk' to me." That says it all.

I have received some touching stories. People who have friends in hospitals will write to me, saying that they read my e-mails to these friends who are ill. They claim that these people have made miraculous recoveries.

During the week I receive between 55,000 and 60,000 visitors to the site. The peak usage time is between eight and ten in the morning, and then they don't come back for the rest of the day. It's like having dessert in the morning. They need that little pick-me-up, that little cup of coffee, that boost, to get them started.

Ray's success with Joke a Day is proof that, by using the power of the Internet, creating an alternative to the "day" job is a real possibility.

Don't let anyone say that it can't be done. I can't begin to count the number of times that I was told I couldn't make a dime telling jokes on the Internet. I began with eight subscribers, and it is a success by any standard you want to apply to it. I love to make people laugh. I love even more that I get paid for it.

I want to keep adding different features to the site to make folks smile even more and, more importantly, to bring them back the next day. Looking back, my site has been phenomenally successful, certainly more so than I ever imagined. Of all of the people I know doing similar humor mailing lists, I can count on one hand the number of people making a living off of this. I'd love to be the Microsoft of Internet humor someday. In a sense, my life has been changed by what I have done here. However, the most amazing thing is the way I have changed, and have affected other people's lives.

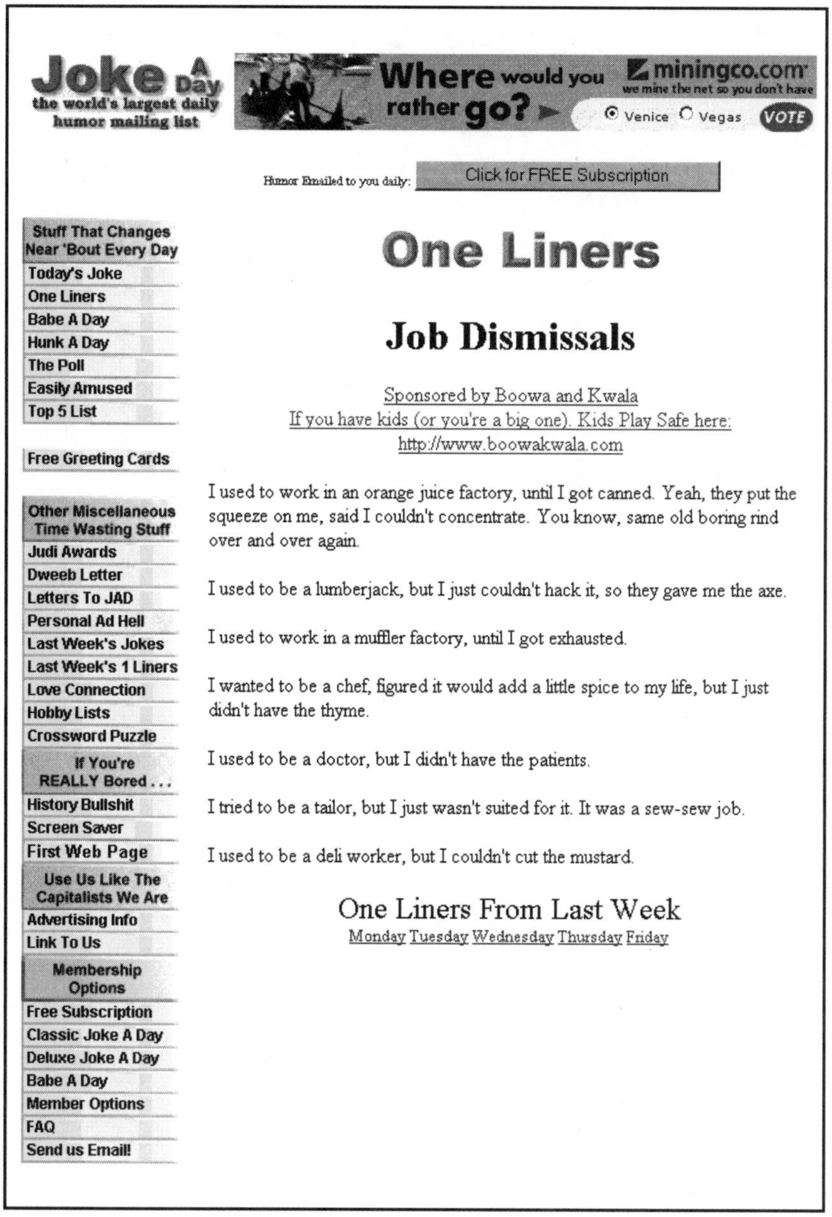

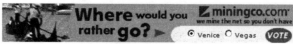

Humor Emailed to you daily: **Click for FREE Subscription**

One Liners

Job Dismissals

Sponsored by Boowa and Kwala
If you have kids (or you're a big one). Kids Play Safe here:
http://www.boowakwala.com

I used to work in an orange juice factory, until I got canned. Yeah, they put the squeeze on me, said I couldn't concentrate. You know, same old boring rind over and over again.

I used to be a lumberjack, but I just couldn't hack it, so they gave me the axe.

I used to work in a muffler factory, until I got exhausted.

I wanted to be a chef, figured it would add a little spice to my life, but I just didn't have the thyme.

I used to be a doctor, but I didn't have the patients.

I tried to be a tailor, but I just wasn't suited for it. It was a sew-sew job.

I used to be a deli worker, but I couldn't cut the mustard.

One Liners From Last Week
Monday Tuesday Wednesday Thursday Friday

Sidebar Navigation

Stuff That Changes Near 'Bout Every Day
Today's Joke
One Liners
Babe A Day
Hunk A Day
The Poll
Easily Amused
Top 5 List

Free Greeting Cards

Other Miscellaneous Time Wasting Stuff
Judi Awards
Dweeb Letter
Letters To JAD
Personal Ad Hell
Last Week's Jokes
Last Week's 1 Liners
Love Connection
Hobby Lists
Crossword Puzzle

If You're REALLY Bored . . .
History Bullshit
Screen Saver
First Web Page

Use Us Like The Capitalists We Are
Advertising Info
Link To Us

Membership Options
Free Subscription
Classic Joke A Day
Deluxe Joke A Day
Babe A Day
Member Options
FAQ
Send us Email!

www.
jokeaday.com

CHAPTER 34

TOPFIVE.COM

www.topfive.com

CHRIS WHITE

www.
topfive.com

Count on Finding the Five Best

About the Site

TopFive (www.topfive.com) is a daily humor mailing list. The site features three humor mailing lists and offers information on how to subscribe for free and how to become a contributor. Visitors can also participate in the Top5 chat room, check out links to other humor sites, and search the archived Top5 lists by month and date.

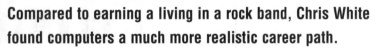

Compared to earning a living in a rock band, Chris White found computers a much more realistic career path.

I am a former musician who eased into various computer jobs after realizing how difficult it is to make money by playing music. I grew up in Houston. While in school, especially junior high and high school, I did a lot of writing, basically parodies for school newspapers. Once I discovered music and found that wearing a guitar attracts women, I kind of set everything else on hold. From the time that I was in high school until my late twenties, I put all my efforts into music. I liked playing, but there wasn't enough money in it, unless you were really good. I struggled for success. At some point, I realized that the people who were most likely to earn a comfortable living as musicians were those who were naturally talented and could easily move on to do something else.

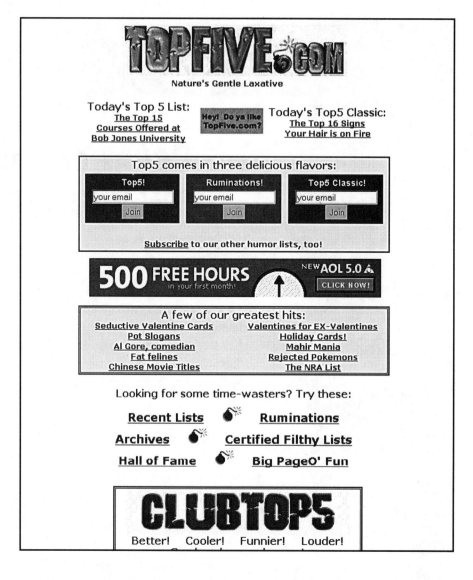

During my time as a musician, I started doing computer programming to get the bills paid. That programming work developed into all sorts of different computer jobs over the years. I've actually been in the PC business since the PC first came out in the early 1980s. I've done sales, repairs, programming, support work, network administration, and analysis. You name it, I've done it.

Chris was never thrilled with the idea of formatting reports in some information systems department cubicle for the rest of his life. However, these positions did provide Chris a place in which to test his creativity. These high-tech jobs offered the perfect opportunity and

setting for Chris to share his sense of humor with office mates via the Web.

I started Top5 in early 1994, when I was working in San Diego. The company with which I was employed had just gotten on the Internet, and I was slowly discovering e-mail. A coworker had gone on vacation, and we decided to fax him a list of the "Top 10 Signs that He Was Being Replaced." I used e-mail to send out that topic to other coworkers and a few friends of his who worked elsewhere. People sent me their ideas, and I compiled the final list from the best of the submissions.

We had so much fun creating this list that we started compiling one daily. I would send out a topic to about twenty people. They would return to me their ideas, I'd choose the best five items for the final list, and e-mail back a completed list later that day, hence, the name, Top5.

All of our early publicity was via word-of-mouth, with most of it coming from postings to various other mailing lists and news-groups. My friends and I started telling our friends, co-workers, and e-mail acquaintances about the list, and it started growing quickly.

After three or four months, *PC Week* wrote an article on us. The magazine ran a column on the list, and within a couple of weeks we had over 6,000 subscribers (and repeatedly crashed my company's mail server). With all the traffic, things really started to get crazy. The momentum began, and we have been picking up over 1,500 subscribers per month ever since.

Unlike most other humor on the Net, Top5 relies on its readers to help shape the daily list itself.

Top5 is unique because it's one of the few humor lists that features only original humor, every day, which is written by various people around the world and submitted via the Net. Every morning, I mail out a topic to the contributors, and they immediately put their jobs on hold until they can develop a few ideas to send back to me. At the end of the day, I pick the best ideas; edit them, if necessary, to give them the highest possible CIQ (comedic impact quotient); and send them out as a list. The most difficult tasks are throwing out good submissions to keep the list short, and deciding the order of the list items.

Chris introduces a broad range of topics to the list each day, challenging contributors to develop new and different types of humor. Recent topics have covered both the

www. topfive.com

**traditional, e.g., ways the royal family can modernize the monarchy,
and the outrageous, e.g., signs your mother is a Spice Girl.**

We did a truly benign list on the topic, "The Top 5 Signs Your Local Girl Scout Troop Hates You," which contained such items as "You find: 'Die, yuppie scum!' spelled out on your driveway in Thin Mints" It was all done very tongue-in-cheek, but Girl Scout troop leaders, who claimed that we were undermining everything they're trying to accomplish, scolded us. We've also gotten reams of complaints and hate mail from people on a couple of other subjects. Any time our list takes aim, so to speak, at the gun control issue, or at the NRA. In particular, we get the most vehement responses, most of which seem to be from people who can't spell.

The topic that generated the most ignorant, hateful responses was our "Rejected NRA Slogans" list. Some of the more interesting NRA slogan submissions were: Fascism—It Ain't Just for Nazis Anymore; 1997 Recipient of the Disgruntled Postal Worker Seal Of Approval; The NRA: Relieving Feelings of Inadequacy for 125 Years; When You Absolutely, Positively Have to Kill Someone; and Who Do You Want to Shoot Today?

Very few things are considered inappropriate fodder for the list. The one glaring exception is that Top5 refuses to make fun of physical characteristics that cannot be easily changed. Things that would be considered off-limits would include making fun of someone's race, gender, or sexual orientation. That's about it.

**Chris splits his workweek between a part-time job gathering
data from Web sites for a publishing company and forty-plus
hours per week working on the Top5 list. Although he spends
the majority of his time maintaining the list, it only accounts
for about a quarter of his overall income.**

I never envisioned making money with Top5, although it does through banner advertising. Even after it started taking up a lot of time, I was more curious to see how big it would get, as opposed to how much money I could make. When it reached the point at which I was spending five or six hours per day on it, I realized that I needed to develop a way of making money on it, or stop doing it altogether, because I didn't need another hobby.

Over the last few years, I've done a lot of cross-promotion with other humor lists, which has paid off for both sides. I'm in discussion with a Web design group that will hopefully help me to move Top5 into an elite status for Internet comedy sites.

I was aligned for over a year with *Windows Sources* magazine, until their recent decision to discontinue the magazine in favor of one with a more corporate slant. My hope is that somebody will want to use Top5 to attract attention to their own Web site and will pay me the big bucks I deserve for having put so much time and effort into building it over the years.

Far from limiting his humor site to a single format, Chris keeps building additional reasons for people to visit the site.

Top5 has over 40,000 subscribers on its e-mail list, and we are averaging about 500,000 hits per month on the Web site. I also run two smaller lists that use the same model: The Ruminations List, a daily collection of original comedic thoughts, to which anyone can contribute; and The Daily Probe, a daily newspaper satire, which is also written by various people around the world. The Ruminations List and The Daily Probe have almost 5,000 subscribers each. I want to tie Top5, The Probe, and Ruminations into some sort of umbrella Web site, so that they can all feed off one another's fans.

Based on my Web sites, I average about 500 messages per day, 100 of those are submissions from my contributors, and another 150 or so are from the actual subscribers. Subscribers write with questions about how they can become contributors, requests for information on the history of the list, and mail to be forwarded to specific contributors.

The participatory writing style, which sets the site apart, is also reflected in the friendships Top5 has helped to develop.

Top5 subscribers, in particular, like to keep track of their favorite contributors and often get fan e-mail sent to them. For that reason, in every list I send out, I include the name, city, and state/country of the different contributors. It's very much like following the baseball box scores to see how your favorite players have done. I also distribute a separate list that allows the contributors to send messages to one another. Some of the contributors "live" on the list and e-mail back and forth all day. Others will pop in for a few days and leave for a week.

I've met many of my contributors, quite a few of whom I consider very good friends at this point. Several of the contributors, maybe three or four, were friends of mine before I started the list. There was a contributor in Chicago who celebrated her thirtieth birthday this year. She posted a

www.
topfive.com

message to other contributors saying that she was having a party and was inviting anyone who happened to be in the area. Out of coincidence, three or four people were going to be in Chicago at that time and some other contributors already live in that area. They attended the party, and I made a point of going, too. I needed to be in Kansas for personal reasons, and thought I would swing up to Chicago on the way back. In the end, a whole bunch of us went to this contributor's birthday party. There was probably eight or nine of us, altogether.

At the Chicago party, we had contributors from seventeen years old to middle-aged. I know most of the people who were at the party from the contributor chat list. Upon my arrival at the party, I already knew most of the people because I'd either met them before or seen their pictures posted on the Web. If you hang out on a chat list like this for any length of time, you get to know the visitor's personalities quite well. After the first five minutes, it was as if I had known these people for a year or more. Everybody shared this same experience. We all felt as if we had been friends for a long time, and were just hanging out at this party. The fact that we had just met in person for the first time didn't really matter. The personalities that I've grown to know are so much like the people that their physical presence really took a back seat—a very strange concept.

Based on my online friendships, I've noticed how the Internet can definitely camouflage conversations quite a bit. One of my contributors is among the funniest, wittiest people on the Top5 list. When I met him in real life, I discovered that he has a very thick speech impediment, which obviously doesn't come across at all on the Net. He's difficult to understand when you are communicating with him face-to-face. It takes him a long time to get his thoughts out, and you must concentrate to understand him. Obviously, this can slow down the communication process. However, over the Net, this difficulty does not exist. You only find an exceptionally intelligent individual. No one can make assumptions or judgments based on the physical characteristics alone.

While helping to bring people together and coming up with some of the best humor on the Web, the Top5 list has also helped some contributors develop their talent for writing.

There are definitely some people who have a knack for writing. Top5 forces them to flex that writing muscle once a day. On the other hand, there are contributors who just send in something when the mood strikes them. I can tell by their submissions that some spend only five minutes working on them. Successful comedy writing is as much about diligent work as it is inspiration.

Every so often, the Top 5 list inducts a contributor into its Hall of Fame. This is an honor of unparalleled distinction, and it goes to the contributor who consistently submitted top-notch ideas to the list, day-in and day-out. In short, a Hall of Famer is a person who takes so much time away from their real job duties that they run the risk of getting fired.

There are over 200 contributors from whom I'll receive between forty and sixty responses on any given topic I send to them. During a three-month span, I get submissions from about half of the contributors, maybe a little more. The model has continued to work well, with over 300 people having served as contributors to the list at some point.

Earlier this year, as part of a celebration of our 500th published list, I invited the Top5 contributors to vote on their ten favorite lists of all time. The votes were as follows:

- Number 10: The Top 18 Anti-Drug Slogans Almost Used by Bob Dole

- Number 9: The Top 17 Rejected Titles for the Movie *Twister*

- Number 8: The Top 20 Cool Things about a Car that Goes Faster than the Speed of Light

- Number 7: The Top 17 Signs NASA Has Hired a Bad Astronaut

- Number 6: The Top 15 Famous Last Words

- Number 5: The Top 18 Signs that You've Hired the Wrong Clown for Your Child's Party

- Number 4: The Top 20 Least Impressive Mafia Nicknames (which is my favorite list)

- Number 3: The Top 20 Rejected Children's Books

- Number 2: The Top 20 Reasons Dogs Don't Use Computers

- Number 1: The Top 15 Latin Phrases for the 1990s (published March 1997)

The Internet has enabled Chris to speak with people he has long admired and build the basis for his future writing work.

I've cyber-met the actor Ed Begley, Jr. I tried to get him interested in becoming a contributor, but he only prefers to read the list. Also, as part of my ever-expanding methods of keeping Top5 fresh, I've been writing the more humorous aspects of my travels and posting them to the Web site.

www. topfive.com

Contains less than 5g of fat

February 25, 2000

~~~ NOTE FROM CHRIS: ~~~
Today's list was compiled from submissions
sent in by our ClubTop5 subscribers.

The Top 16 Things You Don't
Want to Hear on a First Date

16. "No salad for me, but I'll have a couple of those mega-burritos."

15. "You look so much better in person then you do on the
company's hidden bathroom web-cam."

14. "Okay, here's the plan: After you get into the movie, open the
fire door and bang! We save 8 bucks that we can use later on at
Wendy's!"

13. "You think I look good NOW? Honey, I'll look even better when
they finish the surgery!"

12. "I did *not* have sexual relations with that President, Mr.
Clinton."

11. "Hey, wanna hear your name in Klingon?"

10. "It looks like you weren't able to cover up that zit with make up.
Can I pop it for you?"

9. "I do, Mr. Multimillionaire."

8. "Sorry about the cell phone in the theater, but my wife could go
into labor any minute now."

7. "Why don't you want to go to Hooters? What're you, a feminist
or something?"

6. "My imaginary friend wants to know how you feel about
threesomes."

5. "Don't worry about protection, silly -- I'm *already* pregnant."

4. "Mind getting on top? My nose is running."

3. "It seems like only yesterday that Satan welded my crotch
shut."

2. "Heads up, Hon   I *always* get lucky when I'm wearing my
Hulk Underoos."

*and the Number 1 Thing You Don't Want to Hear on a First
Date...*

1. "How strange -- you kiss just like your Dad!"

Originally, the list was a way of passing time and having fun. It's still fun, but has now become my primary means of support, and will most likely function as a springboard into my next career, as a writer. I've strengthened my writing and editing skills with my lists, as well as made many contacts, which should prove beneficial.

In 1993, I began screenwriting, which is where I'm trying to go at this point. As a screenwriter, most of the scripts I do are comedies or romantic comedies. If I can get some other type of writing job, I would be much happier than I am as a computer programmer.

My Web site has given me the opportunity to work and earn an income as a writer based on my three lists and the advertising revenue they generate. I also met my girlfriend of four years on the Web. She is a film studies teacher. In all areas of my life, the Internet has had a profound impact. In fact, a lot of people I've met through Top5 are the type of people whom I'd prefer to have as my friends. It's not easy to find good friends in "real life," and get to know them as thoroughly in the span of a couple months. In most instances, with human communication, you generally meet face-to-face. Obviously, there are people who meet via telephone. But, the Internet allows non face-to-face communication to continue at a low cost to people for indefinite amounts of time. In much the same way, my girlfriend and I knew each other extremely well over the Internet before we had any phone conversation at all.

I enjoy the fact that I give a voice to truly talented comedy writers who otherwise would be heard only by people in the surrounding cubicles in their offices. It's great to receive positive feedback from the subscribers and to add new contributors who seem like that they were born to do comedy writing.

Top5 has reaffirmed for me that the lack of talent that I had as a musician was really the flip side of the natural talent I have as a writer. Top5 has had its ups and downs, but we've done over 600 lists since 1994, and what we're doing today is just as funny as it was back then. I used to sit down with friends of mine who are professional comedians to develop new material and hone it. I was giving many of them help steadily. It wasn't until Top5 came along that I had a venue for doing it everyday.

www. topfive.com

BOB HIRSCHFELD

Humor with Insight

About the Site

Bob's Fridge (www.bobsfridge.com) takes a humorous look at many of the daily issues in the world of politics and current events. The site features an editorial cartoon and satirical stories about issues or personalities in the news. Included in Bob's Fridge is a "cybersatirization" of the Windows operating system, technology, and the Internet.

The first rule of freelance journalism is that you always live at the mercy of an editor. Bob Hirschfeld, creator of Bob's Fridge, was determined to do something about it.

For ten years, I have been writing editorials in major newspapers, which I foolishly thought would be enough exposure to open additional doors and get myself established. However, it really isn't. It seems like people in the media and entertainment fields simply are not that impressed with newspaper columns.

As a satirist, the only way I could reach the public was to hope a column I submitted, along with a bribe, would happen to strike an editor just the right way so it would appear in that paper. Although I was fairly successful in getting columns in *USA Today*, *The Wall Street Journal*, and *The Washington Post*, many times editors neglected a piece until its shelf life expired and was topically stale and useless to submit elsewhere. That's why I fantasized about the ability to reach the public directly on daily basis, without relying on the whims of editors. If only such a thing existed. If computers could interconnect people so that anyone could access my material, it would truly be an amazing world.

The emergence of the Internet as an alternative to traditional media outlets answered all Bob's prayers and changed the situation completely.

I realized that the Web allows me be out there twenty-four hours each day. Anybody can access it, and I don't have to worry about the crankiness or whims of an editor. It creates that feedback that you don't get from other mediums. Over the past decade, I never got any direct feedback from a newspaper column.

Instead of launching a site on the Internet, where in 1995 I didn't see much investment in content development, I went where the online pesos were, notably America Online (AOL). I approached them about creating a daily satirical news feature including interactive features for member involvement. I sent an e-mail to the president, Ted Leonsis, who responded within a few minutes, saying he was interested. A few months later, I launched News Grief.

Allied with one of the biggest players on the Web, Bob thought he had truly arrived on the Internet journalism scene.

I had big dreams, and thought I was on the verge of truly establishing myself as the first cybersatirist, an online Art Buchwald, Russell Baker, or Dave Barry. One problem, however, was that the news and politics channels of AOL refused to put a link to or promote my feature, because the channels were in cutthroat competition for racking up member usage. Since I was under contract with the entertainment channel, they had no desire to help. Forget the fact that properly targeting a feature to members made overall sense for AOL and was critical to success. So, instead of bringing my daily topical feature to the attention of millions of members who went to news and politics, I was relegated to a comedy pub, where you had to decipher the artwork to decide to click on a newspaper lying on the counter next to beer taps.

Ironically, instead of gaining access to a wider audience as a result of his new business alliance, Bob was never afforded the chance to succeed.

www. bobsfridge.com

At that time, AOL's ignorance was revealed. All these channels were competing with each other. They didn't want to help. Therefore, no matter how good my site ultimately was, I couldn't get the attention of enough AOL members to make it a big success. I built a respectable following; however, a year after coming on board, AOL decided to cancel all but the biggest features.

Fortunately, this setback was very temporary, since Bob was already promoting his work independently.

Ironically, I had also created an abbreviated Internet version of News Grief, mostly as a promotional tool, and a week after I finished with AOL, *Yahoo! Internet Life* named it the best site for political humor. This convinced me that it was important to maintain a presence on the Net. Therefore, instead of getting angry about the missed opportunity with AOL, I got humorous and created a parody of the service as part of the subsequent site I created, Bob's Fridge Door, which launched in March of 1997.

My Fridge site was immediately featured in *Newsweek* on their *Cyberscope* page. Soon after, it was reviewed in *USA Today*, *The Washington Post*, *Los Angeles Times*, and many other papers. *PC Magazine* named it a top 100 site. Since then, I have continued to build a readership, positive press coverage, and links to it from search engines and other sites that rate it one of the best on the Net.

I average 25,000 to 30,000 visitors to the site on a weekly basis. I've gotten big bumps from press coverage and, most notably during the first month or so of the Lewinsky scandal. I have on a regular basis about 3,000 to 4,000 visitors per day who return consistently. I'm building a reputation on the grassroots level.

People are writing to me not only to say that they enjoy the site and that they have me bookmarked in their computer, but also to say that they have given my URL to their friends. The Internet is great in that the grassroots support it allows can make a success out of somebody. If people see something they like, they'll pass it around to their friends. More press people know about me now, and interviewers from other sites have approached me.

All of this has been creating momentum for my career. On a practical side, I'm using the Web site to promote a speech presentation I developed. It's a satirical look at the whole digital age. I've created parodies of the Windows operating system, software applications, Internet sites, and e-mail. I've given several presentations already, and I now have a good promotional tape in front of an audience with them laughing, which is essential as I have discovered.

The degree to which people consider whether or not to book me is often based on how others have reacted to me. Usually, the people doing the bookings say "Well, you know I have to show your tape to other people in the company." If they hear a tape of other people laughing, then that is the reassurance they need. "Oh yeah, yeah, yeah, sounds good."

A recent article in *The Wall Street Journal* profiled Bob's site, which considerably boosted interest and activity.

The column gave me another credential and helped bring my site to the attention of a lot more people who, therefore, are bringing it to the attention of even more people. It helps build that Democratic grassroots process on the Internet. I have gotten four or five bookings for speeches since the column. It gives you a great sense of credibility when you're profiled in a major newspaper or magazine. It helped bring my site and me to the attention of many people. This wouldn't be happening if I wasn't offering something that people enjoyed in the first place, but the column has certainly expedited the whole process.

While not likely to generate significant advertising revenue in the short term, Bob does expect that to change as the Internet continues to develop.

In the beginning, I wasn't convinced about the prospects of generating sufficient ad revenue from the site, but now I see long-term potential. The Net is going through an evolutionary period of survival and many, many sites have closed down. That shakedown process, and the continuing acclaim and recognition that my site is receiving, may increase the prospects of advertising as a worthwhile source of revenue.

Readers of Bob's Fridge write to Bob with enormous praise for the high quality of his site and the excellent parodies that he writes.

Every morning, I open my mailbox and always find mail that is full of praise, appreciation, and encouragement for my satire. Also, I've received some touching e-mails from folks who are going through tough times or are depressed and thank me profusely for making them laugh.

I respond to all my e-mail, which surprises a number of people who are used to arrogance on the Web. A number of regulars think of me when they see something bizarre in the news or have a humorous thought, and share it with me. I can always tell the ages of people immediately. Some responses immediately indicate the writer's age. "Hey Bob, your site rocks." Or, "You rule!" I also get a great deal of mail from senior citizens who say that they enjoy finding some intelligent life and humor on the Internet. They often provide me with a little bit about their background. I've heard from ex-news people, journalists, and so forth.

Since I always respond to my e-mail, I'll sometimes get a rapport going back and forth that can last quite a while, an exchange of thoughts. Often people tell me that they are shocked that somebody bothered to reply to them.

Much of Bob's more recent mail and feedback from readers reflects a growing distaste for shock humor.

www.
bobsfridge.com

People are really tired of this in-your-face type of humor. There exists an over-emphasis on all that is lewd and crude. It's not just a matter of moralizing; it's that this brand of humor has been so overdone. It has become boring. Therefore, I receive a lot of comments, such as, "We appreciate the fact that you can make us laugh without having to be outright lewd and crude, and that you treat us with intelligence." Shock humor is just not shocking anymore. Shock humor is actually the easiest humor to express, to have this race to the bottom. You see so much use of expletives, and making fun of somebody's peers. Crude humor can be funny; however, at the same time, there is so little humor on the Internet that isn't of that genre that people find what I'm doing refreshing. I view what I'm doing in the great tradition of satire—trying to be sharp, witty, and funny about current events. Along with making my satire funny and laughable, I also try to make it another form of commentary. That is the real tradition of satire. I think it's a type of humor that appeals across a wide span of generations.

Bob's Fridge has succeeded because of Bob's commitment to deliver consistently high-quality satire.

My success is really a factor of time and effort and word-of-mouth. There is still so much clutter out there. It takes quite a lot of time and effort to find the real quality. That makes it hard for the good sites to really break through.

Ironically, at a time when the news and current events are so full of headlines that are in themselves difficult to believe at times, it's a challenge trying to be "over the top" and, therefore, funny about news that is increasingly so twisted at the start. When I tell people that I try to be tongue-in-cheek about what transpires in Washington, it now sounds more like something an intern does at the White House.

Many mistakenly think that all the craziness in the news would be a heyday for a satirist. Actually, it gets so hard to parody what actually seems like a parody. It pushes you into these creative fits. The news already seems so funny, what is the point in taking it another step? I must intentionally push myself further and further.

Last week, I wrote a column on my site regarding the Serbs. I was reading, yet again, that it is now six years that they have been doing this ethnic cleansing. The country must be immaculate. Therefore, I wrote a piece about how they have actually run out of ethnic groups so they started to attack themselves. Now, they divided themselves along astrological signs.

The Scorpio forces have attacked the Libra forces. But the Libras cannot decide if they should fight back or not.

SKEWPOINT

U.S. WEATHER SERVICE TO SELL CORPORATE SPONSORSHIP OF HURRICANES

Breaking News Beyond Repair

with Cybersatirist

BOB HIRSCHFELD

back to Bob's Fridge Door

write to Bob

Printer friendly version

Skewpoint Briefs from-

January

December

READ 1998 IN RESKEW: THE BEST OF SKEWPOINT FROM THE PAST YEAR

Today's Top Story-

In a move toward semi-privatization, the federally funded U.S. Weather Service is offering exclusive corporate sponsorship of hurricanes. Weather Service spokesman Storm Fields said that several major multinational firms have already put in bids to have storm systems named after them. "This represents an enormous marketing opportunity to reach consumers with natural disasters that receive prominent media coverage. In addition to having their named affiliated with a hurricane, we will include the company's slogan with all the storm related information we release," he said. The hurricane sponsorship program may bring in over half a billion dollars during its first year of operation, enabling the service to fund itself as well as fill federal coffers. Brad Hackliver, a marketing executive from Home Depot, revealed that they are first on the official waiting list. "We believe that when Hurricane Home Depot arrives it will send a powerful message that we are the store people should think of when it comes to rebuilding their homes," he said.

MICROSOFT EXEC DENIES HIS COMPANY EXISTS AT ANTITRUST TRIAL

www.
bobsfridge.com

In the recent past, Bob has been flooded with Monica material and its aftermath.

Janet Reno was holding Congress in contempt for posting pornography on the Internet. It's an amazing hypocrisy. Conservatives have always complained about all the sex and filth coming out of Hollywood and the National Endowment for the Arts grants that support pornography. However, they couldn't wait for the government-sponsored Starr report detailing the Lewinsky scandal to get on the Internet. That was worse pornography than anything to which they have previously referred. It is a very bizarre situation.

As a result of his Web site, Bob has a much better understanding of how his writing is consistently being received. Such information has helped form a broad and loyal audience.

The Internet has provided the ability for me to really hone my talent on a daily basis, to find out what works and what does not. It's a far bigger investment of time and talent than you may initially think, but I believe it is well worth it if you are willing to persevere, because you truly establish grassroots support, and the feedback can be highly motivating.

When I started two years ago, there were many people visiting satire and comedy sites, a lot of them on a daily basis. I think because the technology is easy, at least initially, it lured a lot of people into thinking that running and maintaining a site would be simple. They thought they could just create a site, and update it occasionally. It is only after a while that they start to realize what is really involved. If you're going to run a dynamic Web site on a weekly or daily basis, it's a serious commitment. There is something about the survival of the most interesting. I think through that shakedown, the ones who do survive and have good quality are eventually going to build significant audiences.

As Bob has discovered, no other medium holds so much power or provides such a stage as the Internet.

What I find amazing about the medium is that I alone can compete with Disney, Time-Warner, or any large media site. It's just me and my laptop. When visiting a site, nobody cares if it is that of a big money corporation or simply a lone person, as long as the quality is there. There's no filtering, at least currently. Everybody is equal. If you're good, you can reach people.

Beyond the business side of it, I still have the underlying need everyday to take the news and make people laugh about it. It's probably the most satisfying thing I do.

www.wordmuseum.com

LORI SOARD

Learning to Use the Write Tools

About the Site

WordMuseum (www.wordmuseum.com) is a resource for freelance and professional writers, featuring a dozen genre areas from which to choose. Within each area, visitors will find interviews, previews, author profiles, contests, columns, and writing classes.

Lori Soard, age twenty-nine, is a freelance writer and novelist. She was raised as an only child in Indianapolis. She recalls dreaming up great stories and elaborate tales to help pass the time.

I began pursuing writing as a career about six years ago, after teaching language arts in area public schools for a few years. I started with short stories and articles, and then progressed to novels in the last couple of years. I've been writing since I first learned to form words into sentences. As an adult, a day has never gone by that I haven't written something. You could say that writing is as much a part of my life as eating or breathing.

My favorite type of writing is romance. I like to read and tell stories about how a man and woman overcome all obstacles to find that one true love. I suppose that I'm a romantic at heart. I also write in other genres and have a young-adult novel out right now, *It's Hard to Go Home*, which is available in paperback version through Hummingbird Press. It can be ordered through Amazon.com or Barnes and Noble.

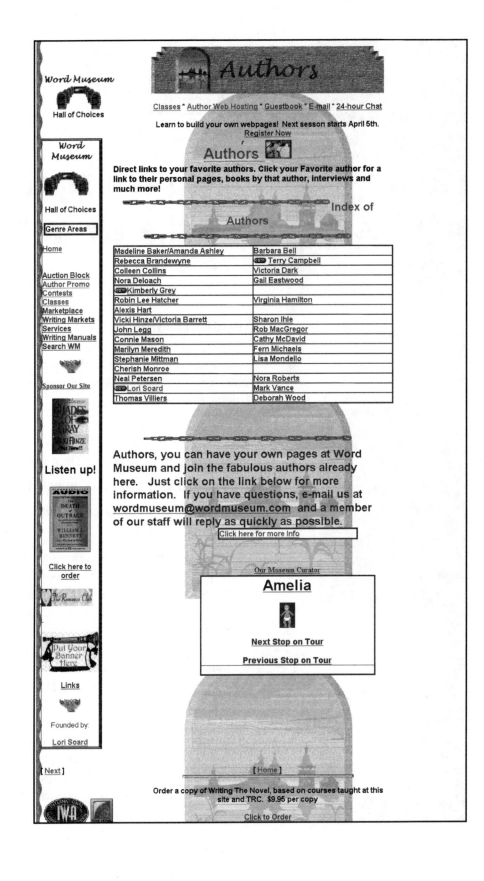

Word Museum
Hall of Choices

Word Museum
Hall of Choices

Genre Areas

Home

Auction Block
Author Promo
Contests
Classes
Marketplace
Writing Markets
Services
Writing Manuals
Search WM

Sponsor Our Site

Listen up!

Click here to order

Put Your Banner Here

Links

Founded by:
Lori Soard

[Next]

Authors

Classes * Author Web Hosting * Guestbook * E-mail * 24-hour Chat

Learn to build your own webpages! Next session starts April 5th.
Register Now

Authors

Direct links to your favorite authors. Click your Favorite author for a link to their personal pages, books by that author, interviews and much more!

Index of Authors

Madeline Baker/Amanda Ashley	Barbara Bell
Rebecca Brandewyne	NEW Terry Campbell
Colleen Collins	Victoria Dark
Nora Deloach	Gail Eastwood
NEW Kimberly Grey	
Robin Lee Hatcher	Virginia Hamilton
Alexis Hart	
Vicki Hinze/Victoria Barrett	Sharon Ihle
John Legg	Rob MacGregor
Connie Mason	Cathy McDavid
Marilyn Meredith	Fern Michaels
Stephanie Mittman	Lisa Mondello
Cherish Monroe	
Neal Petersen	Nora Roberts
NEW Lori Soard	Mark Vance
Thomas Villiers	Deborah Wood

Authors, you can have your own pages at Word Museum and join the fabulous authors already here.   Just click on the link below for more information. If you have questions, e-mail us at wordmuseum@wordmuseum.com and a member of our staff will reply as quickly as possible.

Click here for more Info

Our Museum Curator

Amelia

Next Stop on Tour

Previous Stop on Tour

[Home]

Order a copy of Writing The Novel, based on courses taught at this site and TRC. $9.95 per copy

Click to Order

I got the idea for Word Museum while helping a friend who has her own romance site. Since I enjoy writing in both romance and other genres, I began considering a multi-genre site to offer something not available at the time. I was trying to find a site for all the information I needed as a multi-genre author. There wasn't one. I also love to read and wanted a site where I could sometimes read stories or about new authors. At the time, there was nothing that fit with what I wanted in a site.

Word Museum started in November of 1997, but I've been on the Net, playing or working, for nearly eight years now. I wanted to provide a site for writers unlike anything out there. When Word Museum came out, most other resource sites for writers focused on a single topic. That isn't necessarily a bad thing. But if you are a writer who focuses on more than one style of writing, it can be time consuming to search all of these individual sites. I created Word Museum to fill that void, to provide multi-genre writers like me with every category and writing style imaginable. The site offers interviews, reviews, author pages where you can get to know an individual author better, free chats, contests, regular columns, writing classes, and whatever else I decide to add. When we get our new chat rooms, we will offer Internet Relay Chat (IRC) in addition to Java-based chat for the serious to talk about writing. We will have the controls to ban other users, kicking them out if they have other intentions. However, this really has not been a problem for us, yet. Most of the people who use our chat rooms are serious about writing.

In the early days of the site, Word Museum was much smaller than the several hundred pages and the dozen genre areas it now includes. We had fewer genre areas and less content in the beginning. We hadn't yet started the contests or free workshops, and our author base was smaller. I created the site by myself, and now spend between ten and twenty hours per week working on it. I put in more hours, depending on seasonal updates and new content that needs posting. Since I didn't know any better at the time, I tried to do everything by myself in the beginning. When it became overwhelming, I sent out feelers over the Web for help. The response was incredible. The site has grown to such an extent that I now have about ten staffers. The staffers include writers, readers, family, and friends. Some work as volunteers, although we trade services with them, and others are paid. Some contributors with whom we trade services are looking for author pages or editing of manuscripts, and others want revenue from banner ads. I discuss the needs with each writer and base the arrangement on this discussion. So far, they've all been

www.
wordmuseum.com

pleased with the setup. Those who help with the site are really helping it grow and become a success. I couldn't do this without them.

The Word Museum has expanded since day one as a result of the tried and true, low-tech method of word-of-mouth. One person visits the site and likes it, and then tells three or four friends, who tell three or four friends, who tell others in an endless process. After a while, it starts to amount to a lot of visitors. It's easy to forget that the Internet is amazingly small compared to the number of people on it. Rumors, including both good and bad commentary about a site, can spread quickly. If someone is on a listserv and mentions that they found a great new site, they might post the link and twenty of their friends will visit. Those people pass on the exciting, new contest we're offering or other features. The process happens very fast since everyone is so accessible to one another. E-mail and online chats accelerate the speed of information.

Although we offer free workshops, including author promotion and writing classes, people are constantly writing in to comment about the new free chats and contests. Folks seem to particularly enjoy these features of Word Museum. I think visitors keep returning to check the site because high-quality content is always being switched. I keep it very dynamic by doing these updates on a daily basis. Visitors are always curious about what we've added.

Lori goes to great lengths to keep Word Museum both fun and informative.

We have a museum curator, Amelia, who appears in different costumes throughout the site. Amelia will also take newcomers on a guided tour. I'm willing to try just about anything on my site that will help writers or interest readers. I also consider what is suitable for our younger readers, as well. Plus, some of the best content I post is a result of old-fashioned trial and error. If something doesn't have a good response, it goes and is replaced it with something new. I have no hesitancy about dropping one thing in favor of another. For example, when we started, we had a songwriting area. It got about three hits in three months. So, we ditched it and replaced it with ethnic fiction. We've had a big call for a Christian fiction area, too. Plans are in the works to be adding that soon.

As Lori likes to point out, the site was not started for the sake of making money. It was meant only to be a general resource for the Internet writing public.

I am reluctant to admit it, but we actually claimed a loss last year. I support the costs of running the site from income I receive by writing articles. Three examples of some recent pieces I've done are "Growing Up in El

Salvador," as published in *Faces*, November, 1998; "Growing Up in Kenya," as published in *Faces*, January 1999, and "Hook, Line, and Unsinkable," as published in *Lover's Knot*, October 1999. Some of my short stories include, "The Trouble with Twins," as published in *Writer's Corner*, November 1998, and "Once in a While Romantic," as published in *Bower*, an online magazine, November-January 1998/1999. Writing will never make me rich, but it does help keep the Word Museum running.

I take seriously the responsibility of being a writer in a public forum. We're involved in projects for literacy and other valuable initiatives that I feel are important to help broaden our impact on the Web and beyond. Literacy is a cause that is near and dear to my heart. It is a cause that Word Museum, and I as a writer, will continue to support and through which we can try to make a real difference. Word Museum is releasing an anthology this spring. All of the short stories and poems in it were donated by the authors to help this cause. All profits will be donated to various literacy groups. On another level, I participate in school online exchange programs where I speak with students about reading and writing and try to create fun exercises to promote a lifelong interest in reading. I believe this will build a love of the written word. We also help promote new authors with fresh, exciting voices. I believe readers want something new and innovative. Word Museum never disappoints on this score.

Although Lori never would have expected it, the site has received over a million hits since it first opened in 1997.

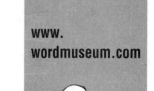

www.
wordmuseum.com

The Word Museum receives about 10,000 hits per week at this point, and I can expect to receive about 100 e-mails per day. People write to comment on a particular article that touched them or was helpful. Others just write to say how much they enjoy the variety of useful services we offer. Contests, open to all the main writing genres, have been successful for us and always generate a good amount of interest. I've never run a contest that didn't receive a terrific response. Our audience really likes to have the chance to win books or other writing/reading prizes. Then there are the readers who wish to be put in touch with authors. Interestingly, in terms of these requests, the reigning favorite is Nora Roberts. In the vast majority of cases, I am able to oblige.

Lately, I've been trying to market Word Museum directly. I did a radio interview recently with *Home Biz Weekly*. The topic was home-based businesses. I corresponded with the host, and he asked me to be on his show. I thoroughly enjoyed it, and, as a result, got about four times the typical number of hits that week. Currently, I have several contacts and will be trying to line up local and national shows in the summer. I also am trying to promote my books, so where I can tie the two in together is quite a benefit. In terms of partnering up in some business alliance, I wouldn't consider that path. I would much prefer to work by myself, be overworked, and be totally accountable for the results of my efforts. That's what works for me.

Lori has successfully transferred her writing and creative skills from the author's page to the computer screen through a strong desire to learn.

I was familiar with Web page building based on the computer classes I took as an undergraduate. I gained the vast majority of my Web skills through continuously experimenting with different designs and formats, and practicing on my own. It also helps that I had a strong basis in computers and how they work on the end-user. Through my own experience, I believe that anyone can learn to do this if they're willing to take the time to read and experiment.

To keep up with the latest technical news, I subscribe to several PC magazines and belong to an HTML writer's guild. I also frequent other sites and belong to mail lists that specialize in technical training for writers. More than simply reading, I find that just experimenting teaches you a lot, too. Once, I tried to create a fairly advanced drop down menu with a dynamic design. I thought it looked terrific, and was so proud of it. The problem came when those visitors to my site with older browsers couldn't access the feature. If you're going to offer it, you need to offer an alternative for those with slower or older systems. From out of nowhere, I received about 600 e-mails from people frantic that they couldn't get to one area or another, or stating that their screen was freezing up on them. So much for advanced technology.

While the Internet's limitless access and ease of use is an endless resource for writers, it also makes a tempting target for anyone determined to copy a successful format.

I really work hard to make certain that the Word Museum is kept fresh and original. At the same time, I find that if, on my own, I get a great design, another site will suddenly have the same design posted. Staying one step ahead of this piracy is a lot of work, since I like to be unique. Immediately, I'll start redesigning.

Being able to connect with long-admired authors has been one of the biggest benefits Lori has gained through her site.

The Word Museum has enabled me to meet a lot of authors that I've admired over the years. Being a romance writer, I love the writings of Fern Michaels, Vicki Hinze, and Nora Roberts. Not only are they talented, but they are warm, caring women who contribute to society through donations, scholarship programs, and appearances. There are so many wonderful folks out there doing great things. I count myself as being lucky just to have met many of them through the Word Museum.

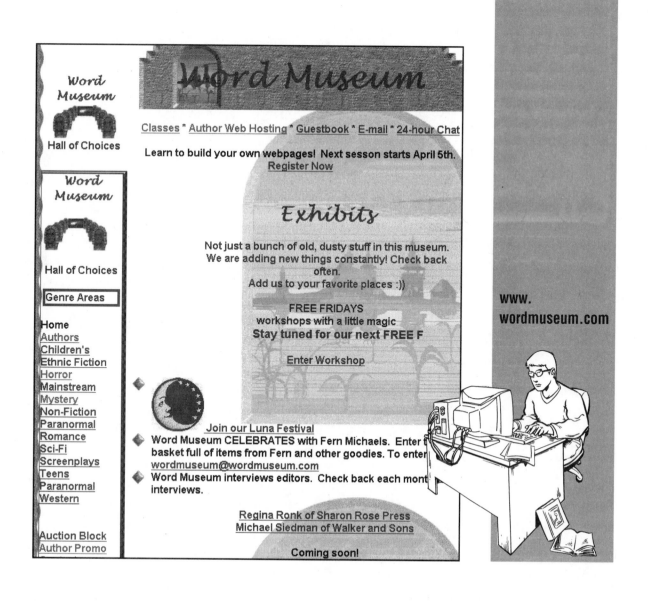

Word Museum
Hall of Choices

Word Museum
Hall of Choices

Genre Areas

Home
Authors
Children's
Ethnic Fiction
Horror
Mainstream
Mystery
Non-Fiction
Paranormal
Romance
Sci-Fi
Screenplays
Teens
Paranormal
Western

Auction Block
Author Promo

Classes * Author Web Hosting * Guestbook * E-mail * 24-hour Chat
Learn to build your own webpages! Next session starts April 5th.
Register Now

Exhibits

Not just a bunch of old, dusty stuff in this museum.
We are adding new things constantly! Check back often.
Add us to your favorite places :))

FREE FRIDAYS
workshops with a little magic
Stay tuned for our next FREE F

Enter Workshop

Join our Luna Festival
Word Museum CELEBRATES with Fern Michaels. Enter t basket full of items from Fern and other goodies. To enter wordmuseum@wordmuseum.com
Word Museum interviews editors. Check back each mont interviews.

Regina Ronk of Sharon Rose Press
Michael Siedman of Walker and Sons

Coming soon!

www.
wordmuseum.com

Epilogue

Now that you have read about the creators, do you feel motivated? Are you going to build a site or visit a new one? As you've seen, it is not just computer nerds who have established a presence on the Web, but people with a wide range of talents and interests. The only commonality is their dedication to constructing and maintaining a vibrant place on the Internet.

This dedication has transformed not only their lives, but also the lives of their viewers. While the Webmasters continually meet new people through their sites, their contributors and readers get to meet each other. The site developers have spawned communities and close friendships among people who have only met over the computer and probably never would meet in the physical world. Shrinking distance and building forums for people with common interests proves the Web is a friendly place to meet and get to know real people.

The preceding chapters were a sampling of some of the real people on the Web. As you explore the Internet and wonder who is behind a certain site, don't feel intimidated about e-mailing that site's Webmaster. Almost all of them appreciate the contact. It's how we created this book. Getting a sense of the individual who brings each site to life can make your visit to that space more intriguing and sometimes can explain a site's quirks.

Due to the pace of Internet time, sites change quickly. In weeks, sites can grow from being completely unknown to being a very popular destination, while others may be completely modified to try to continue to hold onto their current audience. Still other sites come and go within the span of a few days. Even with all this change, one thing is constant; you'll always find a Webmaster who brings a unique personality to the creation of a site. These individuals are the net.people.

Web Sites
Mentioned in the Book

Amazon.com	www.amazon.com
Breakupgirl.com	www.breakupgirl.com
Women.com	www.women.com
Third age.com	www.thirdage.com
Careguide.net	www.careguide.net
Stretcher.com	www.stretcher.com
The Free Site.com	www.thefreesite.com
Lockergnome.com	www.lockergnome.com
Horse-Country.com	www.horse-country.com
Rec.equestrian	http://rohan.sdsu.edu/
Cyberdocs.com	www.cyberdocs.com
Wing.Net	www.Wing.Net
WayCoolWeddings.com	www.waycoolweddings.com
Gananda Community Church	www.ganandacc.org
Net.Humor.Religion	www.usenet2.org
Vikingunderground.com	www.vikingunderground.com
Gridirongrumblings.com	www.gridirongrumblings.com
MVPgames.com	www.MVPgames.com
Solar Productions	www.solarproductions.com
Pro Baseball Weekly	www.probaseballweekly.com

Ballparks.com	www.ballparks.com
Coolrunning.com	www.coolrunning.com
RoadsideAmerica.com	www.roadsideamerica.com
ATT.com	www.ATT.com
Travlang.com	www.travlang.com
FrequentFlier.com	www.FrequentFlier.com
WebFlyer	www.webflyer.com
frequentflyer.com	www.frequentflyer.com
Bmonster.com	www.bmonster.com
MovieJuice.com	www.moviejuice.com
Findagrave.com	www.findagrave.com
OnRamp Communications	www.orci.com
BeanieMom.com	www.beaniemom.com
HappyToy.com	www.happytoy.com
Toymania.com	www.toymania.com
Comicbookresources.com	www.comicbookresources.com
Fishlinkcentral.com	www.fishlinkcentral.com
Centre for the Easily Amused	www.amused.com
Forkinthehead.com	www.forkinthehead.com
KissThisGuy.com	www.kissthisguy.com
The Birdhouse Arts Collective	www.Birdhouse.org
Seriousgamers.com	www.seriousgamers.com
AllGames Guide	www.allgame.com
GameStats News Network	www.gamestats.com
Web Wonders	www.escape.ca/~wonders/
RiotGrrl	www.riotgrrl.com
GrrlGamer	www.grrlgamer.com
TeenGrrl	www.teengrrl.com
chickclick.com	www.chickclick.com

Fray.com	www.fray.com
Kvetch.com	www.kvetch.com
Derek Powazek's personal site	www.powazek.com
San Francisco Stories	www.sfstories.com
fray.org (real-life version of the fray.com)	www.fray.org
TheSmokingGun.com	www.thesmokinggun.com
Fierce.com	www.fierce.com
Thisistrue.com	www.thisistrue.com
Jokeaday.com	www.jokeaday.com
TopFive.com	www.topfive.com
Bob's Fridge.com	www.bobsfridge.com
WordMuseum.com	www.wordmuseum.com

More CyberAge Books
from Information Today, Inc.

The Extreme Searcher's Guide to Web Search Engines
A Handbook for the Serious Searcher
Randolph E. Hock

"Extreme searcher" Randolph (Ran) Hock—internationally respected Internet trainer and authority on Web search engines—offers straightforward advice designed to help you get immediate results. Ran not only shows you what's "under the hood" of the major search engines, but explains their relative strengths and weaknesses, reveals their many (and often overlooked) special features, and offers tips and techniques for searching the Web more efficiently and effectively than ever. Updates and links are provided at the author's Web site.

Softbound • ISBN 0-910965-26-9 • $24.95
Hardbound • ISBN 0-910965-38-2 • $34.95

Design Wise
A Guide for Evaluating the
Interface Design of Information Resources
Alison J. Head

"Design Wise takes us beyond what's cool and what's hot and shows us what works and what doesn't."   —Elizabeth Osder, *The New York Times on the Web*
Knowing how to size up user-centered interface design is becoming as important for people who choose and use information resources as for those who design them. This book introduces readers to the basics of interface design and explains why a design evaluation should be integrally tied to what we trade cash for and fire up for everyone else to use—in settings of all kinds and sizes.

Softbound • ISBN 0-910965-31-5 • $29.95

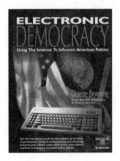

Electronic Democracy
Using the Internet to Influence American Politics
Graeme Browning

Here is everything you need to know to become a powerful player in the political process from your desktop. Experienced Washington reporter Graeme Browning (*National Journal*, Center for Democracy & Technology) offers real-world strategies for using the World Wide Web to reach and influence decision makers inside the Beltway. Loaded with practical tips, techniques, and case studies, this is a must-read for anyone interested in the future of representative government and the marriage of technology and politics.

Softbound • ISBN 0-910965-20-X • $19.95

Internet Blue Pages, 2001-2002 Edition
The Guide to Federal Government Web Sites
Compiled by Laurie Andriot

With over 1,800 Web addresses, this guide is designed to help you find any agency easily. Arranged in accordance with the US Government Manual, each entry includes the name of the agency, the Web address (URL), a brief description of the agency, and links to the agency's or subagency's home page. For helpful cross-referencing, an alphabetical agency listing and a comprehensive index for subject searching are also included. Regularly updated information and links are provided on the author's Web site.

Softbound • ISBN 0-910965-29-3 • $34.95

Great Scouts!
CyberGuides to Subject Searching on the Web
Nora Paul and Margot Williams • Edited by Paula Hane
Foreword by Barbara Quint

Great Scouts! is a cure for information overload. Authors Nora Paul (The Poynter Institute) and Margot Williams *(The Washington Post)* direct readers to the very best subject-specific, Web-based information resources. Thirty chapters cover specialized "CyberGuides" selected as the premier Internet sources of information on business, education, arts and entertainment, science and technology, health and medicine, politics and government, law, sports, and much more. With its expert advice and evaluations of information and link content, value, currency, stability, and usability, *Great Scouts!* takes you "beyond search engines"—and directly to the top sources of information for your topic.

Softbound • ISBN 0-910965-27-7 • $24.95

Millennium Intelligence
Understanding & Conducting
Competitive Intelligence in the Digital Age
Edited by Jerry Miller

With contributions from the world's leading business intelligence practitioners, here is a tremendously informative and practical look at the CI process, how it is changing, and how it can be managed effectively in the Digital Age. Loaded with case studies, tips, and techniques, chapters include *What Is Intelligence?; The Skills Needed to Execute Intelligence Effectively; Information Sources Used for Intelligence; The Legal and Ethical Aspects of Intelligence; Corporate Security and Intelligence*...and much more!

Softbound • ISBN 0-910965-28-5 • $29.95

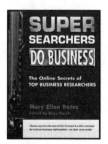

Super Searchers Do Business
The Online Secrets of Top Business Researchers
Mary Ellen Bates • Edited by Reva Basch

Super Searchers Do Business probes the minds of 11 leading researchers who use the Internet and online services to find critical business information. Through her in-depth interviews, Mary Ellen Bates—a business super searcher herself—gets the pros to reveal how they choose online sources, evaluate search results, and tackle the most challenging business research projects. Loaded with expert tips, techniques, and strategies, this is the first title in the exciting new "Super Searchers" series, edited by Reva Basch. If you do business research online, or plan to, let the super searchers be your guides.

Softbound • ISBN 0-910965-33-1 • $24.95

Electronic Styles
A Handbook for Citing Electronic Information
Xia Li and Nancy Crane

The second edition of the best-selling guide to referencing electronic information and citing the complete range of electronic formats includes text-based information, electronic journals and discussion lists, Web sites, CD-ROM and multimedia products, and commercial online documents.

Softbound • ISBN 1-57387-027-7 • $19.99

Super Searchers on Wall Street
Top Investment Professionals Share Their Online Research Secrets
By Amelia Kassel • Edited by Reva Basch

Through her probing interviews, Amelia Kassel reveals the online secrets of 10 leading financial industry research experts. You'll learn how information professionals find and analyze market and industry data, as well as how online information is used by brokerages, stock exchanges, investment banks, and individual investors to make critical investment decisions. The Wall Street Super Searchers direct you to important sites and sources, illuminate the trends that are revolutionizing financial research, and help you use online research as part of a powerful investment strategy. As a reader bonus, a directory of top sites and sources is hyperlinked and periodically updated on the Web.

Softbound • ISBN 0-910965-42-0 • $24.95

Law Of The Super Searchers
The Online Secrets of Top Legal Researchers
T.R. Halvorson • Edited by Reva Basch

In their own words, eight of the world's leading legal researchers explain how they use the Internet and online services to approach, analyze, and carry through a legal research project. In interviewing the experts, practicing attorney and online searcher T.R. Halvorson avoids the typical introductory approach to online research and focuses on topics critical to lawyers and legal research professionals: documenting the search, organizing a strategy, what to consider before logging on, efficient ways to build a search, and much more. *Law of the Super Searchers*—the second title in the new "Super Searchers" series edited by Reva Basch—offers fundamental strategies for legal researchers who need to take advantage of the wealth of information available online.

Softbound • ISBN 0-910965-34-X • $24.95

The Modem Reference, 4th Edition
The Complete Guide to PC Communications
Michael A. Banks

"If you can't find the answer to a telecommunications problem here, there probably isn't an answer." —Lawrence Blasko, *The Associated Press*

Now in its 4th edition, this popular handbook explains the concepts behind computer data, data encoding, and transmission; providing practical advice for PC users who want to get the most from their online operations. In his uniquely readable style, author and techno-guru Mike Banks (*The Internet Unplugged*) takes readers on a tour of PC data communications technology, explaining how modems, fax machines, computer networks, and the Internet work. He provides an in-depth look at how data is communicated between computers all around the world, demystifying the terminology, hardware, and software. *The Modem Reference* is a must-read for students, professional online users, and all computer users who want to maximize their PC fax and data communications capability.

Softbound • ISBN 0-910965-36-6 • $29.95